Case Problems in Personnel and Human Resource Management

Case Problems in Personnel and Human Resource Management

Randall S. Schuler
New York University

Stuart A. Youngblood
Texas A&M University

West Publishing Company
St. Paul   New York   Los Angeles   San Francisco

Production Credits

Cover Design: Alice B. Thiede

Copyediting: Rosalie Koskenmaki

Composition: Cumberland Valley Offset

Copyright © 1986 By WEST PUBLISHING COMPANY
50 West Kellogg Boulevard
P.O. Box 64526
St. Paul, MN 55164-1003

Printed in the United States of America

Library of Congress Cataloging in Publication Data

Schuler, Randall S.
  Case problems in personnel & human resource
management.

  1. Personnel management—Case studies.
I. Youngblood, Stuart A.   II. Title.   III. Title: Case
problems in personnel and human resource management.
HF5549.S2483   1986   658.3   85-13622
ISBN 0-314-93508-8

1st Reprint—1986

To our friends in the world of work who practice PHRM daily, our students who will soon join them, and our colleagues who are helping them do so.

Contents

Preface

Case Problems in Personnel and Human Resource Management, was written to provide a single source of many types of cases useful for personnel and human resource management courses. While this casebook contains a few classic cases such as "Lordstown Plant of General Motors" and "Chandler's Restaurant," most of the cases are of recent vintage. Several of the cases appear here for the first time. Whether new or classic, however, all the cases were included because of their usefulness in personnel and human resource management courses at the undergraduate or graduate level. This casebook contains forty-eight cases of varying length to provide variety.

The cases depict several organizational settings from public to private sector, from mines to banks, and from relatively small companies such as the one in "Traveler Import Cars" to rather large companies such as the ones in "C Company I and II" and the "Lordstown Plant of General Motors." Thus a great many timely personnel and human resource management topics that represent a variety of organizations are presented. The cases can be analyzed and actively discussed by students having relatively no background in personnel and human resource management as well as by those having extensive background, either from previous course work or personal work experience. Fritz Roethlisberger observed that the thoughts, assumptions, and feelings that students bring to the class discussion of a case may be as important as the critical facts presented in the case. More ideas on how to use and analyze cases are contained in the "Guide to Case Analysis" immediately following the Preface. This casebook can be used not only in personnel courses in business administration, but also in hospital administration, social work administration, personnel psychology, and labor and industrial relations. Because the cases in this book are taken from copyrighted material, it is not possible to change their wording, and readers will notice some sexist language. However, these cases have been included here because they are significant and valid even if some of their language is not.

Case Problems in Personnel and Human Resource Management has been organized into seven sections that correspond to topic areas usually covered in PHRM courses: Human Resources Planning and Strategy; Staffing; Appraising and Improving Performance; Compensation; Training, Organizational Improvement, and Personnel Research; Career Development; and Employee Rights and Collective Bargaining. Although our assignment of cases to topic areas may at times seem arbitrary due to the systemic nature of PHRM activities, we beg our colleagues' and contributors' forgiveness in the hope that this organization proves useful in learning more about effective personnel and human resource management.

A great many colleagues have been especially helpful to us in the preparation of this casebook. Several sent us some of their favorite cases and others made invaluable suggestions about the content of the book and the instructor's manual. Based upon the majority of the suggestions, we decided to incorporate all objectives, questions, and comments for each case in the instructor's manual.

Many colleagues indicated this would give them the greatest latitude in using the cases in the book. In addition, where possible, solutions or follow-ups to cases were included in the instructor's manual. Several authors of the cases graciously provided us with these solutions or follow-ups. We are grateful to them.

We wish to thank and recognize those colleagues who provided us with their cases: D. Jeffrey Lenn, Neal Nadler, and James Thurman, The George Washington University; Steve Stumpf, Thomas Mullen and Hrach Bedrosian, New York University; Joe Martocchio, Michigan State University; Susan Zacur and Sue Greenfeld, University of Baltimore; Elmer Burack, University of Illinois at Chicago; Robert J. House, University of Toronto; J.R. Rizzo, Western Michigan University; Noel Tichy and Susan E. Jackson, The University of Michigan; Charles Fombrum, University of Pennsylvania; Mary Anne Devanna, Columbia University; David Balkin, Louisiana State University; Antone F. Alber, Bradley University; William Fitzpatrick, Syracuse University; Hak-Chong Lee, Yonsei University; W.F. Whyte, Cornell University; Vandra Huber, University of Utah; Ed Schuler, Tetley Tea; Rebecca Baysinger, Bruce Kiene, Mitch Fields, Len Bierman, and Marybeth DeGregorio, Texas A&M University; Lynda Goulet and Peter Goulet, University of Northern Iowa; James C. Hodgetts, Memphis State University; George Cooley and Bruce Evans, University of Dallas; Molly Batson, Nancy Sherman, and Jeffry A. Barach, Tulane University; Don Parker, University of Wyoming; Martin Moser, Clark University; Jan Muczyk, Cleveland State; I.B. Helburn and L.J. Ardeleau, The University of Texas at Austin; Donald T. Barnum, Texas Tech University; Isabel Cordova, Howmet Turbine Components Corporation; James W. Thacker, University of Windsor; Magid Mazen, Illinois State University; Hugh French, E-Systems, Inc.; John T. Wholihan, Loyola Marymount University; and E.B. Krinsky, Madison, Wisconsin.

In the instructor's manual we have included several articles on the use, teaching, evaluation, and application of cases. Several colleagues indicated they had never used cases before, and would appreciate some basic guidelines to get them started in the right direction. It was a combination of this feedback and the suggestions of many colleagues that resulted in the inclusion of the articles on using cases.

We would also like to thank Bruce Kiene and Pat Fandt of Texas A&M University and Joe Martocchio of Michigan State University who not only served as contributors to *Case Problems in Personnel and Human Resource Management,* but also assisted in the gathering of permission requests and follow-up necessary to meet our production deadline. We would like to thank Lisa Palmisano, Dick Fenton and Esther Craig of West Publishing Company for their support from the beginning to the completion of this project. Finally, we would like to thank Eddie Roberts for typing the Instructor's Manual and for the support of the staffs at New York University and Texas A&M University.

RANDALL S. SCHULER
New York City

STUART A. YOUNGBLOOD
College Station

Guide to Case Analysis*

Students of biology, chemistry, and the physical sciences learn their fields through practicing and experimenting with theories and materials in the laboratory. As a student of personnel and human resource management, your laboratory will exist in the case problems and experiential exercises presented in this book. The cases and exercises provide the opportunity to experiment with real organizations in the classroom setting.

Personnel and human resource management, like any field, can be learned at three different levels: memorization, understanding, and application. Memorization is the lowest level of learning and involves the simple recitation of facts and simple concepts. Understanding involves deeper learning. It includes the ability to deal with relationships among concepts and to deal with concepts in different contexts. Application is the highest level of learning. Concepts have to be very well understood to apply them to the real world. Mastery of concepts sufficient to solve problems or to diagnose real organizational situations is a significant accomplishment. Learning to understand and apply personnel and human resource management concepts can be effectively and pleasantly accomplished through case study.

Cases and exercises do not replace the textbook and lectures. The personnel and human resource management textbook, readings, and/or lectures provide a theoretical background. The material in this casebook is a supplement; it extends the learning process to the real world. The goal of studying personnel and human resource management with cases is to enable you to apply what is taught from a textbook to a real situation, a reconciliation of theory with life. Managers use theories and models in their day-to-day management of organizations. Often these models are intuitive and implicit. Sometimes they are explicit, just as in a personnel and human resource management textbook. Whatever the nature of the theory or model they use, managers must react to situations relying on past experience and acquired skills to analyze and assess the issues and arrive at a solution. Case study develops your skill in analyzing problems and generating solutions based on your understanding of the theories and models of organization processes and behavior.

---

*Reprinted from *Organization Theory: Cases and Applications* by Richard L. Daft and Kristen M. Dahlen, copyright 1984 by West Publishing Company. Reprinted with permission.

This book contains a variety of case materials and experiential exercises. The cases can be categorized by the educational objective of the instructor and the role of you, the student. The two educational objectives and the associated learning processes are summarized in Exhibit 1. The first type of case learning is theory application/illustration. In this type of case the problem or issue outlined in the situation has usually been solved, and it is your responsibility to analyze the outcome and its consequences. Cases selected for this type of analysis may not emphasize any problem, but present real-life situations that can be used to explain and illustrate theories and models of personnel and human resource management. The facts in the case may be focused toward specific theories, but seemingly irrelevant material will also be included. Sometimes you will be asked to evaluate the solution in the case and to propose an alternative solution if necessary. The second type of case educational objective is problem analysis. Cases used for this objective may be relatively complex. Your role will be to analyze and interpret the situation. You will have to sort out the facts of the case, determine the cause-and-effect relationships, and design a solution and plan for implementation. The primary goal is to solve the problem. The illustration of theories and models is not the primary goal of the case, but theories and models will be used to help identify alternatives and justify your solution.

Another approach to learning personnel and human resource management (PHRM) is through experiential exercises. Experiential exercises engage you directly in the material. Cases require intellectual analysis of an external situation. By contrast, you become an ongoing participant in the PHRM situation when you are involved in an exercise. Experiential exercises require intellectual involvement and critical thinking, but are designed to also engage your real-life experience in the analysis. You are required to become involved in a PHRM situation, either in terms of an assigned role or as a participant observer. After the exercise is completed, the skills you will use to interpret your experiences are similar to those used with other case studies: problem analysis skills help you separate cause from effect and arrive at timely solutions, and theory application skills require you to recognize concepts and relationships in the context of the PHRM situation. A few of the exercises require role-playing in which individuals will be assigned specific identities within an organization situation. You will have

	Theory Application/Illustration	Problem Analysis
Learning Focus	1. Understand concepts. 2. Develop skill in use of concepts.	1. Develop skill in identifying and analyzing problems. 2. Develop skill in designing solutions and plans for implementation.
Learning Procedure	1. Identify examples of theories through relationships in case. 2. Determine inconsistencies with theory. Use concepts to evaluate behavior and predict outcomes.	1. Gather and interpret relevant facts, diagnose critical problems. 2. Use concepts to develop and support a solution and plan of action.

EXHIBIT 1. The Educational Objective and Learning Processes Associated with Case Analysis

the opportunity to test your analytical and conceptual skills in responding to your role and in discussing your interpretation of the unfolding drama.

As you develop your analytical and conceptual skills through cases and exercises, you will be able to master the understanding and use of personnel and human resource management. Many of the cases combine more than one objective. A specific case might be used to practice the application of theory, or to engage you in the identification and solution of the problem. Exercises can also be approached through problems to be solved or the application of theories and models. For any of these materials to enrich your learning experience requires your involvement. An integral part of the learning process is your commitment to preparing the analysis or application and becoming involved in class discussion. Remember, the cases serve a dual purpose: to develop your skills in problem solution and to increase your ability to apply theory to real situations. To assist you in achieving these learning objectives, we suggest the following steps as a guide to get you started.

Theory Application/Illustration

This casebook is intended to be used in conjunction with a textbook or a collection of readings that defines and outlines theories and models of organization. In studying the theories of personnel and human resource management, the cases enable you to see examples of the dimensions and relationships within the theories to be used when solving real problems. Applying theory to the case gives you a deeper understanding of how the theory works in the real world. Theory application enables you to relate the facts of the PHRM situation to theoretical predictions about PHRM processes. The cases and exercises provide you with practice in testing theories from your textbook or readings against the real world.

The application of theories and models to cases is an art that has to be developed through practice and creativity. The framework presented in Exhibit 2 illustrates the three steps required to move you through the process of theory application. The basic elements are identification, relationships, and inconsistencies.

Identification. What is the major emphasis of the case in terms of personnel and human resource management? The primary conceptual topic will be identified by the section heading under which the case appears. However, few cases are limited to one concept. Within the general topic area, what set of variables,

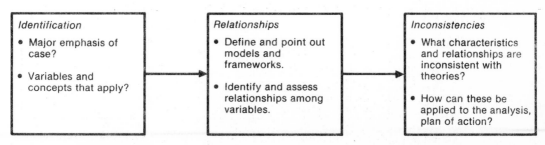

EXHIBIT 2. Steps in Using Cases for Theory Application/Illustration

ideas, and topics from the textbook are illustrated within the case? You must be familiar with the relevant theories and descriptions of PHRM frameworks. Then you should review the processes described within the case, the interactions of the participants, and additional facts that may relate to the theories and models. Try to find as many illustrations of the theory as you can within the case.

Relationships. After identifying the specific concepts relevant to the case situation, describe the relationships among variables. Try to determine whether the predictions made by a theory are illustrated in the case. For example, do the number of rules and procedures reflect the organization's size and stage of development? Is the observed decision-making process what you would predict based on the level of uncertainty confronting managers? Is the organization's structure appropriate for the rate of change in the environment? Does internal organization culture reflect the values symbolized by top management? One test of an organizational theory is whether predicted relationships occur within organizations. By examining theoretic relationships you can understand cause-and-effect relationships and test whether the theory helps you understand the situation. If so, knowledge of one variable will enable you to predict and have knowledge of other variables. Understanding relationships is necessary for determining the impact of contextual factors on the organization under discussion.

Inconsistencies. When discussing relationships among variables, are there instances in which the relationships in the case are inconsistent with theoretical predictions? Perhaps formalization is not consistent with the organization size, or structure is not consistent with the environment. Situations in real life will not identically mirror theory from the textbook, although situations will be similar enough to theory to be useful in understanding the theory. Inconsistencies are an opportunity to challenge and refine your understanding of a theory. Perhaps a model applies only in certain situations. Perhaps other variables are at work that are overwhelming a specific relationship. Identifying inconsistencies and then digging into why they exist is an excellent way to both test and increase your understanding of the organizational theories and models. Occasionally there will be a case that defies theory, possibly presenting familiar variables with inconsistent results or outcomes. In your analysis, bring out these anomalies.

Problem Analysis

Problem analysis frequently requires greater involvement in the case than does theory application. Problem analysis includes and goes beyond the application of theory. Theory application can be accomplished without identifying and solving problems in the case. Problem analysis goes beyond theory by asking students to analyze the situation and propose a solution, as illustrated in Exhibit 3.

An important lesson in identifying and solving problems in a case is to realize that one reading of the case is not sufficient for fully understanding the issues presented. You should allocate your time so that at least two readings will be possible. The first time through, read to get an overall sense of the situation.

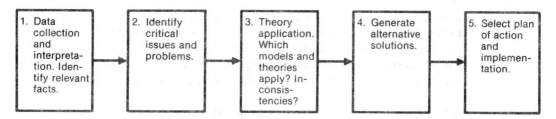

Exhibit 3. Steps in Using Cases for Problem Analysis

You may initially assess all the variables involved, and the relative importance of each, and the nature and scope of the situation. After you interpret the facts of the organization, you will be able to move on to the following steps.

Data Collection and Interpretation. After carefully reading the case, make note of the data that will be useful in determining the state of the situation and the issues to be dealt with. The purposes of this step are to sort out irrelevant from relevant data and to develop a diagnosis of the current situation.

Critical Issues. After diagnosing and analyzing the facts of the situation, you will need to isolate the critical issues or problems to be solved. One way to think about problems is to look for factors that threaten the survival, goals, or performance of the organization or its major departments. Without identifying the real problem, any suggestion for solution will be inappropriate. Isolating the main problem can be quite frustrating, and you may never be absolutely certain you are correct. With careful attention, constant questioning, and practice, your skill at identifying critical issues will improve.

To begin with, think in terms of cause and effect; do not confuse the symptoms with the problem. Dig beneath the surface and determine if something more basic is generating the problem you have identified. For example, you may observe such things as intergroup conflict, a seemingly inappropriate organization structure, poor control, or lack of communication. But to conclude the problem is intergroup conflict or poor control is ignoring the roots or causes of these issues, and thus reduces your chances of finding a successful solution. After identifying the problem or issue, write it 'n a one-sentence statement that concisely conveys the main concern. By reducing your thoughts to one sentence, you force yourself to focus on a primary issue.

Theory Application. Having identified the critical issue, consider your analysis in light of the work you may have previously done with the theories and models that related to the case. Can the theories be used to understand the problem? Are the relationships clearer when viewed in light of the models? If the situation appears to be inconsistent with the theory, is this part of the problem? How can knowledge of the theory assist you in generating possible solutions?

Generating Solutions. Based on the issue or problem you have identified and the theories and models you have studied, brainstorm a list of possible solutions. In brainstorming you should write down every possibility. Do not evaluate the feasibility or rationality of each; just write them down. You should not limit yourself to the strict amount of information provided in the case, i.e., be creative in dealing with the situation.

Having generated a list of wide-ranging possibilities, review your problem statement and identify those alternatives that have a direct link with solving the problem. Combine similar suggestions and begin eliminating alternatives based on your earlier analysis of the situation: constraints of the organization, theoretical concepts, goals and objectives, interacting variables.

Selection of Course of Action and Plan for Implementation. Using your narrowed list of alternatives, begin a detailed analysis of each. Determine the criteria you will use in evaluating each solution. What requirements must a course of action meet? Are there cost constraints? What about timeliness? Resource availability? Are there constituents to consider? Future shock waves? List the pros and cons of each course of action in terms of the criteria you have specified. It may be necessary to make inferences and judgments based on the data provided in the case; this is encouraged as long as you also develop sound and logical arguments to support your interpretations.

The next step of the analysis is to select the best course of action based on the pros and cons and logical assessment of each alternative. You should state the specific steps you recommend and why. You should be sensitive to the arguments against your decision and should be prepared to refute any challenges to your reasoning. Be willing to take risks that can be supported by your analysis of the situation. Indeed, a bonus to solving problems in cases, compared with solving "real world" problems, is that you can take risks without having to answer for the consequences. Be creative and imaginative in developing your answers, but be aware that you will have to logically defend your solution.

Your recommendation should also include a plan for implementation. Consider personnel, time frames, and the sequence of events. In designing the implementation plan you will again be forced to consider your problem definition and analysis. Will your plan address the problem? What are the ramifications of implementing this plan? How will you address them? Many solutions die because no one considered how to introduce the solution or did not consider the possible roadblocks.

Conclusion

An observation you will make all too quickly when studying the cases in this book is that there is never enough information to make the right decision. You can't be certain you have identified the best answer. Other students may have developed different solutions and may present effective arguments for them. There is no perfect answer to a case problem. Each solution may be effective to some extent, but none will be 100 percent accurate. Moreover, no one ever has all the information that would be useful or desirable when analyzing a problem or making a decision. You will just have to make do with what you have, draw logical inferences and assumptions from the available data, and support your arguments with evidence found in the case and theory. Remember, you are being asked to deal with "reality," and there is a lack of information in the real world too.

As you progress through your personnel and human resource management course and the casebook, relate the material, concepts, and theory to your life beyond the classroom. Continue to develop and refine your analytical skills when viewing situations in which you live and participate every day. Look for examples of the theories and models in your own environment. In the classroom, be prepared for discussion, be involved, offer your insights, make constructive criticism, and expect to receive the same from your peers. The case method of learning is most effective when everyone is involved in the analysis and discussion and is willing to experiment with the application of theoretical concepts to the real world. Our intent in designing this casebook has been to challenge, stimulate, and facilitate your learning of personnel and human resource management. We also hope that you find this collection of case materials and exercises interesting, and that you can find the learning process enjoyable. Case problems provide a laboratory setting for your experimentation, and the laboratory is often the most exciting part of the learning process.

Case Problems in Personnel and Human Resource Management

Part I

Human Resource Planning and Strategy

Cases Outline

- Northeast Data Resources, Inc.
- Deft Research and Development, Inc.
- The National Insurance Company
- Human Resource Information Systems at World Wide Utilities
- R.F. Insurance

1. Northeast Data Resources, Inc.*

George Wellington closed the door behind him and slumped into his desk chair with an air of resignation. He had just returned from a meeting of the Executive Committee of Northeast Data Resources where personnel layoffs had been decided upon. As director of personnel at NDR, he realized that he would be responsible for both developing the process by which the layoffs would take place and assisting the managers responsible for the actual implementation. It wasn't a pleasant task, particularly in light of the human resources program that he had begun to implement over the past four years.

Wellington pulled out a pad of paper from the top desk drawer and began to scribble notes. He had found that in times of pressure it was best to get some perspective on the situation before taking action. The drastic character of this situation required a review of the growth of Northeast Data Resources from its inception in 1969 to the present. It was the first crisis the young company had been forced to face.

Background of the Company

In 1969, four young engineers formed a partnership to form the basis of NDR. Three of them had worked for a large, national data-processing company. They had recognized the high potential in the computer industry particularly for a product which filled a vital need in this growing field. Another engineer working in a research program with a large university was asked to join them because of his expertise in the computer field.

Jack Logan was the prime mover of the new company. He had been working for nearly five years on a project within the large company to develop ways to protect its computer systems from being copied by competitors. The primary objective in this project was to ensure that a customer would have to purchase the entire system rather than being able to make use of a number of different systems. Jack saw the opportunity to sell a service to customers that would do just the

*D. Jeffrey Lenn, School of Government and Business Administration, The George Washington University. This case is not meant to be an example of effective or ineffective personnel and human resource management but an example for teaching and discussion purposes. Reprinted by permission.

opposite—provide a mechanism that would link various competing systems into an integrated unit.

He and a colleague, Charlie Bonner, developed a "black box" which had the capacity to connect at least two types of computer systems already on the market. They had worked in Jack's basement over a two-year period to perfect this instrument. Another six months of testing found that it was very effective. The two other engineers had begun to work with them in order to expand the box to tie together three other systems with which they had experience.

The four men decided to strike out on their own and found that their innovation and daring paid off. The first two years were both exhilarating and demanding. NDR subcontracted the production of the black box to a small manufacturing company while the partners divided responsibilities between marketing and continuing research. Jack and Charlie carried the marketing and organizational functions while George Miller and Al Grant worked to streamline the instrument itself.

Early success in securing contracts with some key customers and fears about loss of the exclusive information about the unpatented invention led to a decision to go into full production. An old plant was leased and renovated and workers were hired to begin the process of building the black box for distribution. Within two years the company had grown from four partners to nearly 100 people. By 1976 NDR had expanded to about 700 people and had become the focus of attention for a number of investors. The invention, now dubbed Omega I, had become a product competitors emulated but with little success.

Logan assumed the responsibilities of chairman and president with Bonner as executive vice-president in charge of operations. Miller and Grant stayed in the lab with more interest in research and development, being willing to act more in advisory capacity on managerial decisions.

Logan saw the need to consolidate and expand the overall operations of the company. Production and distribution now overflowed into three buildings separated by nearly ten miles. He negotiated a contract with the economic development committee of Newbury, a New England town about forty miles away, to help construct a new building to house headquarters and plant. The town agreed to help NDR through reduced taxes, water, and sewage hookups at a minimal charge, arrangements with local banks to secure a loan for construction of the plant, and development of a federal grant to train new workers at the plant. In exchange NDR agreed to move its entire operation to Newbury within the next two years. It helped Newbury in its search for new industry while assuring NDR of a secure base of operations for the future.

The Newbury headquarters was only forty miles from the old facilities so NDR lost few of its present staff because of the change. But the growth in business demanded an increase in personnel. Engineers with sophisticated skills in computer science were hired to expand the system capability. Often, international engineers were the only ones available and the importation of English and Australians with a spattering of Europeans gave an international flair to the small company. New factory workers from Newbury and surrounding towns were hired so that the production shifts could be expanded from one to two. The training grants secured by the town helped to equip new workers and the integration with more experienced workers moved smoothly. Empty managerial slots required hiring from the outside mostly. A new vice-president of manufacturing came from a large industrial company in the Midwest. The new vice-president of finance had a solid resume which included most recently financial experience with a large conglomerate but before that two stints with growing companies much like NDR. The staffing of the growing company proceeded professionally.

Future of the Company

The phenomenal growth of NDR in old industrial New England rivaled the computer companies developing in California's Silicon Valley. The workforce had evolved from 4 in 1969 to 100 in 1971, 700 in 1976, and 1,350 by 1982. Sales increased from two small initial contracts in 1969 of $75,000 to nearly $59 million by 1982. In 1975, NDR went public and was listed on the New York Stock Exchange in 1980. The opening price of 7 moved to between 8 and 9 and hovered there in 1981. But a feature article in a national stock advisory report about NDR led to an upward move in the summer in 1982 to 15. Even without paying a dividend in its thirteen years of existence, it had become an attractive investment.

Logan had taken time during the summer of 1982 to begin the process of strategic planning. Convinced that he and his executive committee could and should do this alone, he decided not to engage outside consultants to develop a costly set of plans. His projection was that the computer industry would grow nearly ten times in size over the next decade. Conservatively the company could expect to hold its share of the market which meant a doubling of sales in five years to $120 million and up to $210 million by 1992. Expansion was the key to maintaining market share and holding its own against the handful of competitors which had begun to appear by 1982.

In shaping the strategy, Logan began to map out a new marketing plan which would guarantee NDR's position in the national market instead of the eastern market alone. He saw new customer possibilities in the fields of insurance, financial institutions, and state and local governments. He negotiated an option to buy the factory of a watch company moving South. Its building was about thirty-five miles away in the heart of another old industrial New England town with a pool of skilled workers available to be retrained. He began to develop some ideas about how many new staff would be needed and the kind of capital necessary to finance this expansion.

George Wellington's Career at NDR

George stopped his writing and reviewed the rapid growth of NDR up to this point. He remembered vividly his first few months at the company in 1977. He had moved to a nearby town to retire in the serenity of New England. His career had begun immediately after completing his MBA from a leading eastern university where he had concentrated on management and personnel. He had begun work in the personnel area with a major corporation located in New York. Six years in the field had led him next into marketing and then strategic planning with another company. The last seven years had been with a prestigious consulting firm in New York where he had focused on a variety of problems for a host of clients. His decision to retire had been prompted by a dislike for traveling and a desire to settle down in the area where his children had located.

While retirement continued to bring part-time consulting work, George still found the travel excessive. But his ideas of relaxation in retirement quickly exposed his own need to be fully active in business to be happy. His search for a part-time job was successful as Jack Logan met him at a Chamber of Commerce luncheon in Newbury and hired him as a consultant to help with the transition from the old to the new facilities. He remembered the challenges associated with coordinating not only the efforts of NDR personnel but outside contractors and town officials as well.

The flawless nature of the transition into the new plant made the president recognize that he needed George full-time. Wellington agreed to stay only another six months as a special assistant to Logan. He carried out a variety of projects for Logan and quickly became an integral part of the management team at NDR.

The president called in George one day and showed him an organization chart which he was reworking. "George, I know that your six months are nearly up but I need you around here on a permanent basis. I just don't know where to put you on this chart. How about becoming director of personnel for NDR? That is the only important position which we haven't filled here in the past few months and it would allow me to have you close at hand for help on those big decisions."

George asked for some time to think through his decision and within a week agreed to a full-time position. While Logan still saw personnel as a somewhat unnecessary staff function, there would be a chance for George to help him understand the importance of human resources to this company.

Wellington began immediately to develop a plan for human resources at NDR. Logan encouraged him but wasn't excited about the use of the term "human resources." "I don't understand why you have to complicate this whole business of personnel with a new name. Why not still use the old 'personnel' for the department?" Logan asked. George saw a futile battle in this naming process so he clearly defined his function as that of director of personnel.

His plan for that function at NDR had three major elements:

The Program

Gathering Employee Information. He had his staff develop a file on each employee with a record of hiring date, previous experience and employers, salary, job title, etc. This was stored in a computer so that he could have rapid recall for evaluation.

Performance Appraisal System. He developed a new appraisal system which incorporated a three-page form to be completed twice a year by immediate supervisors. The annual review was tied to salary and bonus decisions. He experimented with it in two engineering sections over a two-year period and then was able to get Logan to mandate it for all of NDR beginning in 1981. The results from the 1981–82 year were compiled and filed for future use.

Personnel Policy Manual. In 1981, a new personnel policy manual was developed that detailed the policies and procedures as well as benefits for all personnel at NDR. There was some initial negative reaction by those who had enjoyed a variety of benefits from the early days of the company. But the imprint of Logan on the manual quelled the complaints and ensured uniformity in the policies.

EEO and Affirmative Action (AA) Program. The highly technical character of the NDR business and its presence in a small New England town made both EEO and AA difficult to pursue. A visit to Wellington by an EEO field investigator regarded the case of a former worker led him to move quickly to formulate this program. The data was gathered on minority hiring and promotion and then a plan designed for increasing the percentage of minorities in all categories and the number of women in management in particular. Logan resisted the immediate implementation of the program with the argument that the Reagan administration would soft-pedal civil rights in employment so that business people did not need to worry. George accepted this decision with reluctance but got an agreement to update the plan periodically as well as pursue informally a goal of more integration of the workforce.

Management Development Program. The rapid growth of NDR created many new managerial positions. Hiring from the outside became one method by which to increase the number of managers, but George believed that the key to the company's future lay in developing them from within. He negotiated a contract with a professor of management at a local university to design and teach a course in management for selected employees. George and the professor team-taught a six-week course for twenty middle level managers in 1980. Its success led to an offering three times a year to both managers and potential managers.

The Staff

George became director of personnel in the spring of 1979. He selected four professionals and two secretaries to work with him. Two professionals came from outside of NDR and two from within. All four had human resources management experience but needed more training. One was encouraged to enter an MBA program on a part-time basis with a concentration on human resource management. The other three were sent to local and national seminars to upgrade skills and understanding in the various areas of HRM. But at the heart of their training was George Wellington, drawing on his vast experience and encouraging his younger colleagues to learn through experimentation and discussion.

The Office Location

The final design of the NDR headquarters had not been decided when George became a consultant to the project so he had taken primary responsibility for the design of the corporate office area. Later, as director of personnel, he negotiated some changes in the office assignments so that personnel was located at one of the major entrances and exits of the building. It was a primary thoroughfare for engineers and managerial personnel arriving in the morning and leaving at night. It was also a stop along the way to the new cafeteria that had just opened.

George had chosen this location for a reason. He felt that human resources departments must have high visibility and availability. Being in the middle of a key thoroughfare allowed people to recognize the central function of personnel in the operation of NDR. It encouraged questions about policies and procedures. It also gave the HRM staff the chance to get to know all of the managers and professionals within a short period of time. This provided instant recognition and a capacity to deal with problems on a much more personal basis. George himself was always at his desk working before most of the staff arrived and usually left after 6:00 P.M. This gave him considerable visibility with managerial personnel who often worked late.

The images of the first few years were succeeded by thoughts about the past two months with his staff. He had begun to engage them in the planning process by asking them to think about NDR for the next five years. He had sketched out the growth projections of Logan and then provided some parameters within which to think about staffing. Each of his professional staff was to develop a short presentation on four consequences for HRM:

1. Impact on the size of our workforce
2. Impact on the mix of skills needed in the workforce
3. Impact on the recruitment efforts from outside NDR and development efforts from within
4. Impact on the working conditions within the company itself, both physically and organizationally.

The first meeting four weeks ago had produced some very good reports. With one exception, the four had done a lot of homework and some imaginative thinking about the future with regard to how HRM plans would fit into the NDR overall strategic plan. George had collated and refined the projections and redistributed them to the professional staff asking for further thought and more specific targets for the next five years. He asked for input for his own report to the president, which he had hoped would be ready by December 1982.

The Present Dilemma

That work had now come to an abrupt halt although he had not alerted the staff to the discussion taking place within the executive committee until the day before. Logan's projections about the future had been overly optimistic.

Two weeks ago, Logan had asked George to meet him at 8:00 P.M. He laid out a report on the results from the first quarter of this fiscal year and then a chart which traced the sales of the last nine quarters. The last two quarters showed a significant decline. Logan indicated to George that, "The decline is now a trend and not simply a blip on the screen as I had thought." The loss of five key contracts totaling nearly $5 million dollars over the past six months plus the entry of a new competitor in the southeastern market had been responsible for the dramatic sales drop. At the same time, profits had suffered as well because of the increased expenses from a decision to increase the size of the engineering and financial service departments. The president admitted that his projections had been too optimistic and that something had to be done immediately. The cash flow problem had emerged as the most important pressure in this situation. The budget had to be pared while efforts to increase revenue were intensified.

George studied the figures carefully and agreed reluctantly to both the conclusions and recommendations reached by Logan. The two men took some time to sort through the various options available but it always came back to drastic cuts in personnel. He urged Logan to call a meeting of the executive committee in the morning and provide the data to them with encouragement to diagnose the problem and solutions to it. He argued that any solution must be a product of consensus of the committee.

The meeting caught everybody by surprise as they had accepted the president's projections of growth despite a temporary decline in sales. Two weeks of intensive debate among the executives led to the meeting this morning which defined the exact personnel cuts to be made. It was agreed that twenty-five engineers, fifty production personnel (workers and supervisors), and twenty-five others from various departments would be laid off within the next two weeks. In addition, fifteen new marketing and sales personnel would be added as soon as possible to carry out a new marketing thrust aimed at a different market segment.

There had been heated discussion about the exact number to be laid off and hired, with considerable friction between the vice-presidents of production, engineering, and marketing. The blame for the crisis was shouldered by Logan who asked that the executives recognize that they had to work together to resolve this problem if the future of NDR was to be assured. Wellington as the director of personnel was given the task of coordinating the identification of the people to be laid off although the actual decision would rest in the hands of the three vice-presidents. There were no criteria for the decisions although all agreed that loyal and trusted employees who had been with NDR for a number of years should be released only as a last resort.

The Director's Responsibility

The acrimonious debate of the morning still echoed in George's ears that afternoon. He tore the pages on which he had been writing off the pad and began a new one as he started to determine how the layoffs should be handled. It was a far cry from the exuberance with which he had begun the process of developing a five-year human resource plan just two months ago. Cutbacks in personnel demanded the same precision and careful thought in planning and action as hiring and promotion. There was less excitement about retrenching than growing because it affected the livelihood of so many people.

George jotted down the important questions in three different areas as he mapped out his thinking on this problem.

1. *The Layoffs*
    - Criteria to be used?
    - Data available on employees?
    - Impact of EEO and AA on decisions?
    - Severance pay and benefits?
    - Procedure for layoffs?

2. *The New Hires*
   - Skills needed in marketing and sales?
   - Available resources for positions?
   - Salary and benefit package?
   - Procedure for hiring?
3. *The HRM Plan*
   - Immediate impact on HRM five-year plan?
   - What if only temporary reversal of growth trend? (Commitments to rehire or not?)
   - Impact on employee morale now and in future?

George recognized that he had a lot of work to do. He struggled to regain his sense of professionalism as he began to detail the options available to each of the questions. His days as a consultant and manager had given him little experience in the arena of layoffs. But Logan had given him the responsibility and he knew that the future of NDR would depend heavily on how it handled this crisis.

2. Deft Research and Development, Inc.*

Karl Rhodes sat back in his chair. On his desk was a short memo from DR&D's new President, Glenn Richards, announcing the upcoming Management Committee meeting of all the DR&D Vice-Presidents and the President to discuss the future plans for the Personnel function.

Rhodes beamed as he looked at the green countryside outside his corner office. It he stood, he knew that the President's office would come into view, a mere 400 yards down the quiet country road that crossed the rural setting which DEFT had chosen ten years ago as the ideal site for its R & D facility.

A look of great anticipation washed over his face as he thought about Personnel's role in helping the company plan and carry out its ambitious strategic plans for the 1980s. He reached for the phone and began dialing. In a few seconds he would have the President of DR&D on the line.

The time is now.

Background

DR&D is a high-technology subsidiary of a large multinational corporation (DEFT Co.). As the research and development arm of the total corporation, it employs some 3,000 scientists and engineers.

---

*A human resource management teaching case prepared by Charles Fombrun, Noel Tichy, and Mary-Anne Devanna for use in class discussion rather than to illustrate either effective or ineffective handling of a particular situation. Names were changed to protect confidentiality.

Personnel, the department of DR&D in charge of employee matters, is headed by a manager who oversees some fifty professionals with functional managers of Recruitment, Labor Relations, Compensation and Benefits, Manpower Planning, Affirmative Action, and Training and Development. Exhibit 1 diagrams the formal structure of Personnel and its reporting line in DR&D.

The founding of the Personnel Department is attributed to Robert McKinnon, a very creative and controversial scientist employed by the former Consolidated Development Company. While holding a high-level position within the organization, McKinnon began building the personnel function in the mid- to late-1930s. This signified forward thinking for its time, reflecting McKinnon's paternalistic orientation toward the function. At the same time that this HR function was developing, DR&D was becoming the first major industrial research company.

During the 1940s and 50s innovative employee relations policies and programs were developed, which at the time were considered to be at the cutting edge of personnel management.

With the creation of scientific personnel salary scales and a maturity curve system, technical employees could now climb the rungs of a dual

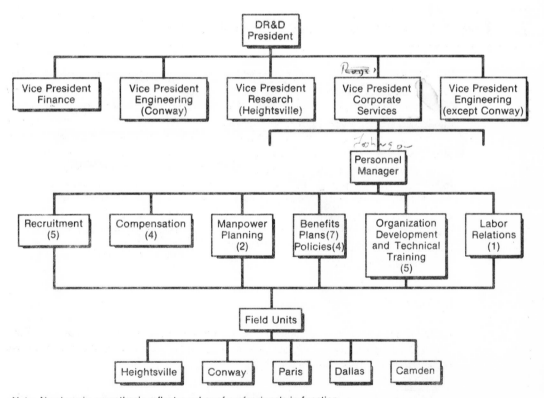

Note: Numbers in parenthesis reflect number of professionals in function.

Exhibit 1. Formal Structure, Personnel Department of DR&D

career/recognition ladder. New and rewarding opportunities became available to them; talented scientists were able to get recognition without becoming managers themselves. This allowed DR&D to attract and retain top individuals within their fields. Textbooks were written about the DEFT system by former personnel employees.

Throughout most of the innovative period and/or through the '60s, Lyle Johnson served as the manager of HR. He ran a dynamic, "hard hitting" department, continually producing innovative employee policies and programs. Organization Development (OD) was the key practice of the Johnson era. "All of the big names in the field either worked or consulted there." In fact, only TRW was doing as much in OD as DR&D at the time.

Although Johnson and his staff were energetic and dedicated, they were also unpredictable and unconventional. Johnson's image was far from professional: he was said to call staff meetings by the blow of a whistle as he paced the corridors, occasionally wearing his volunteer fireman's uniform or his hunting outfit from a weekend camping trip. There were a number of internal political controversies towards the end of his tenure which ultimately contributed to his decision to leave in 1965. Apparently Personnel, as a function, both prospered and suffered under Johnson's leadership.

The late '60s served as a transition phase for the Personnel Department. Alan Boyden followed Johnson as acting Personnel Manager for the next one and a half years. Boyden lost a number of good professionals from Johnson's staff and the personnel function was forced to adjust to a new and very different image and style.

Two critical events followed Johnson's departure. First, all four members of the Personnel Department's OD function left DR&D to form a consulting company (commonly referred to as the "Brown-Frasca split-out"). The OD function was not rebuilt. As a result, division heads at DR&D expected to carry on with OD efforts on their own or with the help of outside consultants. Everyone felt that the dissolution of OD was a disaster for Personnel. Most thought that OD in the hands of line managers would spell "chaos."

The other critical event that followed Johnson's departure was the decentralization of the Personnel Department. Field units were created in the late '60s to provide employee services on site instead of relying on a single corporate staff. Corporate staff had mixed feelings about the decentralization, complaining mostly of a loss of control and dysfunctional relationships with field units. However, Personnel staff in the field units, as well as technical employees, felt that Personnel could respond better to employee and line management needs by the creation of the field units.

Matt Dembinsky was named Manager of Personnel in 1967 and stayed until his retirement in 1977. Characterized as "competent and nice," Dembinsky led the department through a series of budget cutbacks, reduced resources, and other recessive measures.

After a rare layoff of DR&D in 1972, manpower needs increased sharply in 1973. This demand together with the advent of additional federal legislation (EEO, Affirmative Action, ERISA) increased hiring in Personnel.

At the same time, Personnel corporate staff moved from Conway to Heightsville, closer to the main research site of DR&D.

Personnel Today

Karl Rhodes became Manager of Personnel in January of 1978, eight months after the arrival of DR&D's new President, Glenn Richards. The transition from Dembinsky to Rhodes was characterized as "smooth and well-managed," partially due to four months of overlap by the managers. The impact of the change was, however, enormous. With Rhodes came a new definition of the role of Personnel—from a reactive, maintenance role to a proactive, growing, and fast-paced one.

During Rhodes' first few months as Personnel Manager, several significant events occurred. Many of these events have been interpreted as being indicative of Personnel's future role in the company.

- Reopening of the Organization Development unit; Ray Wiggins returns to head the function, Wiggins having been on the OD staff in DR&D at the time of the Brown-Frasca split-out.
- Bob Kopcke transferred into Personnel to renew activity in EEO and to start a Manpower Planning Area.
- Establishment of new Personnel field units on site in Paris, Dallas, and Camden.
- Expansion of the Personnel staff.
- Budgets increased, producing a marked contrast when comparing ability to operate today to the cost control of the previous ten years which precluded anything but maintenance of established programs.
- New compensation and performance appraisal systems introduced (DEFT Company policy changes).

Consultants Called In

Aware of difficulties he would face in turning the function around, Karl Rhodes sought guidance from a team of consultants with expertise in human resource management. At their request, Rhodes called an exploratory meeting between the consultants and the eleven administrators of Personnel (see Exhibit 1).

As the meeting progressed, it became clear to the consultants that the administrators had different visions of Personnel's role in DR&D, and the direction it should go in. To explore the differences, they used a round-robin nominal group technique to generate a list of goals for the department. When the tally was done, the only clearly agreed-upon goal for the department was stated by Rhodes as:

> Have the Personnel Department become (and be perceived as) an influential force in the management of human resources at DR&D.

The Administrator's Viewpoint

The consultants talked with a few of the administrators. Although Karl Rhodes seemed widely respected, a few other comments were made:

Rhodes, hell, he's still on his way up in DEFT. He'll relate well to the Management Committee since he's tied in so well, but I'm worried that he will be looking for a promotion before he is completed here and leave us cold.

How much he has our interest at hand, I don't know. He wants change and more influence for the department which may end up just making our life a little more difficult. He's quite political, but also a very knowledgeable and expert personnel manager.

Some were distressed at the changes taking place. One administrator captured a common feeling when he said:

I can't assimilate the changes fast enough. Never mind new ideas—let's try to catch up with last week's plans. There is an incredible work-load—good for the most part, but also a lot of pressure.

The consultants explored further the different Personnel goals and strategies that had been put forth at the exploratory meeting.

Fred Perella, in charge of Training, saw Personnel as a service department.

Our job is to implement programs which come through the system and to provide advice to line management on the spectrum of Personnel topics.

Maurice Flint, Administrator of Labor Relations, saw Personnel's role as primarily a question of negotiating a good contract. "As long as I keep the big unions out of DR&D, then I'm doing a good job."

Field Unit Personnel Staff

Two field units had existed when Rhodes arrived: at Conway, on site with the refinery, and the major field unit at Heightsville (down the road) where most of DR&D's research was done.

Soon after his arrival, Rhodes started three new field unit operations in Paris, Dallas, and Camden, with one or two professionals in each.

Exhibit 2. Personnel's Mission Statement

Personnel Department's overall role is stated as follows:

The Personnel Department advises and assists line management in the effective recruitment, development, utilization, and motivation of human resources needed to achieve Company objectives.

Discharge of this responsibility requires an understanding of the immediate and long-range goals of the organization and the effects of the internal and external environment on the attainment of these goals. Within this framework, the Personnel Department will develop policies, programs, and plans to create an environment which will optimize employee motivation.

In order to advise and assist line management on the best means of utilizing human resources, the Personnel Department must be knowledgeable of the line organization's business plans and objectives, and develop human resource strategies in support of them.

The Heightsville field unit had a staff of twelve professionals and ten support personnel. Ricky Maier was the Personnel Administrator of Heightsville, reporting to Rhodes.

In conversations with corporate administrators, the consultants discerned some problems in the relationship with field units, especially Heightsville.

> Field units act like we don't exist. They want complete control. Rhodes tells me I'm in charge of compensation for all of DR&D, but the next thing I hear is Maier making unilateral promises to his line managers in engineering that are 10 percent or 20 percent above DEFT guidelines.

> Maier runs a one-man show down there. But Karl's not going to put up with it. The problem is he wanted Rhodes' job and was pretty disappointed when he didn't get it. Turns out Maier had worked for Rhodes ten years back in Dallas. Back then he was Rhodes' fair-haired boy. Now he wants to show off to daddy, so to speak.

Jerry Hall, head of Recruitment, thought Personnel's most vital function was to make sure the company got the best people it could. "DR&D's only resource is its people. So we'd better make damned sure it's got the best."

The consultants spoke with Karl Rhodes in his office. As they began discussing the role of Personnel, Rhodes reached into a drawer and pulled out a sheet of paper. "It's all here." Exhibit 2 presents the formal mission statement Rhodes had developed and was about to distribute through the department.

Corporate Personnel Jobs

In talking with the different administrators and other employees, it was clear that the jobs in Personnel were varied. Administrators coordinated the jobs of professionals under them, and had support staff to assist with clerical work.

Most of the administrators did not shy away from actually doing the grunt work in the department. At peak periods, they pitched in. Some professionals even thought they did too much.

One young professional, who had recently joined the Organizational Development group, blamed the older professionals for not wanting to change.

> A number of people here are POPO's (Pissed On and Passed Over). They have nowhere to go. It would be great if we could just get rid of them, but of course it's not the DEFT way. So we have to carry the driftwood right along with us.

Each function had its own schedules, with peak periods that varied throughout the year. Recruitment, for instance, faced its heaviest activity from June to September. August and September were especially hectic in running training sessions for all the recruiters drawn from DR&D (about 100 volunteers for one week each year). Throughout October they were out on the road, interviewing potential DR&D recruits across North American campuses.

Support staff seemed somewhat alienated from the professionals. When asked to comment on some of the recent events in Personnel, one secretary responded:

> I haven't the faintest idea what they're up to. They just put me in recruiting and told me to type my letters.

Human Resource Audit

In order to more systematically assess the internal dynamics and the effectiveness of the Personnel Department *vis à vis* its clients and users, the consultants undertook a comprehensive HRMA.[1] The HRMA is designed on the premise that all organizations have a range of service needs in the human resource area. The audit, therefore, takes an overall organizational perspective, focusing on the human resource function as a service unit in the organization, delivering these services to an internal market place of client users. Exhibit 3 depicts the outlook that guides the HRMA.

At the core of the model is the human resource strategy of the organization which guides the kind of human resource function that is created. The human resource strategy stems from and intersects with other elements of the corporate strategy of the organization.

The human resource or personnel function is depicted as an organization in its own right. Tasks have to be done (selection, training, compensation), people are hired to do them, placed in a structure, make decisions, get into conflict, build their own networks. The result is a distinct package of services that are provided to the clients. These clients in turn evaluate them and provide a mechanism for assessing their performance. Presumably, the more "compatible" (or the higher the "fit" between them) the people, task, structures, and processes are, the more effective the human resource organization is likely to be in servicing its clients.

The HRMA uses this framework to try to answer such questions as:

1. Is the personnel organization's mission and strategy designed in keeping with its environment—both its external environment and its internal markets?
2. Does the design of the human resource organization enhance its ability to accomplish the strategy?
3. Are the kinds of people in the human resource function good choices for the ongoing tasks, structures, and processes?

Data Collection.   The data collection involved three distinct steps. The first was an assessment of the human resource organization. Data were collected using interviews, questionnaires, documents, and observation.

The second step consisted of surveying the clients of the human resource function. Questionnaires were used to assess areas of agreement and disagreement over work priorities, activities, and the role of the human resource function in the larger organization. Finally, the third step consisted of interviewing upper line management around issues related to the personnel strategy of the whole organization, and perceptions of the personnel organization's role.

Vice-Presidents' Viewpoint

As part of the HRMA, the Vice-Presidents of DR&D were interviewed by the consultants. Questions were asked that dealt with five areas: Personnel's mission in DR&D, appropriate activities for it to pursue, how Personnel's performance

---

1. Human Resource Management Audit. See M.A. Devanna, C. Fombrun, N. Tichy, "Human Resource Management: A Strategic Approach," *Organizational Dynamics,* 1981, *9,* no. 1.

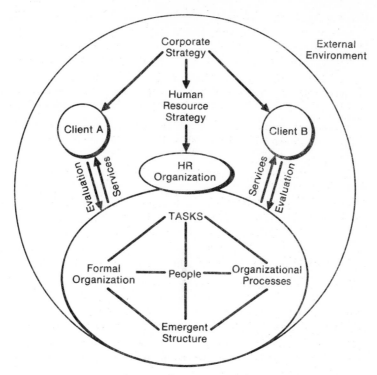

Description of Components

Corporate Strategy: This includes the organization's reason for being, its basic approach to carrying out its mission, its strategy, and its criteria for effectiveness.

Tasks: This refers to the technology by which the organization's work is accomplished.

People: This includes the characteristics of the manners of the organization, background, motivational patterns, managerial style, etc.

Emergent Structure: These are the structures and processes which inevitably emerge in the organiza-

tion and link together individuals and groups.

Formal Organization: This refers to the explicitly designed social structure of the organization. It includes the organization of subunits, communication, and authority networks as well as structural mechanism for integrating the organization.

Organizational Processes: These are the mechanisms (communication, decision-making, conflict management, control, and reward) which enable the organization to carry out the dynamics of work.

Exhibit 3.   The Human Resource Audit

should be evaluated, its strengths and weaknesses as an organization, and the Vice-Presidents' overall impression of Personnel.

The consultants were surprised at the diversity of the responses from the five Vice-Presidents. Exhibit 4 summarizes the results of the interviews.

The Vice-Presidents were asked what criteria should be used to evaluate Personnel's performance. The responses covered a wide range. One Vice-President felt the same criteria used to evaluate DR&D's performance should be used to evaluate Personnel—productivity, creativity, and cost effectiveness. Another implicitly rule out creativity when he stated the criterion should be "How well do they perform delegated tasks." Two Vice-Presidents suggested that the

Exhibit 4. Summary of Vice-Presidents' Perceptions of Personnel

PERSONNEL'S MISSION

DR&D Vice-Presidents were asked to read Personnel's role statement (see Exhibit 2) and comment on its appropriateness. Two of the five Vice-Presidents interviewed said that the role statement reflected their beliefs about what Personnel should be doing and stated that a Personnel unit operating with that role statement could effectively meet their needs. One Vice-President felt it did not reflect his beliefs and would not meet his needs. Two Vice-Presidents did not respond to the scaled question because they felt there was some ambiguity in the role statement. They commented, "The basic problem is that they think they have major charter but they are fighting a 'no win' battle unless Glenn supports it." "Are they servants or are they going to lead? Glenn will resolve it."

PERSONNEL ACTIVITIES

The Vice-Presidents were asked to evaluate the appropriateness of twelve activities Personnel is pursuing over the next year. Four of the five Vice-Presidents responded to the scaled questions. Of the twelve activities, only four considered appropriate by *all* respondents. These were:

- Bring about an ongoing salary communications program tied to orientation of new employees and training of new managers/section heads.
- Conduct studies assessing impact of the Ossipee move on DR&D work force.
- Help DR&D management make effective use of human resources, and have employees believe this is true.
- Establish and actively maintain an effective relationship between management and the bargaining agencies representing company employees.

One was viewed as inappropriate by all four Vice-Presidents:

- Redesign starting level and early career assignments in a manner to make them attractive and challenging for DR&D employees.

The seven remaining activities reflected a lack of consensus on the part of the Vice-Presidents.

---

information or advice Personnel provides to management is the critical factor—"should give us advice on salary levels of scientists." ". . . how promptly they give us advice and how quickly they can do a study to support it." One stated that his criterion for evaluating Personnel's performance was "Do they make my life easier."

The Vice-Presidents were asked about the strengths and weaknesses of Personnel. Some of the items viewed as strengths by some were thought by other to be weaknesses, reinforcing the pattern of "mixed messages" from the Vice-Presidents.

The underlying differences in the pattern of responses is reflected in the comments made by the Vice-Presidents when they were asked their overall impression of Personnel. For some the impression is basically negative as borne out by the following responses: "They don't stand out—arrive at 8:30 and leave at 4:30." "They haven't won our confidence—(they) don't always do their homework." This contrasts with one Vice-President who stated, "Overall, I would give them a 4 on a 5-point scale." Another said "I think they are quite good but they are hampered by the fact that they frequently do not get the support they need—especially from the Managerial Board."

Exhibit 5. Summary of Audit for Components of Model

Component	Summary Diagnosis
Environment	Quite complex and changing, multiple markets with need for multiple services.
Mission/Strategy	Formally written mission quite organic, not fully understood or agreed to by many staff and not seen as accurate by many clients and users. Strategy same as mission.
Tasks	OK at the operational level (mechanistic and appropriate). At the managerial and strategic levels not well developed.
Prescribed Organization	Generally mechanistic, reliance on simple integrating mechanisms. Some medium-range integrating mechanisms but no complex ones.
People	Technically competent at the operational level (with a few exceptions); motivational needs not well matched with organizational rewards, especially career mobility. Lack strategic orientation.
Emergent Networks	Non task-related; very separated by professional vs. support; few participants.
Processes	Conflict OK, communication around goals needs to be improved, rewards need to be changed, control needs to be upgraded.

Summary of Audit Results

The consultants summarized their findings from the HRMA in Exhibit 5.

The consultants had shared these reports with Karl Rhodes and his administrators and were now ready to propose an action strategy for Karl and his Personnel Department.

A Surprise Telephone Call

Eager to discuss the results of the audit with Rhodes, the consultants headed straight for his office. As they entered they found him pacing back and forth, an angry frown on his face.

> How the hell are we going to have an effective strategic role with the Management Committee if we can't even get this shop running right. You know what just happened? That idiot Maier just quit on us, now that we need him in Heightsville! I should have listened to everyone and fired him a long time ago.

The consultants sat down. It was going to be a long meeting.

3. The National Insurance Company*

Jerry Taylor has been involved with the administrative functions of the National Insurance Company for almost twenty years. About three months ago, Jerry was appointed group manager of the Policyholder Service and Accounting Departments at the home office. Before he actually assumed the job, Jerry was able to get away for a three-week management development program at the State University College of Business. One of the topics covered in the program was the concept of job enrichment, or job redesign. Jerry had read about job enrichment in several of his trade journals, but the program was his first opportunity to think about the concept in some detail. In addition, several of the program participants had had some experience (both positive and negative) with job redesign projects.

Jerry was intrigued with the idea. He knew how boring routine administrative tasks could become, and he knew from his previous supervisory work that turnover of clerical personnel was a real problem. In addition, his conversations with the administrative vice-president and Joe Bellows, the personnel manager, led him to believe that some trials and redesigning the work would be supported and favorably regarded.

Description of the Work

Group Policyholder Service Department

The principal activities undertaken in this department are the sorting and opening of incoming mail and then matching to accounting files; reviewing of group insurance bills from policyholders; and coding required changes to policies (e.g., new employees and terminations). These activities are carried out by approximately twenty-eight people; 53 percent of them are over age thirty-five, 82 percent female, 89 percent high school graduates, and 53 percent have less than two years' experience in their current job.

Organizationally, the department is headed by a manager. The employees are grouped into the four functional categories of clerical support, senior technician, change coder, and special clerk. The general work flow and a more specific list of the tasks carried out within each functional category are shown in Exhibit 1.

The Group Policyholder Service Department shares the same physical working area as the Accounting Department. The people within Policyholder Service who work in the different functional categories are in very close proximity to one another, frequently just one desk away. The files for the department are located at one corner of the work area and the supervisors have offices along one side (see Exhibit 2).

*This case and the analysis are adapted (with permission) from Antone F. Alber, *An Exploratory Study of the Benefits and Costs of Job Enrichment,* Ph.D. dissertation, The Pennsylvania State University, 1977. Several figures are reproduced directly, and major portions of the text are quoted directly. The case was written in conjunction with Henry P. Sims, Jr., and Andrew D. Szilagyi, Jr.

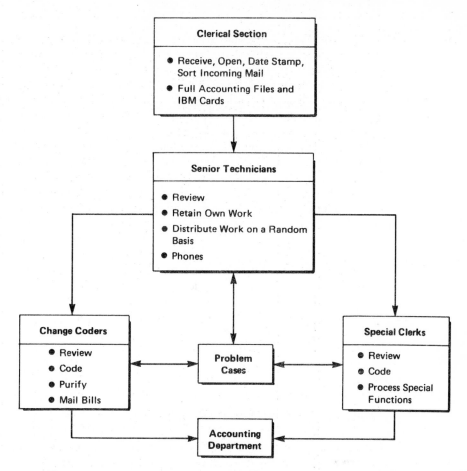

Exhibit 1. Policyholder Service Department Work Flow and Tasks

In the last few months, Jerry has observed that the functional breakdown and the accompanying physical arrangement of people and files lead to a number of problems. Since work is assigned or selected on a random basis, there is no personal accountability for it. Files are at one corner of the work area where they can be retrieved by the clerical group and distributed to a senior technician who randomly distributes them to be processed. After a file is coded, it is placed in a holding area for processing by the Accounting Department. Here, assignment of work is also done on a random basis. It is difficult to respond to phone calls or written requests for information promptly, because it is frequently difficult to find a file. In fact, several people are kept busy doing nothing but looking for files.

The typical employee performs a job which consists of two tasks on approximately an eleven-minute cycle. All work is cross-checked. The training for the job is minimal and there are a number of individuals performing the same set of tasks on files randomly issued. A clerk occasionally corresponds with a policyholder, but all correspondence goes out with the manager's signature on it. The manager thus receives all phone calls and correspondence from policyholders.

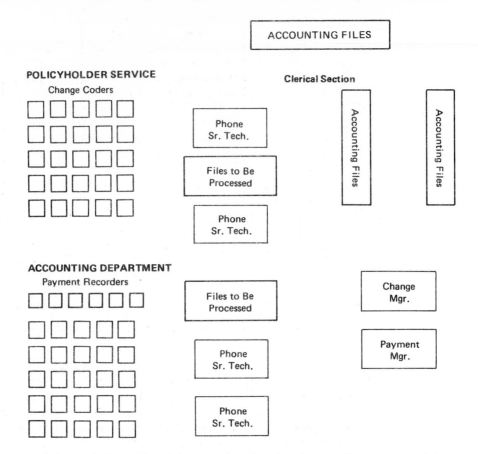

Indicates relative positions and not actual number of employees or floor space occupied.

Exhibit 2. Policyholder Service Department
and Accounting Department Physical Layout

Because of the random distribution of work, individual performance is difficult to measure. There are spot checks on some completed work by someone other than the doer, but it is difficult or impossible to determine the specific individual who was responsible. Consequently, it is not possible to provide specific information to individuals at regular intervals about their work performance.

Accounting Department

The Accounting Department processes the files, bills, and checks received from the Group Policyholder Service. Premiums are posted on IBM cards and worksheets. Necessary adjustments are made to accounts and the checks, cards, and worksheets are balanced. Approximately twenty-eight people are employed

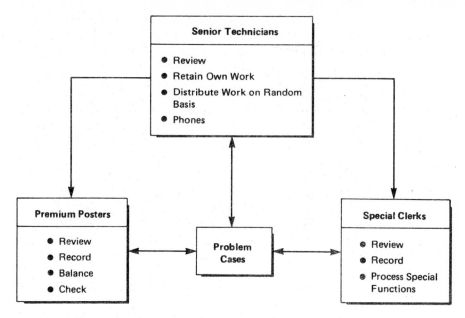

EXHIBIT 3. Accounting Department Work Flow and Tasks

at any one time performing these tasks. Seventy-seven percent of the work force are under thirty-five years of age. Everyone has at least a high school degree and 54 percent have less than two years' experience in the job they were performing.

The department has both a manager and a supervisor. The employees are divided into senior technicians, premium posters, and special clerks. The general work flow and tasks carried out in each of these functional areas are shown in Exhibit 3. As shown in Exhibit 2, the Accounting Department shares its work and files with Policyholder Service.

Work is selected on a random basis. Clerks go to a bookcase file and choose the cases they wish to do. Occasionally, correspondence with a policyholder is necessary, and is signed by the manager.

The Problem of Change

Jerry believes that if the work in his department can be *properly* redesigned, then departmental effectiveness can be improved. In addition, he believes that substantial improvements can be made in terms of individual employee work satisfaction.

In thinking about redesigning the work, Jerry has separated the problem into two parts. First, he is concerned about the *process* of change. How can he best accomplish a job redesign project? Second, Jerry has been concerned with the arrangement of the tasks themselves. Before he begins such a project, Jerry hopes to have at least some preliminary ideas about the feasibility of such a change.

Let's help Jerry out.

First, *as an individual,* how would you actually redesign the work in Jerry's department?

_____

_____

_____

_____

_____

_____

Second, *as a group,* how would you redesign the work in Jerry's department?

_____

_____

_____

_____

_____

_____

4. Human Resource Information Systems at World Wide Utilities*

Substantial advances in human resource planning and development systems have been critically dependent on the generation and maintenance of useful data or information. This data information base and the systems it supports are far different from those developed for functional usage or analysis in the past. However, as these systems have emerged, oftentimes too little attention has been directed towards their design to meet both current and future organizational needs. We have found it highly instructive to study a number of these systems, and frequently as much is to be learned from the successes as from the failures. The World Wide Utilities situation provides a good illustration of the problems encountered in letting a system evolve with insufficient focusing.

Development at World Wide Utilities

World Wide Utilities just completed its twentieth year of operation and fifth year of very profitable performance. Organized to capitalize on the new communications opportunities offered by satellites, skillful management guided the company into a number of profitable business undertakings. Their services

---

*Elmer H. Burack, Ph.D., A.P.D., Professor of Management and former Head of the Management Department, University of Illinois at Chicago.

included private communications networks between Europe and the United States via satellite and special communications systems to service remote locations. World Wide's organization grew rapidly and included more than 3,000 people of whom many were professionals. Some 30 percent were engineers, scientists, and systems specialists. World Wide's newest "brainchild" was an employee career program built around the motto, "There's a Career for You at World Wide Utilities."

The new career program was not altogether altruistic—in fact, a few skeptics said it was really self-serving. Attracting and retaining capable people was difficult. The job often required extensive travel to sometimes remote locations. Good employees were hard to find and keep, despite an attractive pay program with a special bonus for overseas or remote duty. The company hoped to find an answer to these personnel problems with its new career program. It was felt that a career program tuned to the ideals of the day—the desire of young people for the opportunity to achieve and to move into challenging assignments—would successfully meet the challenge of finding and keeping capable people. The career program contained three main features:

1. A joining of overall corporate business planning and human resource planning.
2. An individualized approach to career planning based on personal desires, abilities, and opportunities.
3. A skill bank to be used in conjunction with the computer system to facilitate the match of individual desires and abilities with business opportunities and needs.

The Vice-President of Personnel and Human Resources, Tim Adams, dropped by the office of his friend Serge Baranski who was in charge of engineering for World Wide. Adams told him that now that the career program was finally put together, he was starting to wonder if it would really do as much as they had expected. His friend's response was, "We've got to make some kind of a move, Tim—we're getting a regular parade of new employees through my division and it seems we can't hold onto them long enough to even get to know them."

Human Resource Planning and Careers

The career planning approach proposed by Tim Adams was intended to integrate directly into World Wide's corporate planning program (Exhibit 1). Organization goals and priorities reflected long-range business and economic developments, new technological changes, market shifts, new product developments, and competitive moves. These general *demand* factors were further modified on the basis of forecasts of environmental trends concerning government policy and legislation, productivity, and union developments.

However, organization goals and priorities were also affected by World Wide's ability to *supply* needed human resources—sufficient numbers properly trained and at the right time. Consequently, the organization had to take into account currently available personnel, their abilities and growth potential,

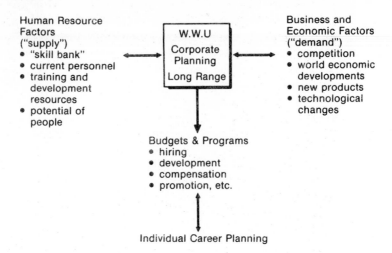

EXHIBIT 1. Overview, Corporate and Career Planning System

training and development capabilities (often considering remote locations), loss of key people, mobility of people, personal career priorities, and attitude towards work. The joint resolution of the supply and demand factors described then became the basis for company budgets and programs in such areas as recruiting, compensation, promotion, and individual development. Individual career plans were to play a specific role in the program design to meet corporate needs. In situations of specialized or critical talents required by certain prospective undertakings, the lack of the abilities might force a change in corporate plans. Where the particular form of business developments did not permit full accommodation of individual preferences, revised programs were to be developed with the individuals involved. Exhibit 2 illustrates the connection between individual career interest, job openings, and the Personnel (Human Resource) Information System planned. Personal data supplied by individuals about their interests and ambitions for the future became a key part of the career planning approach.

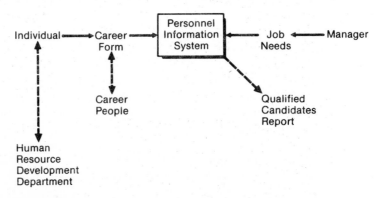

EXHIBIT 2. Career Opportunity System and the Personnel Information System

The following section outlines key features of the personnel career data that were to become a central part of the career planning system.

Personnel Career Data

A major goal of the World Wide career program was that it was to become a key part of its recruiting and internal efforts. Main objectives were:

- Facilitate a policy of internal promotion.
- Provide explicit recognition of individual capabilities and interests.
- Accommodate individual career interest when possible.
- Provide opportunities for individual movement to positions where development was possible.
- Permit regular review of individual abilities and desires in conjunction with business needs.
- Determine which work assignments made best use of individual abilities.
- Better meet Equal Employment Opportunity needs.

The career data forms that were to be provided to individuals contained seven major sections plus supporting code information for the computer system. Wherever possible, standardized codes were to be used for work experience, work preferences, and so forth, in order to facilitate processing of information. Aside from basic personal information such as name, social security number, and job starting date, major data sections were designed to bring out important skills, abilities, and preferences of the individual. These major data sections include:

- *Section 1—Previous Employment:* A summary listing of former employers, employment dates, job titles, and a few words describing main responsibilities.
- *Section 2—Education:* Degrees received, school year, and dates.
- *Section 3—Military Experience:* Experience, military schools, rank at discharge, dates.
- *Section 4—Company Experience:* Record of skills gained in company employment. Here each major skill was listed (by code number), years of experience in area were recorded, and last date of work was noted. An example of this section is provided in Exhibit 3 for assistant department head in the marketing division.
- *Section 5—Job Expertise:* Occupational and work specialties in which the individual would feel highly qualified are identified (up to four are to be selected). See Exhibit 4. The individual would rate each one on (a) specialist knowledge and (b) level of responsibility currently achievable.
- *Section 6—Training and Development:* Individual lists job-related courses, programs, and various self-improvement activities. Each entry shows activity, the year it was done, and the length of the course (hours, days, or weeks).
- *Section 7—Supplementary Information:* Applicants are asked to supply all additional information that would provide insight into an individual's personality, interests, capabilities, or desire to move ahead.

EXHIBIT 3. Company Experience, Section 4

Experience Area	Description	Skill*	Year(s)	Last Year	Individual Preferences
Sales-marketing	Market analysis	SM	1	'69	Second Choice
	New product planning	SM	1	'71	
	Sales forecasting	SM	2	'75	
	Model building	SM	2	'72	
	Product pricing	SM	1	'71	
	Technological forecasting	SM	3	'79	
	Price analysis	SM	1	'70	
Management and administration	Marketing management	MA		'76	First Choice
	Financial planning	MA		'68	
	Project leadership	MA		'82	
	Business administration	MA		'68	Third Choice
Technical	Control systems	TEE	2	'66	
	High voltage distribution	TEE	1	'65	
	Telemetry	TEE	2	'65	
Other experience, abilities	Teacher	P 20	3	'62	
	Flying	P 20	12		Current
Professional licenses	Institute for Electronic and Electrical Engineers	PM 22	10		Current
Professional memberships	American Management Association	PM 156	10		Current
	American Marketing Association	PM 170	5		Current
Area, location preference (foreign?)	Europe,	ALP 100			Current
	Middle East,	ALP 300			Current
	Japan	ALP 800			Will consider

*Refers to specific technical competencies detailed in company documents, a book of 20 pages.

Exhibit 4.   Major Areas of Individual Ability and Expertise, Section 5

Job Area	Priority	Level of Ability*	Responsibility†
Marketing management	1	2	A
New product planning	2	1	S
Business administration	3	3	M

*Ability level: 1 = expert; 2 = very good; 3 = working knowledge.
†Responsibility level: S = specialist; M = managerial; A = administrative.

Keeping the Information File Current

Keeping the information file current was recognized as a major design problem for the career system. Adams felt that information would have to be updated annually through the submission of "annual update" cards by employees. The responsibility for data submission was to be that of the employee—they were to judge whether new items should be added to their file. Each professional employee was to receive a card automatically at the end of each year for update purposes, regardless of location.

5.   R.F. Insurance*

In 1984, as an assigned project, three graduate students from a Behavioral Factors course decided to assess job design, career development, and job motivation in a district office of R.F. Insurance. Initially, the District Office Manager received the team enthusiastically, confident the team would produce a favorable, if not glowing, report. Contrary to expectations, problems arose immediately after the team's first visit to the district office.

Corporate History

R.F. Insurance, an aggressive carrier, handles only commercial risks, primarily in worker's compensation, fire, commercial automobile, general liability, crime cover, and umbrella coverage for medium to large companies. The current strategy is growth, trading off a reduced profit margin for increased sales volume by offering deep discounts to businesses with a large dividend to policyholders.

Coverage policies are solicited and written by the corporate sales force, but a large number of policies are also placed by brokerage firms. The firm is licensed in thirty-four states with its core operations on the East Coast.

*Sue Greenfeld, University of Baltimore. Reprinted with permission.

District Office Operation

The district office is located on the second floor of an office complex in a suburban shopping center. In personnel it is typical of most district offices for R.F. Insurance, and contains one District Office Manager, a sales force of twelve, five claims adjustors, one loss prevention engineer, one account executive, and eight clerical workers. The District Office Manager reports directly to the Regional Headquarters. While the sales forces are physically located in the district office, they do not report directly to the District Office Manager. The claims adjustors and the clerical staff do, however, have a direct reporting relationship to the District Office Manager (Exhibit 1).

The office operation seems to involve three basic groups: the sales force, the claims adjustors, and the clerical staff. In addition, there is a Loss Prevention engineer who visits clients, helps them ensure safe work practices, and who evaluates the riskiness of the potential client.

The first group, the sales force, uses the information obtained by the Loss Prevention engineer. The salesperson draws up an appropriate policy based on the applicant's needs, reviews it, and completes the sale. The account then becomes serviced by the district office. At this point, the sales force is no longer involved with the account.

The District Office Manager evaluates the policy in terms of type, size, and complexity, and assigns the account to a claims adjustor, one of the second group in the office. This assignment is based upon the Manager's evaluation of the account and upon the experience and capabilities of the adjustor. The assigned claims adjustor delivers a claims kit, i.e., reports and forms needed to file a claim, to the insured. This account is now the responsibility of the claims adjustor until the account is dropped or cancelled. The claims adjustor handles all inquiries, complaints, and service requests. He or she also investigates, evaluates, and concludes account claims for payment, in essence handling the entire account after the sale.

The third group, the clerical staff, consists of seven clerks and one lead clerk. Each clerk has a special set of jobs such as medical payments or sales. At the end of each day, the clerks turn in a daily work sheet to the lead clerk. On Fridays, the lead clerk compiles a time standards report from this work sheet. At the time of the team's investigation, this office reported over 100 percent productive in clerical work time standards. The clerical staff are required to do all the typing and filing in the district office. They are not responsible for the work of any particular account or of any particular person and see very little of the entire task.

Layout of the District Office

The layout of the local office (Exhibit 2) is straightforward. Individual offices for various functions surround a larger room with desks. In this inner area, all the clerks perform their work. The clerks' desks are arranged in two rows. The office has very little in the way of extras. The team described their first impression of the office as "antiseptic, bland, and stark . . . a typical no frills business office . . . well kept and organized, uncluttered and generally a functionally adequate facility." The waiting room has no receptionist to greet any potential visitors.

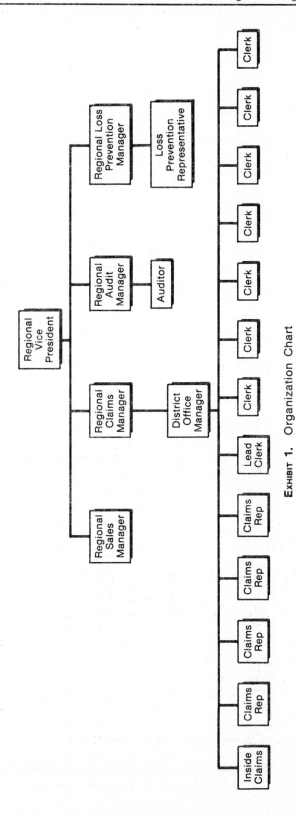

Exhibit 1. Organization Chart

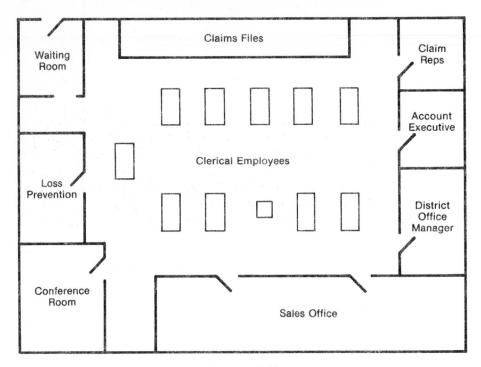

EXHIBIT 2. Present Office Layout

Team Analysis Begins

While very receptive to the project, the District Office Manager also wanted enormous control and veto power over the student surveys. Ideally, both questionnaires and interviews were to be used. Further discussions limited the team to questionnaires only, which included a modification of the Job Characteristics Inventory, and a twenty-four question survey designed by the team. The District Office Manager immediately expressed concern over the modified Job Characteristics Inventory and allowed no one of the clerical staff to take this questionnaire. Of the twenty-four questions composed by the team, the District Office Manager vetoed the following six questions for use in the study:

  6. I have a great deal of say over what changes are made in my work place.
  7. I have a great deal of freedom to run my own job.
12. People who get ahead in this part of the company deserve it.
13. In this part of the company, getting ahead is based on ability.
17. I really expected to make more job progress than I have up to now.
18. I feel I deserve to have been promoted higher by now.

The team felt quite discouraged by the actions of the District Manager who also distributed the research instruments. In total, five sales personnel and four claims adjustors completed both the modified Job Characteristics Inventory and the team-designed questionnaire (minus the six vetoed questions). Only three of the eight clerical workers completed the survey they were given.

Results

The limited number of respondents made analysis very difficult but, as expected, the nine professionals consistently reported more positive replies (better job development, better utilization, more influence, more advancement, more career progress, and better work group relations) than did the three responding clerks. Inferences would have to be made about the five remaining clerks.

The nine professionals also reported very positively on the modified Job Characteristics Inventory in the following rank order: Autonomy, Feedback, Task Significance, Task Variety, and Task Identity. Only in the case of "this job is arranged so that I have the chance to do a job from the beginning to the end (i.e., a chance to do the whole job)" were the respondents less positive, but even there most felt the statement was slightly true. As mentioned previously, the clerical staff were not allowed to fill out this instrument.

Part II

Staffing and Equal Employment Considerations

Cases Outline

- Reliable Insurance Company
- Compusystems Job Search
- The Office (A) (B) (C)
- Promotion to Police Sergeant
- A Case of Black and White
- "Perfectly Pure Peabody's"
- Peoples Trust Company
- Sunday at Al Tech

6. Reliable Insurance Company*

Company Background

Reliable Insurance Company is a management firm that provides businesses and individuals with insurance for unique and often unprecedented risks. Gross premiums written have increased from $325,000,000 in 1980 to nearly $775,000,000 in 1985.

A diversified facility of insurance professionals, Reliable was formed in 1956. A 1975 acquisition of the Diamond Insurance Group, Reliable is headquartered in San Francisco, California (Exhibit 1). As a management agent, Reliable provides all of the staffing and oversees the activities of two insurance companies titled Bay State and Ace Company.

In order to achieve a high degree of responsiveness to the needs of clients' concerns, branch offices are located in six major United States cities including Atlanta, Boston, Chicago, Los Angeles, New York, and San Francisco.

Formed to write Surplus Lines, Special Purpose, and Reinsurance, Bay State has been providing coverage for unusual risks that other carriers often avoid. In addition to commercial property and casualty coverages, Bay State provides concerns with errors and omissions coverage for financial institutions.

Ace Company operates two divisions, Circle, a treaty underwriter, and York, specializing in facultative business. In operation since 1960, Ace has been writing insurance for primary insurers (reinsurance) for the following reasons: (1) increasing capacity to cover larger individual risks; (2) protecting against catastrophes; (3) reducing net liability to a level consonant with a company's own financial strength.

Reliable currently employs 510 individuals. Of these, 155 serve as corporate officers. Approximately 90 employees maintain branch operations. All internal functions, referred to as "cost-side" departments, including administrative services, data processing, financial control, payroll, personnel, and purchasing, are rendered to all branches from the home office.

*Joseph J. Martocchio, Michigan State University. This case is based upon a real-life situation. It should serve as the basis for classroom discussion. Its purpose is not to convey what is effective or ineffective management. In this spirit, all proper names, dates, and vital information have been changed.

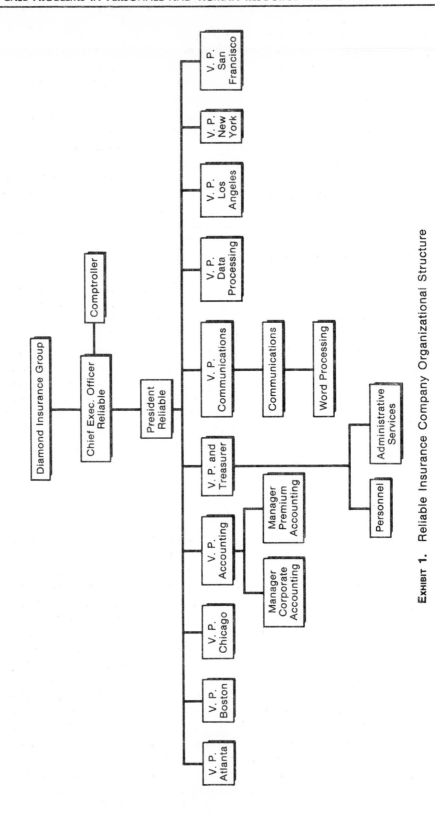

Exhibit 1. Reliable Insurance Company Organizational Structure

Reliable's corporate culture is best expressed by (1) Controlled Aggressors. While growth is a fundamental objective, it will not be pursued at the expense of service or financial stability. (2) Endurers. No matter how unreasonable or impossible risks may be, they are studied in depth for the purpose of providing protection at a fair premium. (3) Innovators. By listening to the ideas and needs of brokers, of intermediaries, and of clients, underwriters may effectively respond to the most demanding interests. (4) International in scope. Since the world economy is interdependent in nature, insurance needs have been satisfied in Europe and the Far East.

According to John A. Ritz, Vice-President of Personnel, "Reliable is known as the 'Cadillac' of the insurance industry. It is not widely known by people whose insurance needs do not exceed the norm."

Corporate Strategy

With "high tech" firms sprouting at exponential rates, the need for high-risk coverage has been one main reason why others are now competing for a piece of the pie. Given the situation, Reliable has directed its energies toward cultivating and nurturing its most profitable accounts, creating new ones only if service to existing accounts is not impaired. In this light, the firm is striving to achieve as well as maintain branch recognition as a quality and dependable service by these new entities. According to Ritz, "quality, not quantity" is where the emphasis lies.

While quality is a must, management envisions "a future whose possibilities for advancement and growth are necessarily limited only by the vision and confidence of the people operating the company. We have the talent and the enthusiasm required, along with the resources and facilities, to accomplish our most ambitious goals."

Human Resource Strategy

Due to the highly specialized nature of the business, two distinct philosophies exist with regard to personnel selection. Reliable searches for experienced individuals with extensive backgrounds in insurance for the top management positions. For this reason there is no formal training program offered.

Staffing on these levels is maintained primarily by promoting individuals who have made a significant contribution to the company either by being instrumental in retaining company-established objectives or by exhibiting entrepreneurial creativity in paving a new avenue upon which the company may prosper.

Reliable believes that it possesses a responsibility to satisfy the professional achievement needs of its employees by bestowing a greater and more diverse responsibility upon those who have reached the limits of a particular position. If the situation warrants it, an employee may be promoted to satisfy professional achievement needs while also serving the management needs of the company.

Given the need for individuals with specific experience, Reliable also seeks to attract "professionals" through executive search agencies as well as by "staying tuned" to informal industry contracts for insurance professionals who may have plans to leave their present employers.

Recruitment for technical and clerical support staff members as well as for "cost-side" managers is initiated when such an employee voluntarily or involuntarily terminates from the company, or, as a particular department experiences an increased work flow that is expected to characterize everyday operations. Individuals are also recruited when a department diversifies, assuming a totally new function.

The Personnel Department

A highly centralized operation, the personnel department at Reliable is comprised of four individuals who recruit. They include John Ritz, Vice-President of Personnel, age 55; Virginia M. Skinner, Personnel Manager, age 46; Stephanie Turner, Administrative Assistant, age 29; and Joe Perini, personnel intern from a local business college, age 21 (Exhibit 2).

Each of these individuals has distinct responsibilities in addition to their recruiting functions. In the recruiting mode, Ritz works with other company executives in planning human resource strategy. He also recruits for exempt-level personnel including computer programmers, staff accountants, and policy underwriters. As a human resource recruiter, Ritz determines whether a candidate's professional aspirations are compatible with that which the organization offers. Compatibility is also a function of a candidate's salary needs and other benefits including vacation time, medical and life insurance, and desire to attain advanced professional training through tuition reimbursement. If compatibility exists in this respect, the hiring department interviews the candidate for technical and interpersonal skills in order to further judge fit.

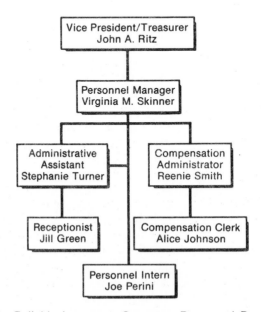

Exhibit 2. Reliable Insurance Company Personnel Department

Ritz also works with the personnel manager in establishing personnel guidelines including salary administration, affirmative action, payroll budgeting, and assorted other functions unique to the personnel area.

As personnel manager, Skinner serves as the core in personnel operations. Virtually all day-to-day decisions are made by her. Skinner initiates structure for her support staff, prescribing that which needs to be accomplished by each.

Crucial to the personnel manager's function is the ability to listen. Skinner must be available to any employee who feels dissatisfied in a particular position whether it be for personality conflicts, salary gripes, the lack of or even too much job responsibility. In addition, she must serve as the administrator of disciplinary action.

Skinner also shares responsibility in recruiting for all levels when time permits. She advises the administrative assistant and intern on marginal candidates.

Turner, the administrative assistant, works to implement many of the plans developed by Ritz and Skinner. For example, a job posting program was recently created to afford the opportunity to current employees of obtaining more advanced upper-level positions before "outsiders" were interviewed for these positions. In addition, Turner maintains records for the medical and life insurance options that are part of the company's benefits package.

In the recruiting mode, Turner recruits for clerically based positions that are classified as non-exempt. When a position opens, she prescreens candidates sent by employment agencies. She also consults with the hiring department about prospects, conducts the reference check, and makes employment offers.

In recent months, Reliable has experienced a significant increase in turnover of clerical employees. Turner's efforts to attract, select, and place individuals in these job vacancies have not been sufficient to satisfy the demands of the hiring department's managers. Most of the complaints stem from the inability of several departments to process the clerical aspect of the work, thus hindering Reliable's responsiveness to the needs of its clients. If this condition persists, there are likely to be negative consequences, ultimately evidenced through deterioration in competitive position.

Aware of the potential implications, Ritz decided that an additional individual would need to assist Turner in recruiting, selecting, and placing job candidates. Reviewing the work of the personnel department staff, he realized that he and Skinner would be tied up in several meetings with department managers and compensation specialists from Diamond's home office. Therefore, Ritz selected Perini as the one to assist Turner.

Perini was hired by Reliable to design and construct a database of employee information for use by the personnel department. Once the program is constructed, Perini will train personnel's clerical staff members to extract information needed by Ritz, Skinner, and Turner. In addition to his knowledge of microcomputers, Perini is in his final year of undergraduate study in which he has taken several courses related to personnel and human resource management. Given Perini's qualifications, Ritz feels that Perini will be able to assist Turner in recruiting.

Perini has eagerly accepted the opportunity to work with Turner. He is particularly excited about relying upon his knowledge gained in his personnel courses as a guide to working effectively and efficiently. After meeting with Turner to discuss the company's guidelines, Perini realizes that several discrepancies exist between Reliable's recruiting policies and procedures and those which he had been taught in his personnel courses.

Perini has such thoughts going through his mind as:

- What are the legal issues that affect personnel recruiting, selection, and placement?
- In what ways are human resource management planning and corporate strategy related?

Perini's first interview is scheduled to begin in forty-five minutes.

7. Compusystems Job Search*

While it does not offer a complete line of computer products, Compusystems sells a wide range of computers and auxiliary equipment, including printers, carrying cases, modems, and disc drives. Additionally, the retail, consumer-oriented store carries a reasonable assortment of software for the machines it stocks. In business for more than five years, the store has relied primarily on its small business customers for its $850,000 plus monthly sales. However, recently the number of home-use computer purchases has also increased. And just recently, store manager Dick James successfully negotiated a contract with the local university. The contract stipulates that the school will buy all its personal computers from Compusystems. In exchange for this high volume of business, Compusystem will give university faculty, staff, and students a 10–30 percent discount on products.

Because of the expected increase in business, Dick has decided that his service staff needs to be expanded. While his force of salespeople should be able to handle the increased workload, a technician's assistant is needed to help set up computer systems for customers. At present the store employs a senior technician, Doug Jones. Doug coordinates service and repair operations. He supervises two technician assistants and three junior technicians who service equipment. The addition of a third technician's assistant will bring the service department staff up to seven.

Job Description

The primary duty of the technician's assistant is to set up computer systems for customers who have purchased a system from the store. First, the technician's assistant must assemble all component parts as specified on the salesperson's order slip. Prior to delivery, the entire system is assembled and tested at the store.

---

*Vandra L. Huber, Assistant Professor, University of Utah. Reprinted with permission.

Any defects must be found and corrected before the computer is delivered to the customer; otherwise it won't operate correctly. Once the computer system passes this inspection, it is disassembled, taken to the customer, and reassembled on-site. Following set up, the technician's assistant must demonstrate basic system operations to the customer. Although this often entails a demonstration of how to load software, it does not include instruction in how to use specific programs—that is the job of the sales force. The store also has an elaborate in-house training program. Each month a variety of training classes on word processing programs, spread sheets, and data management are conducted. Individuals who buy the software get a discount on the courses.

An entry-level position, the technician's assistant position pays a base salary. After completion of a six-month probation period, a technician's assistant also earns one share of the store's profit. While the career path is limited, a technician's assistant can advance to the position of junior technician when and if an opening occurs. Should Doug Jones ever quit (he's been with the company from its inception), a technician could eventually advance to senior technician. While a career path is in place, turnover has been relatively low at Compusystems.

Qualifications for the Position

Because the position includes routine, basic skills that can be acquired on the job, no specific prior training is needed. As Dick James explains, "It's important that the individual have an interest in computers. However, they don't have to be programmers. Most of what needs to be known to service the equipment can easily be taught on the job. What I am concerned about is finding someone who works well with the public. Once the computer is sold, it is the technician's assistant who deals most with the customer. If he or she cannot explain how the system works, answer impatient, impolite, and often stupid questions from fussy, anxious, or computer-phobic customers, then that person won't do well in the job. For this position, as well as others at Compusystem, the basic requirement is good communication skills. I look for people who are relaxed, calm, enthusiastic, and outgoing. They must be willing and not afraid to learn."

Advertising Campaign

To find the "right kind of person" Dick decided to place an advertisement in the local newspaper (see Exhibit 1). Experience has taught him that display advertisements usually do best. The advertisement was written purposely vague, rather than specific. "I didn't want to lock into too many specifics. Qualified applicants might be discouraged from applying if the standards were too rigid," he said. The advertisement (Exhibit 1) appeared in the paper for one week.

Overwhelming Response

The response was overwhelming. More than 200 letters, applications, and resumes were received. One current employee left an envelope on the manager's desk containing a resume and put a note on it reading, "My husband just got laid off

```
┌─────────────────────────────────────────────────────┐
│                                                       │
│              TECHNICIAN'S ASSISTANT                   │
│                                                       │
│   We need a fast learner to assemble, test, and      │
│   install micro computer systems for our local        │
│   customers.                                           │
│                                                       │
│   This is an entry-level position that does not       │
│   require a technical background, but does require    │
│   an interest in computers and an ability to deal     │
│   with people in an organized and efficient manner.   │
│                                                       │
│   Send resume to: Manager, Compusystems: 831          │
│   Techwood Drive, Ithaca, N. Y. 14850                 │
│                                                       │
│   NO PHONE CALLS PLEASE                               │
│                                                       │
└─────────────────────────────────────────────────────┘
```

Exhibit 1. Advertisement for Technician's Assistant

and would like the job. We're broke can you help us out?" A customer wrote a letter thanking Dick for the new computer she had just purchased for her agency. As a postscript she said, "Oh yes, if you haven't filled the technician's assistant position, next time I come in to make another big order, I'd like to talk with you about hiring my son. It sounds like just the kind of job he needs."

Another person sent in a letter, three unsolicited letters of recommendation, his Army discharge papers, his certificates of professional electronics competency, and his last performance appraisal rating from his prior job. Another letter was written on a piece of torn-out notebook paper. Throughout the letter, the individual talked about "coputers." In several cases the individuals were clearly overqualified (e.g., Ph.D's in computer science and engineering). Others sent vitas with inappropriate career objectives such as "to obtain a position in Personnel and Labor Relations utilizing my practical capabilities in the labor relations field" or "to gain experience in the field of automotive repair."

After hours of carefully reading resumes, Dick sorted them into three piles of acceptable applications marked "A," "B," and "C" and a reject pile. At the end of this exercise, Dick had six resumes in his "A" pile (see Exhibits 2–7). He decided to call the six persons in for interviews. Your task:

1. What criteria would *you* use to narrow down an applicant pool that is too large, or is Dick James' approach adequate?
2. From this point forward, how should Dick James proceed? (a) Describe your selection procedure, outlining components of the system. (b) As well as describing any selection tests you would use, indicate the weight you would assign to the tests, and the sequence and order of tests. Explain your rationale.
3. The manager wants to interview at least one applicant. What should be asked in the interview to best aid the manager in the selection decision? Be specific as to what you would ask and why.
4. Because 200 applications of varying degrees of quality were received just by placing an ad in one newspaper, no alternative recruitment sources were considered. Was this justifiable?
5. Based solely on the resumes (see Exhibits 2–7), whom would you hire and why?

R.D. # 1
Beaver Dams, New York 14812

June 30, 1983

Manager
Compusystems
831 Techwood Drive
Ithaca, New York 14850

Dear Sir:

Enclosed is a brief resume which was requested through your advertisement in the Ithaca Journal.

I am very interested in computers and feel that my past record regarding the ability to deal with people is excellent.

Please consider me for an interview with your company.

Thank you for your attention to this request; it is greatly appreciated.

Sincerely,

Thomas F. Cofer

Thomas F. Cofer

Enclosure

Resume

Name:	Thomas F. Cofer
Address:	R.D. # 1, Beaver Dams, New York 14812
Telephone:	(607) 555-0513

Personal

Marital Status:	Married; two children
Date of Birth:	December 22, 1946
Military Status:	Honorable Discharge—United States Army

Employment
Experience:

1970-1976	Morton Salt Company, Himrod, New York Duties included heavy equipment operation
1977-1981	Kirby Vaccuum Cleaners, Elmira, New York Hasting Brothers, Horseheads, New York Spaulding Bakeries, Horseheads, New York Duties for the above included sales and distribution of products and home demonstrations. Accurate records for sales of products and operational techniques were included with the vaccuum cleaners.
1982-1983	Fenix and Scission, Watkins Glen, New York Duties include equipment operation
Education:	Horseheads High School—Graduate BOCES Adult Education—Drafting and Welding Elmira College Adult Education—Psychology courses
Hobbies:	Softball, bowling, reading

EXHIBIT 2

Ruthie Davidson
901 Grover Lane
Ithaca, NY 14850
(607) 277-1485

WORK EXPERIENCE

Frederick & Nelson, Seattle, WA   Sept., 1974 - Apr., 1983

Department Selling Manager (Full Time), Sept., 1982 to Apr., 1983 - Responsibilities included: Coordination of activities between store managers, buying and selling staffs; staffing, training & supervising personnel for normal sales activities; coordination of special projects, e.g., inventory, extraordinary sales, special events.

Merchandise Supervisor (Full Time), March 1977 to Sept., 1978 - Duties included: inventory control, special order buying, forecasting staff requirements.

Intermediate time has been as a part time sales clerk while attending school.

Monet Jewelers, Seattle, WA   Sept., 1979 - November, 1981

Duties included: conducting promotion seminars, inventory maintenance, and general customer relations for four major department stores.

Houk, Wold and Trunkey, Seattle, WA   Sept., 1973 - Sept., 1974

Dark Room Technician, part-time.

PROGRAMMING EXPERIENCE

- Languages: COBOL, BASIC, PASCAL, VAXJCL
- Operating systems: VAX/VMS, NOS
- Database system: RIM
- Hardware: VAX II/730, Cyber 170/750, HP 2000
- Applications: Created data entry and inquiry screens, defined and updated database systems, designed a software package, dynamic data structures.

EDUCATION

University of Washington   Bachelor of Arts, June, 1982

Business Administration degree with concentration in Quantitative Methods.

Highline Community College   Sept., 1977 - March, 1978

General Business

ACTIVITIES

- Volunteer Usher, ACT Theatre
- Member, Forum on Science and Human Relations

References available upon request.

EXHIBIT 3

754 Rynes Road
Ithaca, NY 14850
July 7, 1983

Manager
Compusystems
831 Techwood Drive
Ithaca, New York 14850

Dear Sir:

I would like to apply for the advertised job of Technician's Assistant with Compusystems. I have been working with computers as a user for a number of years and would welcome the opportunity to learn about the operation and assembly of small systems.

I have a knack for understanding computer systems and feel sure that I would quickly pick up the skills required for this job. I have a lot of experience with teaching and working with people, both in groups and in one on one situations, and am confident of my ability to explain the operation of installed systems to the purchasers and to help them get started.

I have enclosed my resume for your consideration. I hope to hear from you soon. Thank you.

Sincerely,

Joseph Gelletich

Joseph Gelletich

JOSEPH GELLETICH
754 Rynes Road
Ithaca, New York 14850
(607) 555-0808

CAREER QUALIFICATIONS

Data analytical abilities: Design, execute and interpret statistical analyses; techniques include regression and multivariate analysis.

Research: Clearly define a question, develop methods for obtaining needed knowledge, collect data, and produce a report of the results.

Computer proficiency: Interactive computing: CMS, WYLBUR; Statistical software packages: SAS, SPSS, BMDP; Programming: PL/I, BASIC.

Communication skills: Experienced at writing (several published articles), teaching, and speaking before groups.

Ability to synthesize results of diverse and complex analyses, distill important features, and report using an effective combination of written, graphic and tabular materials.

EDUCATION

University of Iowa, Iowa City, Iowa. Master of Science, 1982. Course of study included statistics, data analysis, biological research, and computer applications; GPA = 4.0 (A = 4.0); Teaching-Research Fellowship (4 years).

Wesleyan University, Middletown, Conn. Bachelor of Arts, 1978. Graduated magna cum laude, Phi Beta Kappa; GPA = 3.7 (A = 4.0)

EMPLOYMENT HISTORY

Laboratory Instructor, Ithaca College, Ithaca, N.Y. 1983. Taught laboratory procedures, composed tests and graded students.

Computer and Data Base Worker, Cornell University, Ithaca, N. Y. 1982. Input and helped manage a large data base. Devised procedures for data entry, data management and error checking. Trained others in procedures.

Research Assistant, University of Iowa, Iowa City, Iowa. 1980-1981. Had complete responsibility for carrying out part of a study of tropical fruit dispersal; aided in design and analysis of the experiment.

Teaching Assistant, University of Iowa. 1978-1980. Taught laboratory methods and concepts, lectured, wrote tests and graded students.

Waterfront Head, Cornwall Summer Workshops, West Cornwall, Conn. 1977. (summer). Headed water activities, designed and implemented the swimming program, supervised swimming staff, and taught life saving at a summer camp.

EXHIBIT 4

RICHARD HERNANDEZ

8 Jupiter Street
Ithaca, NY 14850
(607) 555-4244 (home)
(607) 555-3090 (leave message)

CAREER OBJECTIVE:

Pursuing a position in the field of digital and/or analog electronics.

EDUCATION:

Tompkins Cortland Community College
Electrical Technology Program
Associate in Applied Science Degree,
  May 1983
Dryden, New York

Tompkins Cortland Community College
Fire Protection Technology Program
Degree Pending (56 out of 68 credits
  accomplished)
Dryden, New York
Concurrent with Liberal Arts Degree

Embry Riddle Aeronautical University
Aeronautical Science Program
September 1979 through May 1980
Prescott, Arizona
Certified Private Pilot

Tompkins Cortland Community College
Major in Mathematics and Science
Associate in Science
  Liberal Arts Degree, 1978
Dryden, New York

RELEVANT COURSES:

Digital Electronics I and II
Analog Electronics I and II
Computer Circuits
Circuit Analysis
Technical Mathematics I
Technical Mathematics II

Linear Integrated Circuits
Microprocessor Fundamentals
Fabrication and Techniques
Electronic Drafting
Technical Mathematics III
Introduction to Computer Programming

WORK EXPERIENCE:

Service Technician   June 1982-January 1983
Cornell University, Ithaca, New York

> Built, serviced, calibrated electronic measuring equipment.
> Maintained inventory including parts procurement. Supported
> professional staff with projects. Applied through Co-Op Office at
> Tompkins Cortland Community College. University extended work
> through January 1983 to complete program concurrently with
> third semester courses.

Repair and Maintenance Person   May 1982
Booth's Electric, Cortland, New York

> Small engine repair including electrical and mechanical.

AWARDS:

Citizenship award in high school

Spring 1976, honor roll
Fall 1976, honor roll
Fall 1977, honor roll

REFERENCES:

Available upon request.

EXHIBIT 5

34 Lee Dyer Boulevard
DeRuyter, New York 13052

June 29, 1983

Manager
Compusystems
Ithaca, New York 14850

Dear Sir:

I am writing to inquire about the Technical Assistant position you have advertised
in the Ithaca newspaper. I am very knowledgeable in computers and would like the
opportunity to contribute my talents.

I have recently graduated from Morrisville College with an A.A.S. Degree in
Electrical Engineering Technology. I have worked with microprocessors and digital
electronics. I like the idea of travel and feel very confident around people. I feel I
am very well qualified for the position I seek.

I look forward to hearing from you soon about the possibility of joining your staff.
Thank you for your consideration.

Sincerely yours,

Patrick O'Laughlin

Patrick O'Laughlin

Enc.

RESUME

Patrick O'Laughlin

Address until May 19, 1983:
  P.O. Box G3, Apt. 101
  College Hill Apartments
  Morrisville, New York 13408

Home Address:
  34 Lee Dyer Boulevard
  DeRuyter, New York 13052
  Phone: (315) 555-3279

Education: State University of New York, Agricultural and Technical College,
             Morrisville, New York

           Candidate for Associate in Applied Science Degree, May 1983

          Majoring in Electrical Engineering Technology

        Option: Digital Logic Design

Courses in:

  D.C. Theory
  A.C. Theory

Also Courses in:

  Analytical Geometry and Calculus
  Calculus

Solid State Devices	Science and Society
Linear Amplifiers	General Psychology
Linear Integrated Circuits	
Combinational Logic	
Sequential Logic	
Assy Language & Interfacing	
Micro Processor Interfacing	
Mechanical Assy-PC Boards	
Basic Programming	
General Physics	
Advanced General Physics	

Extracurricular activities: Electrical Technicians Club

DeRuyter Central School, DeRuyter, New York–Diploma

Work Experience:

Summer 1981:   Rowes Red & White, DeRuyter, New York

Bag and Stock Boy

Summer 1980:   DeRuyter Central School, DeRuyter, New York

Custodian

Summer 1979:   Jim Hocutt, DeRuyter, New York

Farm Hand

EXHIBIT 6

Steven D. Richeson
50 Augusta Street
Ithaca, New York 14850

June 25, 1983

Manager
Compusystems
831 Techwood Drive
Ithaca, New York

Dear Sir;

I am Submitting the attached resume in application for the position of Technician's Assistant as advertised in "The Ithaca Journal." I have been hoping to find an entry level position in the Computer field for a number of months now and this position seems to meet the bill. My experience with computers is limited to my operation of terminals for inventory input and information retrieval. I am however an enthuisiastic learner and feel that I could make myself an asset to your business. I have become quite proficient in working with the public. The fact that I am locally born, raised and educated for the most part also has certain advantages for me in dealing with the public at large in this community.

I hope that I will be considered as a candidate and that I will be hearing from you soon.

Sincerely Yours,

Steven D. Richeson

Steven D. Richeson

```
┌─────────────────────────────────────────────────────────────────────────────┐
│  Steven D. Richeson                                    50 Augusta Street      │
│                                                        Ithaca, New York 14850 │
│                                                        tel. 5552670           │
│                                                                               │
│  Experience   Ithaca Collge Bookstore, Textbook Office. Temporary     1982-83 │
│               Process Textbook Order and handle public complaints.            │
│               Supervise temporary staff. Use computer terminal for log        │
│               and search operations                                           │
│                                                                               │
│               Volunteer Fund Raiser Ithaca Festival                   1983    │
│               Helped Organize fund raising activities such as the             │
│               Festival Auction and the Festival Button Campaign.              │
│                                                                               │
│               Restaurant Assistant Manager and 1st Cook               1979-80 │
│               Ithaca, New York                                                │
│                  Responsible for organizational planning, cost control,       │
│                  and purchasing                                               │
│                                                                               │
│               Professional Children's Touring Theater                 1978    │
│               Auburn New York                                                 │
│                  One of six member cast. Performed in over fifty              │
│                  communities in New York and Canada                           │
│                                                                               │
│  Education    Instituut Vlieghuis; the Netherlands                    1980-82 │
│               Two year program in Modern Languages                            │
│                                                                               │
│               University of Nottingham; England                       1976-77 │
│               Represented SUNY Cortland in an undergraduate program           │
│                                                                               │
│               SUNY College at Cortland, New York.                             │
│               B.A. In English Literature, August 1982                         │
└─────────────────────────────────────────────────────────────────────────────┘
```

EXHIBIT 7

8.   The Office (A)*

The turnover of secretaries in the Office of the Dean was serious. The Dean and Associate Dean had discussed the situation. Their questions to each other were to usual ones about causes, problems, symptoms, and restrictions they faced in solving the problems. The structure of the College secretarial staff is shown in Exhibit 1.

Betty joined the staff in April, filling the vacancy in the Level-3 position. This position has the title receptionist. Within six months the Level-4 secretary resigned. After completing her probation period Betty was promoted to the Level-4 position, Records Clerk, and a replacement in the receptionist position was sought.

The Dean, Associate Dean, and Administrative Secretary hired the new person with only a small amount of input from Betty. The new person, Sally, had worked

*John T. Wholihan, Dean, College of Business Administration, Loyola Marymount University, Los Angeles, CA. Printed with permission.

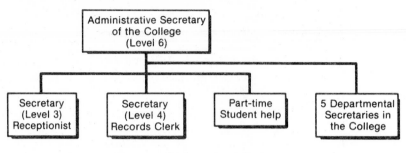

Exhibit 1. College Secretarial Staff

for the College in one of the departmental offices a couple of years earlier. She had resigned before completing her probation period because of the need to be more available to her family. Her husband's job was now insecure and additional income was essential. Sally's work record was clean, she knew the organization and the people she would work with, and was recommended by her former boss. She appeared to be rather quiet but soon was thought to be rather chatty. Sally was not Betty's choice. She was the choice of the Administrative Secretary.

Administrative Secretary

The Administrative Secretary had been in her position for over twelve years. She had served one Dean until his resignation in 1971; an Acting Dean in 1971; a new Dean from 1972 to 1978; an acting Dean in 1978; and another new Dean since 1979. In classic fashion she had made herself indispensable through knowledge of office, college, and university operations. The high rate of turnover meant that no one else was available with her background and knowledge.

The Administrative Secretary controlled most aspects of the office and college. She was the "office manager" and involved herself in everything from building maintenance to student and faculty files. The janitorial staff did not report to her but rather to central maintenance. She supervised the secretaries very closely, requiring submission to her way of doing things, permitting little creativity, issuing corrections for errors in a somewhat demeaning fashion, and therefore had a reputation as a difficult task master.

Secretaries in the departmental offices reported to her on such matters as time cards, reporting days off for vacation or illness, and other kinds of activities. The work of these departmental secretaries was controlled by the department chairs. However, when departmental secretaries were not busy the administrative secretary might indicate that the secretaries could help with the overload in some other office. She usually asked them if they could help out.

The Administrative Secretary saw herself as extremely loyal to the institution, with high work standards, following rules exactly, expecting from others nothing more but also nothing less than she herself was willing to give. The secretaries were not overpaid but the Administrative Secretary had benefited from two of her children attending the university nearly tuition free.

Although the other secretaries were not expected to stay overtime, the Administrative Secretary regularly came in early and left late without extra pay. It had been mentioned that this was unnecessary but, of course, coffee at a 7:30 A.M. meeting was appreciated.

The Administrative Secretary handled all the Dean's personal business including some private family matters. She did not break any confidences regarding these matters. She handled all matters pertaining to college budgets including preparation of all documents concerning faculty salaries. She attended the meeting of the Executive Council of the College (Deans and Department Chairs) not only taking minutes but also injecting her insights and feelings based on her years of experience. The minutes of these meetings seemed to appear in batches when she had time to transcribe and type them herself.

The area around her desk became a source of concern for the Deans. The new desks, room divider, and other office trappings had not produced the appearance the Deans had expected. The Associate Dean had instructed the Administrative Secretary to clean up her area while he was on vacation. He also had asked her for a list of several tasks she could delegate to the secretaries and not control personally, such as segregating the mail for each Dean and opening and stamping it for date of receipt. The clean-up occurred and last briefly. The list of duties for delegation was not forthcoming.

Although Betty was technically in charge of student records, the Administrative Secretary controlled so many of the files and the computer program of student records that it was difficult for Betty to know where certain records were at various times.

The faculty used the Administrative Secretary to get quick answers to their questions or clarify procedures. They openly said in subtle jest that they knew who "runs the college." However, even the faculty were intimidated by her and some were afraid to get on her "wrong side."

Changes Begin

The first secretary not to be totally intimidated by the Administrative Secretary was a young high school graduate who remained in her position of receptionist for two years. As she resigned she made it clear that she had been picked on too much and although she admitted causing some of the problems by being tardy and talking back to the Administrative Secretary, she felt she was being driven away. She complained about being scolded for too many personal calls when the Administrative Secretary actually made and received more personal calls than she did.

Betty was also not at all intimidated. When confronted with unacceptable treatment or obstacles to her performance she went to the Dean and openly complained. She used words indicating bias, ineffectiveness, and insensitivity on the part of the Administrative Secretary. However, such behavior was not exhibited by the Administrative Secretary in the presence of the Deans.

Betty was over qualified for her job. She was a college graduate with honors in English. She would have been a teacher but jobs were unavailable when she graduated. She needed a job and decided to make the best of this secretarial position. She indicated that she could be more effective if given a little freedom. She regularly corrected small errors in letters she typed and made suggestions about improving some correspondence. Her performance was positive. Her work was clean, fast, and accurate. She organized work quickly and allocated her overload to the receptionist and student workers. She had learned to operate the word processor in a matter of a few weeks. In a recent meeting with the Dean she made it clear that if things didn't improve in the office she would leave.

The quality of the work of the Administrative Secretary had been slipping. Errors were more common. Errors on student records that probably existed earlier were conveniently being brought to the attention of the Deans. Her health was not as good as it had been and her husband had been forced to retire early as his job was phased out. She was relieved when he returned to work.

The Administrative Secretary had always received positive annual performance ratings. She had been an essential link as managerial changes took place and no one had reviewed her performance critically.

The deterioration of the Administrative Secretary's performance, Betty's unwillingness to accept her dictatorial managerial style, and the threat of losing a very efficient employee were causing the Deans to consider changes in the office. They felt they were losing the respect of others by having an office where turnover was high and morale was low. As secretaries became unhappy in the office they didn't hesitate to tell others why they were unhappy. The Deans were tired of interviewing secretarial candidates.

Complicating the issue for the Dean and Associate Dean was the way some of the other secretaries and faculty viewed Betty and the Administrative Secretary. Though some were intimidated by the Administrative Secretary and some had made jokes or disparaging remarks about her Napoleonic personality, most were convinced of her usefulness to the College. She *was* the place to go for quick answers because she knew people campus wide, knew whom to call for what problem and usually got good results. This was much faster than going to either Betty or Sally (they would probably have to ask the Administrative Secretary anyway) or even to the Dean or Associate Dean because many of the matters (room assignments, air conditioner problems, etc.) had never been handled by them.

Betty was neither as capable nor as cooperative as the Administrative Secretary and was openly disliked by some of the staff. Some felt that she had her eyes set on the Administrative Secretary's position and, in fact, may have contributed to the vacated position that she now fills.

The Office (B)

The Reorganization

Reviewing the personnel file of the Administrative Secretary, the Dean concluded there was insufficient documentation to release her. Informal conversations had taken place with her regarding turnover, office atmosphere, and management style. The Deans had not "written her up" in the formal sense. She admitted the office operations were not as smooth as she expected, took the blame for some of the personnel problems, but was sure things would be better.

The question was how to bring greater efficiency to the office, reduce conflict, and, in a sense, work around the shortcomings of the Administrative Secretary.

The vacation of the Administrative Secretary was used to examine the office operations and realign positions. New job descriptions for each secretary were developed, and reporting relationships clarified. The new organization structure is shown in Exhibit 1. The new job descriptions are shown in Exhibit 2.

Departmental secretaries no longer reported to the Administrative Secretary but instead reported only to the department chair. Their time cards were turned in to the Dean's office for central processing, which created a problem of who should handle the cards.

At the end of her probation period, Sally learned of a position in another office on campus. The opening was on Level 4, which meant more money. Indicating she had to leave, she did so with reluctance. However, the only person really sad to see her leave was the Administrative Secretary. The Administrative Secretary could not be blamed for this turnover. Sally was the twelfth secretarial turnover in less than five years with two women simultaneously lasting two years each.

Sally's replacement was selected following a new system developed by Betty and the Associate Dean. Betty was to greet each candidate and introduce her to the others. After showing her the office she would take the candidate through the building to meet other secretaries, see the location of the offices, and get a feel for the environment. Next, the candidate was asked to perform several administrative tasks that included setting up, correcting, and typing a paragraph with numerous mistakes in it. Another activity included reading an instruction sheet and

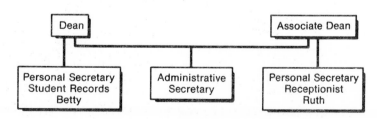

EXHIBIT 1. Office Organization

EXHIBIT 2.   Office of the Dean—Job Descriptions

DUTIES OF THE ADMINISTRATIVE SECRETARY
COLLEGE OF BUSINESS ADMINISTRATION

1. The Administrative Secretary will maintain the master calendar of events of the College and the University and ensure that all official deadlines are met.
2. The Administrative Secretary will be responsible for all matters relating to the use and maintenance of Baker Hall, including classroom assignment, building maintenance liaison, and equipment (capital) purchase and maintenance.
3. The Administrative Secretary will work with the Associate Dean on all matters related to curriculum, including class scheduling, catalog maintenance, and as secretary to the College Curriculum Committee.
4. The Administrative Secretary will maintain the Master Correspondence File of the College updated daily as well as keep all other files currently up to date.
5. The Administrative Secretary will maintain all faculty and staff personnel records, expenses, and salaries. (Student records are excluded from this area of responsibility.)
6. The Administrative Secretary will, in coordination with the Dean, maintain all budgets of the College, assist in their development, projection, and presentation to the departments of the College and the administration of the University.
7. The Administrative Secretary will hire and assign student workers for the optimum efficiency of work in the Office of the Dean.
8. The Administrative Secretary will maintain the copy and mimeograph machines and ensure that proper maintenance schedules are carried out including paper, toner, cleaning, and other operations.
9. The Administrative Secretary will act as liaison with the Computer Center on the modification and/or development of new computerized student letters. The Records Secretary will work with current letters on a day-to-day operational basis, and update them as needed.
10. The Administrative Secretary will perform related duties as assigned and write and maintain an updated description of all tasks performed.

The Administrative Secretary will work with the Associate Dean on all matters related to curriculum and other assigned duties under his administration. The person holding this position will work with the Dean on matters under his purview, such as operating budgets, personnel, and building maintenance. The Administrative Secretary will coordinate his/her activities with those of the Students Record Secretary and Secretary for purposes of smooth communication and operation in the Office of the Dean. The official reporting line of the Administrative Secretary is to the Dean.

DUTIES OF THE STUDENT RECORDS SECRETARY
COLLEGE OF BUSINESS ADMINISTRATION

1. The Student Records Secretary shall be responsible for all personal secretarial duties related to the Dean, including the receipt and distribution of mail, answering of the Dean's telephone line, scheduling of all his appointments, typing and distribution of all correspondence, and other related duties as assigned.
2. Maintain all official student records for the College of Business Administration.
3. Prepare student course and grade information for computer entry. Work with the Administrative Secretary on the maintenance of the computerized letters.
4. Receive and review all transcripts of prospective transfer students.
5. Process student application materials.
6. Assign work to student assistants under your control.
7. Operate word processing and duplicating equipment as required.
8. Develop a Procedures Manual for all tasks you perform.
9. Perform other related duties as assigned.

The Student Records Secretary will coordinate his/her activities with those of the Administrative Secretary and Secretary-Receptionist for purposes of smooth communication and operation in the Office of the Dean. The official reporting line of the Student Records Secretary is to the Dean.

Exhibit 2. Office of the Dean—Job Descriptions *(continued)*

DUTIES OF THE SECRETARY-RECEPTIONIST
COLLEGE OF BUSINESS ADMINISTRATION

1. The Secretary shall be responsible for all personal secretarial duties related to the Associate Dean, including the receipt and distribution of mail, answering the Associate Dean's telephone lines, scheduling of all appointments, typing and distribution of all correspondence, and other related duties as assigned.
2. Serve as relief secretary to the Department of Business Management and Administration when called upon to do so.
3. Serve as the general College Receptionist to faculty, students, staff, and other visitors.
4. Type dictated and written materials from rough draft to final form, subject to review of content.
5. Operate word processing and duplicating equipment as required.
6. Develop a Procedures Manual of all tasks you perform.
7. Perform other related duties as assigned.

The Secretary will coordinate his/her activities with those of the Administrative Secretary and Student Records Secretary for purposes of smooth communication and operation in the Office of the Dean. The official reporting line of the Secretary-Receptionist is to the Associate Dean.

evaluating a transcript by marking it according to the instructions. The Administrative Secretary briefly interviewed each candidate. She was asked for her reactions. The Deans interviewed each candidate. The Associate Dean made it clear to Betty that he wanted her input on each candidate since she would have to work closely with the new person.

The Deans agreed to inform the candidates that two conflicting forces were in the front office. The new person should work, be her own person, and recognize she would report to the Associate Dean as a personal secretary.

The second of the finalists accepted the position. Ruth was single, in her mid-twenties, with a strong personality, considerable work experience, and a good spirit. She took hold quickly and was anxious to prove herself.

The Office (C)

The conflict between Betty and the Administrative Secretary was more than professional or power based. It was, in fact, rooted in a very delicate matter of personal life style. Betty was a lesbian. Her preference began to be revealed within a few months of starting her job. However, her associations were kept out of the office and nothing more was said about it. When the Deans realized the situation they agreed not to use such information against her unless or until it affected her performance. During probation an employee can be released without explanation.

Betty's preference in some ways helped the office situation. Once students, faculty, and others learned of her preference, they did not hang around as much as they would have. Betty was an unusually well-built woman.

Betty called in ill a few times, and occasionally needed a day off. These were unscheduled. On one occasion when she returned to work a noticeable bruise on her face was covered with makeup. The Dean, knowing who Betty's partner was, informed her politely that her personal life was not company business and would not be used against her unless it interfered with her work. Time off to recuperate from injuries from domestic violence was not acceptable.

From time to time Betty returned from lunch obviously having had alcohol. It was not particularly noticeable except periodically there followed a need to leave work a little early. There was some evidence, not substantial or clear, that Betty was sometimes in a daze and appeared to take medicine frequently. Her performance was almost always considered superior. Her new position as personal secretary to the Dean gave her some prestige and power formerly held by the Administrative Secretary.

The Administrative Secretary reported any performance deviations to the Dean. She made it clear that she would do her own job but not someone else's if she no longer possessed the authority. She informed people that she was no longer responsible for a particular activity and that they would have to check with one of the other office staff. Since she had personally advised selected students of her choice and interest, she would turn the students over to Betty usually when she was very busy.

The Dean was quick to point out that his productivity had increased markedly. His mail system improved with Betty's organization of it. She could draft letters with minimal instruction. Her work area was reasonably neat. Student records were improving both in terms of being current and also in terms of being filed properly, which had not always been the case when handled by the Administrative Secretary.

In early November the Dean received a call from Betty indicating she was unable to come to work. It was obvious that something serious had happened. The next contact was from an organization to protect battered women. The Dean was requested to meet the case worker in an obscure location on short notice. Her request was to give the victim time to recover and return to productive employment.

The Deans pondered the situation. Legal, ethical, professional, constitutional, and humane issues were discussed. This was new territory for them. They attempted not to be influenced by the fact that Betty's lesbian relationship also had racial implications. However, the racial issue existed and the partner was now known to have a substantial criminal record. The question kept coming up: Why would a beautiful young woman tie herself up with such a partner? The Dean had tried to ask Betty whether she could leave if she wanted to do so. A clear answer was never given, which suggested that Betty's partner may have had some hold on her beyond that of a lover.

The Dean was trying to decide whether to meet the case worker. The Administrative Secretary was gloating as she saw the end of Betty in sight.

9. Promotion to Police Sergeant*

Until recently selection of candidates for promotion to police sergeants at State University was done unsystematically. Job analysis was not the foundation for selection decisions but rather intuition and subjective judgments. The presence of a legal imperative and a desire to make better and more objective selection decisions resulted in a program to develop new promotion procedures.

State University is a large university with eight campuses spread throughout the state. Each campus has its own police department. Although the eight campuses are fairly autonomous and independent, there is a central administration group which coordinates certain functions, including personnel. Legally the police departments are responsible for their selection and promotion decisions; they are not governed by the personnel group in central administration nor by the campus-based personnel departments. But the chiefs recognize that their expertise is limited and so they regularly seek advice and guidance from the campus and central administration personnel departments.

The eight campuses differ from each other in many ways, including size (from 4,000 students at the smallest campus to 30,000 students at the largest campus), location (both urban and rural), and age or time in existence (from as young as ten years to as old as more than 100 years). Corresponding to these differences among the campuses are differences in the composition, philosophies, and histories of the police department, each run by its own police chief. Of particular importance in 1983 was an ongoing rivalry between two large departments, one in the northern part of the state and the other in the southern part of the state; each was vying for recognition as the "best."

Despite competition among the departments, all eight police chiefs recognized the value of pooling their resources to maintain a single promotion procedure (or test) for selecting sergeants. By having a single procedure, a rank-ordered list of all university police officers qualified for promotion could be developed and made available to all campuses. Each list had a two-year life. During these two years, whenever a vacancy for sergeant came up on any of the eight campuses, the people at the top of the list had first priority for promotion. Approximately twenty vacancies occurred during a list's two-year life, and usually about 150 of the 250 police officers met the *minimum* requirements for promotion (i.e., two years of college credits, two years' police experience, and completion of a state-sponsored management training course).

Because of the attractive small selection ratio, the police chiefs wanted to improve their selection procedures so that the twenty vacancies were filled with the very best of the 150 eligible police officers. Accordingly, the university agreed to pay for a consultant to work with the police and personnel groups to design a high-quality promotion procedure for sergeants. They hired Gerri Smith from a prestigious consulting firm specializing in selection.

---

*This case was prepared by Susan E. Jackson, The University of Michigan. The example used is for teaching purposes only and is not meant to be an example of effective or ineffective management practice.

Getting Started

As with previous consulting assignments of this type, Ms. Smith knew that the development of a new promotion procedure would take time and involve several components. These components, beginning with job analysis, are outlined in the sequence through which Ms. Smith proceeded. This outline is shown in Exhibit 1.

Job Analysis

In 1979, six of the eight police departments had hired a firm to conduct job analyses of all jobs within their departments. The method the firm had used appeared to be the critical incident technique (CIT), but it was difficult to tell for sure because the documentation of the job analysis procedures had been retained by the consulting firm. The police chiefs contacted the firm after Ms. Smith pointed out to them that this documentation would be critical should they ever need to defend in court decisions they made using the results of the job analysis. Unfortunately, the particular consultant they had worked with four years ago was no longer with the firm and the documentation was nowhere to be found.

Neither Ms. Smith nor the police chiefs had anticipated this problem. They had hoped to have their promotion list ready in four months. If they did a job analysis, they knew they might have to wait six or seven months before seeing that list. After discussing the matter at length, the chiefs decided that in the long run it was in their best interest to collect systematic, up-to-date job analysis information, so they asked Ms. Smith to get started.

Phase 1: Determining Job Tasks. Usually, Ms. Smith likes to use an extended CIT method of job analysis but in this case it was not practical. To do so, she would have had to travel to eight locations that were hundreds of miles apart from each other. Both time and budget constraints ruled this out. Therefore, Ms. Smith decided to combine features of the CIT and GOJA methods. This creative solution was possible because the *Uniform Guidelines* recognize that there is no one best

Exhibit 1. Components of the Promotion Test Developed by Ms. Smith

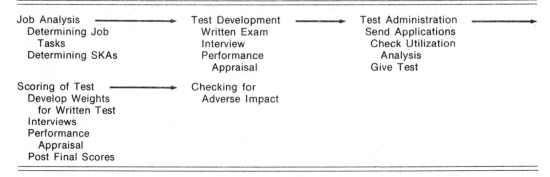

Job Analysis ⟶	Test Development ⟶	Test Administration ⟶
Determining Job	Written Exam	Send Applications
Tasks	Interview	Check Utilization
Determining SKAs	Performance	Analysis
	Appraisal	Give Test

Scoring of Test ⟶	Checking for
Develop Weights	Adverse Impact
for Written Test	
Interviews	
Performance	
Appraisal	
Post Final Scores	

method of job analysis. As long as the method used provided information about the importance, frequency, difficulty, and trainability of one's job tasks, it would probably hold up to the scrutiny of the courts.

Ms. Smith conducted the job analysis for sergeants as follows: First, she asked each police department to send copies of the job descriptions for all of their sergeants. These gave her a general working knowledge of what the job of sergeant involved. Next, she developed a form that she would send to each sergeant to fill out. This form asked the sergeant to list all of his or her job duties and then, for each duty or task, to rate how frequently it was performed relative to other duties, how important it was to the job overall, how difficult it was to perform, and the amount of training that would be needed to teach someone to perform the duty. This form was sent to each sergeant, who filled it out and then reviewed it with his or her commanding lieutenant. If the lieutenant felt any qualifications or changes were needed, these were noted in a designated space. Both the sergeant and lieutenant then signed the form to indicate they had reviewed it together. Finally, the chief reviewed the form, added any comments he felt were appropriate, and signed it. The original copy of the form was kept by the campus police department and a photocopy was sent to Ms. Smith.

Using the information from the completed forms, Ms. Smith generated a list of eight job domains, which she believed, based on the data she had collected, represented the tasks relevant to the job of a sergeant. Then, for each domain, she listed all of the specific tasks that she felt belonged to the domain. For each task, she recorded the corresponding ratings of frequency, difficulty, importance, and trainability *(FDIT ratings)*. This list of domains and tasks was then sent back to twelve randomly chosen sergeants and three lieutenants who reviewed it. Ms. Smith asked these reviewers to study the list she had generated and evaluate whether the domains made logical sense to them and whether the tasks within each domain belonged there. They returned their suggestions for revision to Ms. Smith in writing. She then finalized the list, which is shown in Exhibit 2.

The last step in Phase 2 of the job analysis involved calculating frequency, difficulty, importance, and trainability values for each of the eight job domains. These values were calculated by averaging the FDIT ratings of the tasks within each domain and are shown in Exhibit 2.

Phase 2: Determining Skills, Knowledge and Abilities (SKAs).   Now that the major job tasks had been identified, Ms. Smith needed to determine the SKAs required to perform those tasks. Then methods of assessing applicants' relevant SKAs could be designed for use as a selection test.

To find out which SKAs were important for performing a sergeant's job, Ms. Smith went back to the experts—the sergeants and lieutenants. In order to record their judgments in a systematic way, Ms. Smith designed a simple matrix for the job experts to complete. The headings on the eight columns of the matrix were the names of the domains generated in Phase 1 of the job analysis. The labels for the seventeen rows of the matrix were names of abilities, knowledges, and skills that she believed someone might need to perform well as a sergeant.

This domains × abilities matrix was sent to all sergeants and lieutenants along with a list of the tasks that belonged in each domain and definitions of each

Exhibit 2. Job Domains for the Position of Police Sergeant

		Average Ratings			
		F	D	I	T[a]
Domain:	Law enforcement activities including patrolling, investigating, apprehending.	6.2	5.8	6.3	5.1[b]
Sample tasks:					
	1. responding to call for crime in progress				
	2. cultivating sources of street information				
Domain:	Adaptability to the job, including completing work in a timely manner, attention to detail, willingness to assume accountability for one's work.	6.4	3.3	5.7	4.0
Sample tasks:					
	1. accepting orders or assignments				
	2. keeping up-to-date files				
Domain:	Dealing with the public.	6.7	4.9	5.2	4.1
Sample tasks:					
	1. making death notifications				
	2. talking to news media				
Domain:	Communication, including communicating to others as well as understanding others.	5.5	3.2	6.1	4.2
Sample tasks:					
	1. referring citizens to other agencies				
	2. interviewing witnesses				
Domain:	Personal appearance and demeanor.	6.7	2.7	5.3	2.9
Sample tasks:					
	1. physical fitness activities				
	2. maintenance of uniform and equipment				
Domain:	Supervision and leadership.	4.7	6.4	4.8	6.7
Sample tasks:					
	1. working with a rookie or new transfer				
	2. supervising an investigation				
Domain:	Report writing.	5.9	4.6	5.5	5.1
Sample tasks:					
	1. writing up findings for an ongoing investigation				
	2. writing descriptions of events that occurred during on-site call				
Domain:	Teamwork, including working with other professionals both inside and outside of the department.	5.4	5.1	5.7	4.3
Sample tasks:					
	1. requesting assistance from other officers				
	2. teaching knowledge and skills to other officers				

[a] F = Frequency of task performance; D = Difficulty; I = Importance; T = Trainability.
[b] Ratings were made using a scale of 1 to 7. Values shown are means obtained by averaging across all items in the domain.

ability. The job experts completed the matrix by indicating the importance of each ability for performing the tasks in each domain. Using these ratings, Ms. Smith determined the nine SKAs that were most important to assess in order to predict performance as a sergeant (see Exhibit 3).

Test Development

The police refer to the process through which sergeants are selected as the *Sergeants' Promotional Exam (SPE)*. Traditionally, SPE has three components: a written exam, an interview, and an evaluation of past performance. These three

EXHIBIT **3.** SKAs Assessed by the Sergeants' Promotional Exam

	Skills, Knowledges, & Abilities	I [b]	Exam Component in Which SKA Was Assessed [a]		
			Written	Interview	Performance
1.	Knowledge of State and Federal Law	6.7	X		X
2.	Knowledge of Local Procedures and Regulations	6.6	X		X
3.	Writing Ability	5.2	X		X .
4.	Communication Skills	5.8		X	X
5.	Reasoning Ability	5.0		X	X
6.	Skill in Interpersonal Relations	6.1		X	X
7.	Knowledge of General Management Principles	5.4	X		
8.	Reading Ability	4.9	X		
9.	Leadership Skills	4.8		X	X

[a]An "X" indicates the ability was assessed by that component of the exam.
[b]I = Importance rating of the ability. The value shown is a mean obtained by averaging the importance ratings of the ability for all job domains.

components have always been used by the university police departments and they are typically used by city and state police departments as well. The police chiefs wanted Ms. Smith to maintain the three components of SPE, but they were eager to have the content of each component revised and updated. So, the major questions were: (1) Which SKAs should be assessed by each component? and (2) How exactly should each SKA be measured?

In deciding how to design the SPE, Ms. Smith kept several things in mind: First, she knew that written tests were more likely than interviews and performance ratings to have adverse impact against minorities, especially blacks and Hispanics. Second, she was wary of interviews because she knew they are difficult to standardize and make reliable. Third, she preferred to assess as many SKAs as possible using the most job-related method possible, which in this case was the performance appraisal. Finally, she knew that each of the three methods at her disposal (written test, interview, performance ratings) had both strengths and weaknesses, so the best strategy would be to measure all SKAs using more than one method, if possible.

The three components of the SPE Ms. Smith designed are described in detail below. Throughout these next sections, reference is made to a Task Force. This Task Force was organized to assist Ms. Smith with her task of developing the tests. It consisted of three chiefs and two lieutenants.

The Written Exam.   During Phase II of the job analysis, seventeen SKAs had been rated for their importance to a sergeant's job performance. Of these, nine were judged to be relatively high in importance. Five of the nine were judged to be appropriately assessed in a written exam: *reading skills, writing skills, knowledge of basic management principles, knowledge of state and federal laws,* and *knowledge of university regulations and procedures* as described by the local General Orders manual. The two skill areas had been rated as relatively less important than the three knowledge areas, so the proportion of test items devoted to each skill or knowledge area was adjusted to reflect the importance ratings.

Usually, the most difficult part of developing a written test is writing the test items. Fortunately, the Task Force had the advantage of being able to obtain potential items from a state agency that maintained a bank of thousands of test items for law enforcement exams. Upon request, this agency randomly selected a total of 400 items relevant to the SKAs to be assessed on the exam. Each member of the Task Force then reviewed all 400 questions and noted any objections they had. At a group meeting, the Task Force discussed their evaluations of the 400 items. Their goal was to select a total of 100 of the best items. The decision rule they used to eliminate items from the pool of 400 was to eliminate any item to which any member of the Task Force had objections. This reduced the pool to fewer than 200. Finally, redundant items were eliminated and the final 100 items were chosen to fit the goal of distributing items across the five knowledge and skill areas according to the relative importance of the areas.

As already noted, one disadvantage of written tests was that minorities tend to score lower than whites, resulting in adverse impact for selection decisions based on written tests. Test experts now realize that a major source of unfairness in written tests is that often the reading skill needed to take the test is higher than the skill needed to do the job in question. To decrease the potential for unfair discimination, any written test used for selection should be checked to ensure that the readability level of the test is equal to or below the readability level of written materials typically encountered in the job. Therefore, as the last step in developing the written test for the SPE, Ms. Smith conducted readability analyses of the test and of samples of department memos, regulation manuals, legal documents, and correspondence taken directly out of the record files of current sergeants. This analysis showed the reading skill needed to take the test was somewhat less than the skill needed to read materials from the sergeant's actual files.

The Interview.   In the past, the police department interviewed only candidates who passed the written test. This practice meant that the chiefs had to decide on a cut-off point to define what a passing score would be for the written exam. They had always found this to be an extremely difficult judgment to make and wanted to avoid making that judgment this year. Their solution to the problem was to allow everyone to go through the interview process and not use the written test as a hurdle. This solution fit the chiefs' philosophy that someone who does well in the interview should be able to have that compensate for a low score on the written test, but it creates a practical problem: How could they interview approximately 100 candidates spread throughout a large state in a manner that everyone perceived to be standardized and fair, without incurring prohibitive expenses?

Ideally, it seemed that fairness and standardization could be best attained by having only one interview board (or panel), rather than having one panel at each of the eight campuses. But this would mean unbearably high travel costs—either the board members would have to travel around the state, or applicants would have to travel to the board. The Task Force decided the only practical solution was to set up two interview boards, one in the northern half of the state, and one in the southern half. This solution presented a real challenge to Ms. Smith who had to develop an interviewing procedure so sound it could not be attacked as possibly giving an unfair advantage to candidates in either half of the state. Ms. Smith realized that this challenge could be met only with a structured interview conducted by trained interviewers.

The first order of business was to solicit volunteers to serve as interviewers. The chiefs believed the interviewers should represent the following: the Affirmative Action officers from central administration, the general university community, the local communities by which the campuses were surrounded, the state law enforcement agencies, and their own departments. The group included the people to whom the chiefs felt most directly accountable, the people to whom the chiefs wished to demonstrate the credibility of their departments, and the people for whom the chiefs felt their departments should serve as role models. The Task Force was given the responsibility of creating two interview boards. Each board was to have one member to represent each of the five groups listed above.

After the interview boards were set up, Ms. Smith arranged a one-day training session for the interviewers. Her objectives for this training session were as follows:

- Develop a set of four or five questions that would be used for all interviews.
- Develop standards to use in evaluating candidates' responses to each question.
- Generate consensus among the interviewers about what they were to accomplish with the interview process.
- Give the interviewers an opportunity to role play an interview session.
- Develop an appreciation among the interviewers of the seriousness of their task and the problems inherent in accomplishing it (e.g., rater errors and biases, primacy and recency effects, and possible boredom and fatigue).

In order to accomplish these objectives, Ms. Smith did several things. First, prior to the training session she identified five SKAs (based on her job analysis) that could *potentially* be assessed in an interview. For each of these SKAs, she asked a few lieutenants to suggest interview questions that would tap the SKAs. Using these suggestions, she generated a list of about twenty potential interview questions. She sent this list, along with a short manual on interviewing and a job description for sergeants, to all members of the interview boards. The interviewers were asked to review this material prior to the training session.

At the training session, Ms. Smith reviewed several principles of interviewing and explained her objectives to the board members. She explained her belief that the only way to accomplish the objectives was for the interviewers to spend the day communicating and problem solving together. She turned over to them the task of selecting four or five questions that they all agreed were appropriate, and for which they were able to specify standards to be used in evaluating the candidates' responses. The interviewers struggled for several hours with this task, which they were surprised to find so difficult. By the end of the day, they had developed four questions they could all live with and a conviction that the interview process would be standardized and fair. At the end of the day, one of the interviewers—a twenty-year veteran of a large city's police department—admitted to Ms. Smith that he came to the training session believing the day would be a waste of time because there was nothing he didn't already know about interviewing. To his surprise he came away feeling that every interview board should go through a similar process before they began evaluating candidates, especially since their evaluations can strongly influence the careers of young officers.

Performance Appraisals. The third component of the SPE was a performance appraisal of each candidate. Ms. Smith was happy to learn that the department already had a good performance appraisal procedure that was used for promotion decisions. The system worked as follows: For each candidate, all of the department officers who knew the candidate (this was typically three or four people) filled out a detailed appraisal form. The appraisal form assessed seven domains of job performance. For each performance domain, eight to twelve specific tasks were listed. The officers evaluated the candidate's performance of each task using a ten-point rating scale. These ratings were averaged and multiplied by ten to yield one overall performance score.

Administering the SPE

At the same time the three test components were being developed, Ms. Smith and the Task Force were planning for the administration of the tests. Only internal applicants were allowed to take the SPE, so the recruiting process was simple. All university police officers were sent a letter that described the testing procedures in detail. An application form was sent with this letter instructing all interested persons to apply by a particular date.

Although it was routine practice for the department to use only internal recruiting for the SPE, the chiefs always felt obliged to justify this practice. The major argument against the practice of internal recruiting was that it would perpetuate any existing underrepresentation of minority groups. To counter this argument, the chiefs sent a utilization analysis to the university's AAP officer, who compared this information to their routinely collected availability data. Because the police department had an aggressive recruiting program for entry-level positions, this comparison usually revealed that minority groups were not underrepresented in the pool of potential internal applicants.

The written exam was scheduled for a Saturday morning, and the police chiefs were all instructed to take this into account when assigning duties during that period. All interviewing was conducted the week after the written test. The officers completed their performance appraisals during that week also. Candidates were told the final list of total scores would be posted three weeks after the date of the written test.

Scoring the SPE

Final SPE scores were created by adding together the weighted scores from each component. The written test was weighted 50 percent, and the interview and performance appraisal were each weighted 25 percent. The final list of promotion candidates consisted of a rank ordering of everyone who had completed all three phases of the SPE based on the overall scores. This list was posted in each of the eight campus police departments along with a notice encouraging all applicants to speak with their chief to obtain detailed feedback.

The chiefs chose to weight the written test more heavily than the interview and performance appraisal primarily because they and their patrol officers all believed the written test was the most objective component of the SPE, and thus was the least subject to the criticism that favoritism determined the scores. Initially, the chiefs had suggested to Ms. Smith that the performance appraisal be weighted only 10 percent because it was the component believed to be most subjective. However, Ms. Smith countered that the performance appraisal was the most job-related component and therefore was probably the most valid predictor. The 50-25-25 weighting system was eventually agreed upon to take into account these and other similar types of concerns.

Checking for Adverse Impact

As noted previously, this university's police departments viewed themselves as leaders in the field of law enforcement practice. Consequently, they were particularly concerned about maintaining a force that was balanced with respect to the races and sexes. Recall that it was primarily this concern that led the departments to use a compensatory selection model rather than use the written test as a hurdle and therefore have to impose an arbitrary cut-off score for that component.

Ms. Smith believed that when management is sincerely concerned about the potential discriminatory effects of their selection procedures, the best guarantee for preventing unfair discrimination is information. Therefore, her last task for the police department was to conduct numerous analyses that illustrated the effects certain types of policies could have on their selection process. For example, one analysis involved computing adverse impact figures (using the 80 percent rule and a computer) under the assumption that the top ten, twenty, or thirty candidates, respectively, would eventually be promoted from their list. This analysis revealed that strong adverse impact against blacks would occur if only the top ten candidates were promoted, that using the top twenty candidates would cause less adverse impact, and that no adverse impact would occur if the top thirty candidates were promoted (see Exhibit 4). Similarly, Ms. Smith demonstrated the

Exhibit 4. Analysis to Check for Potential Adverse Impact

Test Component	Asian (n = 23) [a]	Black (n = 37)	Hispanic (n = 11)	Am. Indian (n = 3)	White (n = 71)	Males (n = 118)	Females (n = 27)
	% of Subgroup Who Are Among the Top 20 Candidates						
Written	(5)[b]22%	(2)5%[c]	(1)9%[c]	(1)33%	(11)15%	(14)12%	(6)22%
Interview	(6)26%	(3)8%[c]	(1)9%[c]	(0) 0%[c]	(10)14%	(16)14%	(4)15%
Performance Appraisal	(5)22%	(5)14%	(0)0%[c]	(1)33%	(9) 13%	(15)13%	(5)19%
	% of Subgroup Who Are Among the Top 30 Candidates						
Written	(7)30%	(7)19%	(2)18%	(1)33%	(13)18%	(22)19%	(8)30%
Interview	(7)30%	(6)16%	(2)18%	(1)33%	(14)20%	(24)20%	(6)22%
Performance Appraisal	(5)22%	(6)16%	(2)18%	(2)67%	(15)21%	(25)21%	(5)19%

[a] n = indicates the total number of job applicants in the subgroup.
[b] Values in parentheses represent numbers of applicants.
[c] Indicates that adverse impact defined by the 80% rule exists for the subgroup in comparison to the majority group (whites or males).

adverse impact of each of the three components of the SPE and the effects that changing the weighting system would have with respect to adverse impact. Because adverse impact was associated only with the written test, the adverse impact of the total SPE was directly affected by the weight given the written test— the higher the weight of the written test, the more adverse impact of the SPE overall. To reduce the potential adverse impact of the SPE, the weight of the written test should be reduced.

Ms. Smith concluded her consulting assignment with the police chiefs. It is now up to them to fairly utilize, evaluate, and update the promotion procedures Ms. Smith helped them design. What problems, challenges, and issues face the police chiefs in carrying out the procedures developed by Ms. Smith?

10.   A Case of Black and White*

Karl Kaster sat quietly in the hushed courtroom cradling his head with both hands. For Karl, an associate professor of education at Southeastern State University and director of the Division of Curriculum and instruction in the College of Education, the past week would rank as one of the hardest in his life. Karl wondered how a seemingly straightforward decision to hire Harvey Butler nearly three-and-one-half years ago could have led to the string of events that had now culminated in a week-long Title VII discrimination suit brought by Janice Keim. As Karl waited for Judge Lyle Eastman to return to the courtroom and announce his verdict, he mentally recounted the testimony and events that led to his appearance as a witness and observer of Janice Keim's discrimination suit against Southeastern State and the College of Education that refused to hire her.

Janice Keim first expressed interest in a job at Southeastern State in a letter addressed to Dean Paul Moose in May 1974 prior to the completion of her doctorate degree in Education from Florida State University (FSU) in the summer of 1976. Janice also held an M.S. in Special Education from Trenton State College and a B.A. in Early Childhood Education from College of the City of New York, as well as Teaching Certificates in Early Childhood Education, Elementary Education, Junior College, Varying Exceptionalities, and Mental Retardation in the state where Southeastern was located. Dean Paul Moose acknowledged her letter by promising to keep her in mind even though no jobs were available. In the early part of 1975 Keim applied to the applicant pool, a computerized data base created by Southeastern State, an historically all-black institution.

At the time Keim (a white female) applied to the applicant pool, Caucasians were considered a minority at Southeastern State and were listed as minority employees on the EEO reports submitted to the Department of Health, Education,

---

*This case was written by Stuart A. Youngblood.

and Welfare on behalf of the university system. The computerized data base was created in response to a state-ordered desegregation plan such that qualified applicants could be matched to job openings among the state university system. In theory, applicants could submit their credentials to the Personnel Programs Office (PPO) of the Board of Regents who in turn would prepare the state university system listing and use the computer to list those pool applicants who met the basic minimum qualifications for the advertised position. When a match occurred, the PPO coordinator contacted the campus EEO coordinator with the applicant data.

In August 1976 Karl wrote a position description for slot #00408, which was created when Laverne Strange, a black female, retired. The position description, which was advertised in the state university system listing between August 27 and September 2, read as follows:

> Doctorate in Exceptional Child Education (Special Education) with concentration preferred in Motor Disabilities or related areas. Conduct undergraduate classes in motor disabilities (mental retardation and specific learning disabilities courses may be included if background is appropriate): must advise undergraduate and graduate students and supervise field experience of students. Salary range $11,000–$13,000 for nine-month appointment.

The deadline for filling this position was September 9. When no applications were received in response to this listing, Karl met with Dean Moose and they revised the position vacancy listing for this permanent, nine-month, tenure-track position #00408 to read as follows:

> Ph.D. strongly preferred; MA/MS with 5 years' experience will be considered. Background should include work with motor disabled and mentally retarded children: elementary/early childhood education beneficial.

This listing ran from November 19 through November 25, with the deadline moved to December 3.

Janice Keim did not see the job listing of position #00408 in August, but she saw the November advertisement on November 16. She immediately contacted the PPO coordinator who verified that she was in the system applicant pool and met the qualifications for position #00408. The PPO coordinator further advised Janice to check with Southeastern State. On this advice she contacted the EEO coordinator at Southeastern State who then sent Janice to the personnel office to complete an application for the position. Janice took the completed application to Dean Paul Moose's office where she was directed to take the application form to Karl Kaster's office. During this same day Keim contacted FSU and arranged to have her transcript and letters of recommendation forwarded to Southeastern State. Janice was concerned about meeting these requirements because the top of the first page of the application form read:

> To complete this application we must have on file transcripts of all college or university credits and three letters of recommendation, one of which must be from a former employer and one from your major advisor in graduate school.

To be sure that her credentials were in order, Janice called Karl, who confirmed that the application was complete and in order. Karl also informed Dean Moose that Keim was applying for position #00408.

Harvey Butler, a black male who was subsequently hired for position #00408, holds two M.A. degrees and an Ed.S. from Atlanta University in Early Childhood Education and Special Education and a B.S. degree in Elementary Education from Cheyney State College. Harvey found out about position #00408 through a chance meeting in Atlanta with Virginia Devoe in October. At that time Harvey was employed part-time at a major retail store.

Virginia Devoe, Coordinator in the College of Education at Southeastern State, was later asked by Dean Moose in early November to chair a departmental search committee whose responsibility was to fill position #00408. During the trial Devoe testified that she had not told Harvey Butler about the opening, even though their friendship dated back to 1972, when they met through the Consortium of Southern Colleges for Teacher Education. Needless to say, Southeastern State's cause was not helped when Harvey asserted during the trial that Devoe had informed him during this chance meeting that a position was available.

Virginia Devoe had never previously chaired a search committee, but she had participated in employment interviews. On December 3, the deadline for application for position #00408, Virginia confirmed her committee selections in a letter to Dean Moose. Virginia chose two black female professors whose areas were special education and early childhood education, and Karl Kaster (a white male). On the same day Virginia informed Dean Moose in a letter that was entered as evidence in the trial by Janice Keim that the interview process was underway. In her letter she stated that the selection committee was formed, that she would pick up Harvey Butler if the Dean would inform her of Butler's arrival time, that the conference room could be used for interviewing, and that the two female professors of the search committee "can show him around the setting and further discuss the details of their plans and work with him." The letter concluded with Virginia recommending that a team of professors from Southeastern State attend a conference in Houston, Texas, during January of 1977. One of the recommended names was Harvey Butler.

On December 6, Harvey called Virginia Devoe to discuss the housing situation at Southeastern State. During this same day Dean Moose called Butler to make arrangements for his interview on December 9. On December 9, Harvey Butler was met at the airport by Virginia Devoe, spoke with Dean Moose both before and after his interview, received an application form from Dean Moose, and spent about two-and-one-half hours with the screening committee.

During the interview Butler was told that the position was temporary. Nonetheless he expressed interest in it. When asked by the committee what he could contribute to Southeastern State programs, Butler replied that he was interested in developing a special program for exceptional children. Moreover, Butler noted that he had experience writing grant proposals and that he was a major writer of a project in Pennsylvania.

At the time of the interview things seemed to go very smoothly for Harvey Butler; the recollection of the interview process by Karl Kaster was anything but smooth. At the trial the issue of qualifications was raised, which launched a discussion of Harvey's resume. Because the resume was the only document before the screening committee at the time of the interview, it was examined carefully, perhaps too carefully. An embarrassed Karl mentally recalled the numerous inaccuracies noted with the resume during Harvey Butler's testimony. For example, Butler's resume stated that he was a teacher at Green Valley Elementary School from October 1960 through June 1970. Butler testified, though, that he held that position from October 1969 to June of 1970. Butler's employment at Rogers College was only from March 1973 to January 1974, yet his resume showed employment from June of 1970 until January 1974. Butler's resume stated he was employed by the Pennsylvania Department of Education from March 11, 1973, to August 11, 1976, when he was actually employed there from March 1974 to August of 1976. Finally, Butler's resume conflicted with his transcripts by indicating fulltime employment at Rogers College in 1972 at the same time he was enrolled in fifteen hours of courses at Atlanta University, and fifteen hours of courses at Georgia State University. Karl cringed again as he recalled his own testimony that he "couldn't recall any acknowledgment of these discrepancies by the screening committee." Harvey Butler, when pressed by Janice Keim's attorney, characterized the inaccuracies as "typographical errors."

On the evening of December 9, the day Harvey Butler completed his interview, Karl Kaster decided to telephone Janice Keim and inquire if she had been scheduled to be interviewed for the position. The next morning Janice Keim called Dean Moose to arrange an interview and was referred to Virginia Devoe. Virginia told Janice that she was reviewing applications, scheduling interviews, and that her application was in order. Janice followed up the phone conversation with a letter reaffirming her interest in the position. At the trial Virginia could not recollect the phone call.

On the same day, however, Virginia Devoe wrote Dean Moose on behalf of the screening committee and recommended that Harvey Butler be hired. During the same day Dean Moose called Georgia State to learn that Harvey Butler had not taken his comprehensive exams and was still considered a doctoral candidate at Atlanta University. During the trial Virginia Devoe testified that as of this date, December 10, she was only aware of Butler's application for position #00408. She also testified that she only knew whom to interview by the resumes received from the Dean's office. She admitted, though, that between November and December 3 she did not check with the Dean's office to see if there were other applicants. When Dean Moose received her letter recommending Butler she testified that Dean Moose came to her office and told her, "You're supposed to interview all the applicants."

On December 13, the same day that Butler dated his application form (which was received by Dean Moose's office December 15), Virginia Devoe's secretary phoned Janice Keim, at 9:00 A.M. and informed her that her interview was scheduled for 10:30 A.M. that morning. The screening committee interviewed Janice for one-and-one-half hours. Needless to say, she was surprised to learn the position was temporary but she still expressed interest and volunteered that she would take the job.

Virginia Devoe testified that the committee met on the morning of December 14 to finalize the decision on the candidates and that "Harvey Butler was the one." Kaster, however, did not recall the events as Devoe stated. Kaster testified that the committee used rating forms immediately after the interview to rate each candidate in their field and relative to the other candidates. No meeting was necessary on December 14 according to Karl because the chair could simply tabulate the ratings from the form. Virginia testified that at the conclusion of Harvey Butler's interview three committee members rated Butler favorably and one was neutral (identified as Karl Kaster). Virginia testified that on the morning of December 14, the committee met again and reached consensus that Butler should be extended the offer. Later that day Dean Moose recommended Harvey Butler for position #00408 with a starting salary of $14,500. This was subsequently approved by the vice-president of Academic Affairs. On December 22, Janice Keim received a letter from Virginia Devoe dated December 15 that thanked Keim for her interest and that stated " . . . the Committee did not effect closure on your application at this time." Janice Keim then requested in writing (in accordance with the State's Public Records Laws) that she be allowed to see the application of the person hired for position #00408. Dean Moose refused Keim's request.

Although Virginia Devoe testified that the screening committee had Butler's resume and letters of recommendation before them at the time of his interview, Janice Keim testified that the dates on the letters of recommendation when written were *after* December 9; in fact they were not received by the Dean's office until December 16, 17, and 20. Virginia Devoe then revised her testimony and suggested that perhaps the committee did not have the letters before them.

As Karl concluded his recollection of the trial events, he wondered what impact the final witness, the president of Southeastern State University, would have on the verdict. President Donald Moore (a black male) testified that in 1965 Southeastern hired its first white faculty member. Moore elaborated that Southeastern's heritage was molded by blacks and that he sought to preserve this heritage. His personal goal, however, was modified by the office of civil rights. The creation of a search committee procedure was, as he put it, "a means to vest authority in administrators other than myself." The search committee process was designed to replace the invitational method used when Virginia Devoe was hired. Thus, the committees were given choices; they were to follow the guidelines of affirmative action under the state desegregation plan. Moore testified that his administration discussed the situation of employment of too many Southeastern graduates and too many males. Moore, although evasive, did not dispute the data presented at the trial: white female representation among assistant professors for 1975, '76, '77, and '78 was 8, 9, 10, and 10 percent, respectively. Additional data also indicated that in 1975 eight of the eighty-nine assistant professors were white females, that about 10 percent of the total faculty was white, and that Southeastern was pursuing a goal of 33.33 percent white faculty members.

As Karl reflected on the impact of Moore's testimony, he was jarred back to the present with the court clerk's announcement that the Honorable Judge Lyle Eastman was returning to the court to announce his decision.

11. "Perfectly Pure Peabody's" *

A Case of Affirmative Action for Women

The Peabody Soap Company was founded by Joshua Peabody, a smalltown pharmacist who patented his formula for "Perfectly Pure Peabody's" soap in 1909. By 1973, Peabody Soap had grown from a one-product mail order house to a $100 million publicly-held beauty business with 2,500 employees. The founder's grandson, George Hinton, now chairman and chief executive officer, had masterminded the recent growth, divisionalization, and international expansion of the company.

During the last ten years, Peabody Soap had received national recognition for its achievements in pollution control, community relations, and minority employment. George Hinton was personally responsible for spearheading activities in these areas and he was proud of the company's fine record.

Hinton was known throughout the industry as a business leader with outstanding instincts for developing both quality products and a sound management team. He began his career at Peabody Soap in 1945, having spent a year at a well-known consulting firm after graduation from Stanford Business School. He assumed the presidency in 1956, and became chairman in 1965.

However, in January 1974, the resignation of Chemical Research Manager Sarah Barrington (the company's top-ranking woman) made Hinton aware that he had not adequately addressed himself to a key corporate problem: women in management.

Peabody's Marketing: 1965–1973

Prior to 1965, the company had limited production to a highly successful and profitable line of soap, shampoo, and related skin care products. "Perfectly Pure Peabody's" consistently maintained better than a 20 percent share of the face soap market. In the mid-60s George Hinton decided to expand product lines domestically and open up new foreign markets.

To meet the domestic objective, he promoted Herbert Richardson, a 46-year-old production manager, to vice-president of marketing. Richardson, who had come up through the ranks, was considered a rugged individualist. His energy, directness, and work record made him a prime candidate to succeed George Hinton, who had already announced that the next chief executive officer wouldn't be a "member of the family."

Richardson's first move was to create a market research department. After a year of thorough market analysis by the new department, Richardson recommended that Peabody expand into the hypo-allergenic skin care products

*Reprinted from *Stanford Business Cases 1974* with permission of the publishers, Stanford University Graduate School of Business. © 1974 by the Board of Trustees of the Leland Stanford Junior University.

field. Because the company had experienced little need for research before the decision to broaden the line, its chemical laboratory was inadequately staffed for experimentation. As a result of his industry review, Richardson knew that several companies were experimenting with hypo-allergenics. He was convinced that the growth objective of the company depended on the caliber of the chemical research section and the speed with which it could develop new products. A "blind" ad for a product research manager, placed in several trade publications, *The Wall Street Journal,* and *The New York Times* brought in nearly eighty applications.

Richardson, who prided himself on his young and eager management team, was particularly impressed with one applicant—32-year-old Sarah Barrington, an unmarried research chemist. Barrington had spent the last three years as assistant laboratory director for Peabody's nearest competitor. Born and educated in England, she held a graduate degree in Business Economics and a doctorate in Organic Chemistry. Her total work experience was only four years but she had an outstanding record with both of her previous employers. Furthermore, her salary requirements were low ($15,000 per year) compared with other applicants.

After her initial interview with Richardson, Barrington was sent to the company's industrial psychologist who summarized his findings: "Sarah has good management potential, she is highly results-oriented with the proper balance of deference to authority. If, however, she cannot see the logic of a superior's request, she will seek an honest explanation. She is respectful, but also inquisitive and direct. She is ambitious as well, and will benefit from working toward long-term career goals." (See Exhibit 1.)

On the basis of her work record, the psychologist's assessment, and the knowledge that Hinton would be pleased to finally have a woman on his management team, Richardson selected Barrington for the job. In January 1967, she was named manager of chemical research and given full responsibility for setting up and staffing the lab.

Since fire laws prohibited the establishment of a laboratory in Peabody's headquarters, the research facility was located in a "loft" at a warehouse several blocks away. By March 1967, the laboratory was operational and Barrington hired a senior researcher, five assistant researchers, and a secretary. A year later, after a crash program involving close collaboration among the researchers, Peabody Soap was able to patent a process for the manufacture of "Peabody's Super Sensitives," a line of hypoallergenic products matched product by product to the regular Peabody Line.

The sales increase of 50 percent over the next two years was due, in great measure, to the introduction of the new products. In January 1970, the Company went public to raise much-needed capital for future growth—with funds earmarked for expansion in international markets. No new domestic product research of any magnitude would be required to meet these objectives.

Soon after the development and patenting of the "Super Sensitives" process the research staff was cut in half with the remaining members moving into quality control and analysis of new raw materials. Barrington received a citation from the Board of Directors and won an industry award for her work—but the company was no longer interested in expanding product lines. Realizing that she was at a dead end in her present position, Barrington hired a management trainee in 1970 so that she could prepare someone to assume her position. A year later the trainee

INDUSTRIAL PSYCHOLOGIST'S REPORT ON SARAH BARRINGTON: 1/5/67

Miss Barrington is a conscientious, industrious, dependable woman
who takes herself and her responsibilities seriously. She enjoys
her work, is ambitious for career progress, and is willing to work
as hard as necessary to achieve her goals.

She is alert, intelligent, perceptive of what goes on around her,
and is eager to learn all she can about the processes with which she
works. Her strong points are trouble-shooting and problem-solving;
she is analytical, critical, and objective in her approach to situations of a technical nature. She works at a brisk pace, with strong
focus on tasks and takes pressure well. She plans effectively, is
well-organized and methodical, and can be counted on to meet
requirements. She sets high standards for herself and others and
faces up to issues squarely.

She likes activities that are challenging, stimulating, and rewarding
on which her capabilities will be utilized fully and which will
provide opportunities for further growth. Initiative is readily
available; she welcomes responsibilities and is eager to show what
she can do on her own. She likes to explore wherever clues lead,
will innovate and improvise as warranted, and is not reluctant to
take calculated risks to test the validity of her ideas.

Verbal and social skills are very good. She is articulate, precise,
fluent or terse as necessary, and typically puts people at ease.
While initially reserved with others, there is a warmth and dignity
about her to which people respond favorably. She enjoys working
with and through people and usually gets along with them.
Occasionally, nevertheless, some people may be disconcerted by her
somewhat unfeminine tendency to be forthright and outspoken when
provoked.

On the job she prefers to set her own pace and be in control over her
domain. Direction and criticism are used constructively, but she
dislikes close supervision after assignments are outlined for her.
She is most effective when allowed to participate in planning and
decision-making affecting her activities, given adequate authority
for implementing them, and support when needed. Generally, she
makes every effort to figure things out for herself before presenting suggestions or plans for discussion and approval.

Attitudes toward authority are favorable. She is appropriately
deferent, cooperates fully, and complies and conforms as required to
promote the organization's objectives. However, when directives or
procedures don't make sense to her she will raise questions and offer
her views--tactfully but unequivocally. She needs superiors who are
competent, strong, worthy of her esteem, and who keep communication
lines open. Above all, she needs to be dealt with honestly and fairly,
and be given adequate recognition for whatever she contributes to the
overall effort.

Her outstanding trait, perhaps, is her impelling drive for personal
achievement and career progress. And her strongest asset is indicated
potential for further growth. Thus, while she is young and her
experience is not extensive, and the fact that she's a woman will
make her sometimes less effective, she should be capable of getting
the new unit started.

EXHIBIT 1

was offered a promotion to assistant manager of market research. (Since he would receive more pay in the new position, company policy prohibited Barrington from refusing to let him make the move.) The following year, a similar promotion was accepted by his replacement.

In June 1972, separate product divisions were established. The work of the marketing function was to be phased out to the divisions over the next two years. At the same time, Richardson was promoted to president. John Carlisle, a distribution manager who was nearing retirement, was named marketing director. While most phases of the marketing divisionalization were easily achieved, the lab posed a real problem. Divisions were not interested in the additional overhead of separate labs. Yet, they all insisted that a company lab was necessary. Carlisle had little knowledge of the lab function and did not care to supervise the section. To deal with the situation, he held a meeting of all division managers to determine to whom the lab should report. They decided on quality control and sent Barrington a memo informing her of the new reporting relationship.

Equal Employment Opportunity at Peabody Soap

A family tradition of community involvement was a vital part of Peabody Soap's corporate policy. Joshua Peabody had a personal policy of donating one-quarter of his annual earnings to community organizations. His son-in-law, William Hinton, received nationwide recognition for his successful racial integration of the Peabody factory in the 1950s—long before such actions were required by law. It came as no surprise when, in 1967, George Hinton was appointed one of six Presidential advisors on the blue ribbon committee, "Minority Employment and the American Future."

Although laws requiring affirmative action for minorities were not promulgated until 1969, Hinton had set goals for the promotion and hiring of minority group members as early as 1966. By 1973, every Peabody plant had a workforce which reflected the racial composition of its community.

Finding an effective Equal Employment Opportunity (EEO) manager, however, had been a difficult task. After several men failed at the position, Richard Adams proved to have the necessary qualities for the job. Adams, thirty-five years old, had been a white activist in the Civil Rights Movement in the early sixties. His understanding of the problem of minority employment combined with his ability to establish good rapport with managers led to his success in Peabody's personnel department.

Peabody's workforce had always been about 50 percent female. While production jobs in some industries weren't considered "women's work," cosmetic soap manufacture was an acceptable industry for female workers. Peabody actually assessed potential plant sites based on labor surveys of the rate of female unemployment in the area. If the figure were high and other factors were favorable, the location was selected.

The precision involved in the work, clean working conditions, and low wages had also been cited as reasons why women were employed in the industry. Peabody Soap, like its competitors, had been slow in moving women into management. In 1973, Sarah Barrington was the highest ranking woman in the company—and one of only four women in middle or upper management.

In 1971, federal legislation requiring affirmative action for women was in the wind. George Hinton's own daughter was pressuring him to take a closer look at the underutilization of women and the related issues of day care and job restructuring. Hinton had an "open door" policy—any employee could come directly to him with a problem—and several women within the Company had used it to point out areas for improvement.

As a result, Hinton asked Personnel to add a woman to Adam's staff to handle female affirmative action. In fact, Hinton suggested his own secretary, 27-year-old Brenda Goldman, for the job. "She's been with us for five years now—she's bright, capable, and knows our management," Hinton explained to Adams, "and she's not one of those Women's Libbers. I hate to give her up, but I'd feel more comfortable with her in the job." Goldman became EEO assistant two weeks later. Announcement of her promotion included Hinton's policy statement regarding Equal Employment (Exhibit 2).

From the outset, rapport between Adams and Goldman was difficult.

Goldman: Where do I get started with the women's program, Dick? Guess I should begin by getting an idea of how we're going to be working together. . . .

Adams: I'm looking forward to getting this women's thing started, Brenda. But frankly, we're going to have to hold back on anything big for a while. Right now minorities—blacks in particular—are our biggest problem. That doesn't

---

TO: All Employees   December 5, 1971
FROM: George Hinton

  At Peabody's Soap, we have always been concerned with developing our resources--both in terms of people and products. It has also been our philosophy that discrimination, in any form, will not be tolerated here. We now recognize that women, as well as minorities, have suffered the effects of employment prejudice in the past.

  We are, therefore, establishing a program of Affirmative Action for Women. Brenda Goldman, who joined the company as a secretary in 1968, will move up to become EEO Assistant for women reporting to our EEO Manager. Her responsibilities, aside from the implementation of the women's program, will include counseling, developing recruitment resources, and providing other supportive services.

  In the year ahead we will intensify our efforts in the identification of promotable women.

  At Peabody's Soap EEO is a corporate-wide policy. Every division, department and facility is charged with the responsibility of setting goals and every manager is evaluated on the action he or she takes to insure that our commitment is met. Monitoring the program, providing support services, and insuring that all personnel practices are equitable is the duty of our Equal Employment Section.

  It is my sincerest hope that we will continue to direct our energies toward EEO for women with the same vigor and enthusiasm with which we approach all other pressing business problems.

EXHIBIT 2

mean we're going to forget about women. You know, we've already made real headway. Sarah Barrington's doing a great job . . . she's one of the top twenty managers in the company. Besides, we're letting Carla O'Day and Helen Coates go on half-time jobs because they want to spend time at home with their young children. We've sent ten women to that "Women in Management Course" at company expense . . . we've liberalized our maternity leave policy. . . .

Goldman: You're right, we have taken some excellent steps and most of the innovation came from you, Dick . . . you must admit though, that we still have monstrous problems. Look at the statistics. Women have a worse problem at Peabody's than do minorities.

Adams: I disagree. Black men have always had a tougher time finding work than have women.

Goldman: Dick, we could go around in circles about this. I don't agree with you. Black men and women both have had a tough time . . . and, I hasten to add, so do the other minorities—you forget about Chicanos, Asians, and American Indians. All of these groups are considered "Affected Classes" by the law.

Adams: Look, we've made progress and we'll keep making it . . . but we have to see this thing in perspective.

The conflicts were, of course, private; the reports which reached Hinton showed progress. To his knowledge, the EEO function was being handled well and the company's reputation continued to be virtually untarnished.

Another aspect of the EEO operation of which Hinton was unaware was Goldman's "image" in the company. She had been accepted neither by her "constituency" nor by management.

Barrington's Resignation

On January 15, 1974, George Hinton received this letter:

Dear Mr. Hinton:

It is with deep personal and professional regret that I must submit my resignation, effective February 1, 1974. While Peabody Soap has provided me with the opportunity to make an outstanding contribution in chemical research, I find no room for developing beyond this department.

The recent shift in reporting relationships in my section and the manner in which that shift was accomplished make it clear that my services to the organization are no longer of value. Furthermore, my ability to effect a promotion to other departments has been deliberately inhibited.

I suggest you personally audit your EEO Program for Women. Many problems with potential legal implications exist in the organization.

Thank you for your personal encouragement over the last five years.

Sincerely,

Sarah Barrington

Hinton, alarmed by the letter, called the personnel department and asked them to send up a copy of Barrington's latest review (Exhibit 3) immediately.

EMPLOYEE PERFORMANCE APPRAISAL	REVIEW PERIOD		
	From (Mo-Yr) **DECEMBER 1971**		To (Mo-Yr) **DECEMBER 1973**

Employee Name **SARAH BARRINGTON**	Position Title **MGR. PRODUCT RESEARCH**	No. Months in Present Position **10**	No. Months Supervised by Rater **6**	Seniority Date **FEB 5, 1967**	Field Location **ADJACENT LAB**

Responsibilities Performed (to be written by Employee)	Performance Appraisal (to be written by Rater)
List agreed upon objectives under each responsibility:	Evaluate employee's performance on each responsibility and related objectives
1. COMPLETE LISTS FOR ALL POSSIBLE NEW MATERIALS AND PROCESSES '72-'73.	1. EXCELLENT
2. ASSIST MARKETING GROUP BY NOTIFYING THEM OF TESTS OF ALL COMPETITORS' PRODUCTS.	2. EXCELLENT
3. SUPERVISE STAFF OF 4.	3. SARAH IS A GOOD SUPERVISOR.
4. DEVELOP BETTER EXPOSURE FOR LAB TO OTHER FUNCTIONS.	4. SARAH IS PROGRESSING IN THIS AREA.
5. MAINTAIN PROGRESS ON X-22 PROJECT.	5. X-22 COMPLETED SATISFACTORILY.

OVERALL JOB PERFORMANCE

☐ Unsatisfactory ☐ Fair ☐ Competent ☐ Highly Competent ☑ Exceptional

COMMENTS

Rater's Signature _John Caudle_ Date 12/3/73

Employee Signature _Sarah Barrington_ Date 12/5/73

ADVANCEMENT POTENTIAL

☐ Can Develop Further in Present Position ☐ Adequately Placed ☑ Ready for Advancement Now

COMMENTS

Manager's Signature _John Castle_ Date

Describe Two or More of Employee's Strongest Points:

1. SUCCESSFULLY DELEGATES AUTHORITY.
2. DOES AN EXCELLENT JOB OF TRAINING SUBORDINATES.
3. RUNS AN EFFICIENT LAB, NEEDS LITTLE SUPERVISION.
4. VERY PROFESSIONAL IN HER APPROACH.

List Two or More Areas that Could Profit from Improvement:

1. SARAH IS SOMETIMES AGGRESSIVE... SOME OF THE MANAGERS SHE WORKS WITH FIND THIS "PUTS THEM OFF". IT MAY INHIBIT HER JOB PERFORMANCE.
2. SHE COULD BENEFIT FROM MORE INVOLVEMENT IN MANAGEMENT ACTIVITIES.

What Are this Employee's Career Goals?

FOR SOMETIME, SARAH HAS INDICATED AN INTEREST IN PROGRESSING TO ANOTHER MANAGEMENT POSITION. NOTHING IS AVAILABLE AT PRESENT.

Suggested and Agreed Upon Actions to be Taken for Self Improvement and Achievement of Career Goals:

SARAH IS OUR TOP FEMALE MANAGER AND THEREFORE IS A GOOD CANDIDATE FOR PROMOTION. TO DO SO, SHE MUST HAVE CLOSER COMMUNICATIONS WITH OTHER MANAGERS. SHE WOULD BENEFIT FROM A LITTLE "SOFTENING" TOO.... BEING A BIT MORE GENTLE IN HER APPROACH.

CURRENT SALARY: Weekly **340**	SALARY GRADE **30**	
RECOMMENDED SALARY: Weekly **397** Eff. Date **JAN 1, 1974**	CURRENT SALARY	
	Min Mid Max	

EXHIBIT 3

After a quick reading of Barrington's review, Hinton confirmed his belief that Barrington was an above-average manager in all respects. Next, Hinton asked Richardson to come to his office.

The Hinton/Richardson conversation went as follows:

Hinton: Herb, did you know that Sarah Barrington resigned?

Richardson: No, George, but I did know she was unhappy here . . . it doesn't surprise me. For the last two years she's wanted to get out of the lab . . . but there's nowhere for her to go. She doesn't know any other function . . . and the fact that she's located in that other building just hasn't given her any exposure.

Hinton: Do you think it's because she's a woman?

Richardson: Oh, George, I just don't think that's a problem with Sarah. She's had an excellent job and makes good money for a woman.

Hinton: How have her raises been?

Richardson: Well, since she's been in the same job all this time . . . and this wage freeze has been in effect . . . oh, she makes a little less than twenty grand.

Hinton: Well, where could she go?

Richardson: George, I don't know.

Hinton: Well, what about her reviews?

Richardson: They're great. She's good at what she does . . . we've been very pleased, as you know, with the contributions she's made in research.

Hinton: We've never really talked about her for a promotion, have we?

Richardson: George, I don't think anyone's ready for her to take over a major function as yet. We considered her for that International job . . . but they just didn't think a woman could do the job.

Hinton: Herb, off the record, what do the guys think of her?

Richardson: That's a tough question . . . nobody really talks about her very much. She's effective for a woman. They respect her judgment . . . but we don't know much more about her. Her trouble is that she doesn't sell herself enough. She doesn't socialize. Frankly, George, I don't know what more we can do to keep her here.

Hinton: Thanks Herb, I appreciate your candor. Oh, one more question . . . how do you think Brenda is doing in her new job? You're closer to the action around here than I am. . . .

Richardson: To tell you the truth, George, I've been meaning to speak to you about Brenda. Although the figures are up slightly, I haven't heard anything about an affirmative action program for women, and from what I have seen and heard I think Brenda may be having problems. Just what the cause of the difficulty is, I'm not sure; it may be the set up in that office, or it may be Brenda herself. Let me do some more probing and I'll get back to you.

Hinton: You really think Brenda may be at fault?

Richardson: Well, it's possible. We just may have to move her out.

Hinton: Thanks, Herb. Let me know what you find out.

Hinton then called Barrington and asked her to come to his office. Traditionally brief at his meetings, Hinton decided to break the rule with Barrington to delve more deeply into her side of the story. The relationship between Barrington and Hinton had always been cordial and open.

Hinton: Sarah, I really don't want to accept your resignation. I'd like you to stay on. Tell me exactly why you've made this decision . . . and don't be afraid of chewing my ear.

Barrington: I joined the Peabody Soap Company in 1967 because, as I stated on my application, I wanted the opportunity to grow with a growth company. In fact, I chose to go into industry because I hoped to move from strict chemical research into other related areas of the organization. The reason-ableness of that goal is evident when one looks at the experience of the two trainees I've had. Both men hold degrees similar to mine. I hired them at Herb's urging . . . "You can't get promoted until you have a replacement," he kept stressing. But both Simon and Roger were offered promotions to other parts of the company. They make almost as much as I do now, and their work experiences and the exposure they're getting will make them more valuable to the company.

So much for what might sound like jealousy . . . and if it does, I'm sorry. I'm proud of Simon and Roger because I hired and trained them in the beginning. I mention them only as examples. In fact, my secretary was promoted to a training position in the Soap Division last month—so your Affirmative Action Program does work.

But, back to my problems. Although I've indicated to both Herb and my new supervisor that I want to progress beyond my present job, nothing has happened. Other managers have been promoted from technical to non-technical jobs. Take Frank Everett, he was quality control manager and now he runs the "Super Sensitive" Division.

My reviews have been good and have indicated that I'm ready but when top jobs open up, no one even thinks of me. There was a job open for a research director in the International Division—it would have meant a big promotion in grade, pay, and status. I wasn't even considered, as I found out later, because they "didn't think a woman could do the job." It involved travel and dealing with raw materials suppliers—I do those things in my job now. And I had all the requirements, too. No one thinks I'm "strong" enough to negotiate or wheel and deal.

When Herb left—I had thought that he was my real mentor—things got worse. Carlisle doesn't know me or what we do in the lab, and frankly, he doesn't care. I discussed my desire to be promoted and he simply said he'd get back to me on it; he hasn't.

You wonder why I haven't pursued it further? George, have you seen my last review? *[He indicated that he'd just read it.]* Well, look at the strengths and weaknesses section. Carlisle listed aggressiveness as a weak-ness. If I come on too strong, I'm considered "brassy" or "pushy" . . . and unfeminine. If I'm the least bit reticent, they think I don't have the stuff managers are made of. No one seems to be able to cope with the idea of a woman manager.

Frankly, George, I've been discriminated against for the last few years. I've never been promoted; I've never had much of a raise; I've never received a stock option; I've never been invited to the Annual Management Meeting . . . probably because it's held at the Downtown Club, where women aren't even allowed.

It's harder for people to level with me, too. Herb never gave me many pointers about improvement. I hardly got any feedback, negative or positive.

The other men here won't treat me as an equal either and there aren't any other women even near my level in the organization . . . so I have no one to emulate or consult.

George, there really isn't anything you can do about these things, I know. I don't mean to sound melodramatic, but I'm honestly fed up with having to perform like I'm "Superwoman" . . . and being treated like someone's little sister.

Hinton: I'm glad you've been so frank with me, Sarah. Have you talked to anybody in Personnel about this?

Barrington: Yes, I did give Brenda a call and we had lunch. We've known each other for a long time and I'd hoped she could give me some advice. She suggested talking it over with Herb. I did, but he didn't seem very concerned . . . I think he's lost interest in me since his promotion.

George, Brenda's in an impossible situation. Adams hasn't given her any guidance in counseling, he's jsut made a statistician out of her. She cited two cases where she's afraid we're going to have sex discrimination suits—but she can't get anywhere with Adams . . . he simply sees the women's program as a threat. Most of the women in the company don't even know who Brenda is. In fact, there's an indepedent Women's Group already holding meetings outside the company. It's common knowledge that Brenda is all but totally ineffectual.

At the close of their conversation, Hinton asked Barrington if she'd wait a few days before her final resignation. Barrington agreed and offered a handshake. Hinton then began to consider his course of action.

12. Peoples Trust Company*

The Peoples Trust Company first opened its doors to the public on June 1, 1875, with a total salaried staff of eight members: a treasurer; a secretary; and six assistants (three of whom held the positions of day watchman, night watchman, and messenger). Located in a large, midwestern city, the original company had occupied the basement floor of a new five-story office building with an electric-bell system, steam heat, and steam-driven elevator.

During its early years, the Trust Company had concentrated its activities on providing vault services to its customers for the safekeeping of tangible items and securities. Management had been able to develop the reputation of being a highly conservative trust company that concentrated on a relatively small and select market of wealthy individuals from the local area. In the years following, the vault service had been retained as an accommodation to its customers, but the

---

*This case was prepared by Hrach Bedrosian and is used here with his permission.

company's emphasis had slowly shifted from vault service to a wider range of banking and trust services.

Until the early 1900s, banking services had overshadowed trust services in terms of asset volume. Following the turn of the century, trust assets had begun to grow at an increasing rate. Over the years, the company had been able to achieve an impressive record of sound and steady growth. According to a story often told in banking circles: "Peoples Trust was so conservative that they prospered even during the Depression!"

In 1963, with the appointment of a new president, a new era began for Peoples Trust Company. Between 1963 and 1978, trust assets under supervision rose by $145 million, while deposits increased by more than $20 million. The company entered 1983 with about $2 billion in trust assets and $90 million in savings deposits.

Accompanying this recent growth has been the company's desire to fashion a new image for itself. In 1979, Mr. Robert Toller assumed the presidency of Peoples Trust. In 1982, he remarked: ". . . it should be said that the old concept of a trust involving merely the regular payment of income and preservation of capital is largely obsolete." Accordingly, the Investment Division of the company had been expanded and strengthened. Similar changes had been effected in the Trust and Estate Administrative Group and other customer services. Among these were the improvement of accounting methods and procedures, the installation of electronic data processing systems, and complete renovation of the company's eight-floor building and facilities. Most recently, the company has extended its services into the field of management consulting. This had been acknowledged as a "pioneer" step for a banking institution. The president recently characterized the company as "an organization in the fiduciary business."

At the time these data were gathered, the company had a total of 602 employees. Of this number, 109 were in what is considered the "officer-group"[1] positions of the company. The company's relations with its employees over the years have been satisfactory. The Peoples Trust is generally recognized by city residents and those in suburban areas as a good place to work. The company hires most of its employees from the local area.

In the period before 1980 Peoples Trust had provided satisfactory advancement opportunities for its employees, and it had been possible for a young, high-school graduate who showed promise on the job to work his way up gradually to officer status. Graduates of banking institutions were also sought for employment with the company. Ordinarily individuals were considered eligible for promotion to the jobs above them after they had thoroughly mastered the details of their present positions.

Prior to 1980 the total staff of the company was small enough so that there was no need to prepare official organization charts or job descriptions. Virtually all of the employees knew each other on a first-name basis, and they were generally familiar with each other's area of job responsibility. New employees were rapidly able to learn "whom you had to go to for what."

In 1980 the company management called in an outside consultant to appraise its organizational structure and operations and to confer on the rapid expansion and diversification of banking services that the company had planned. The

---

1. Membership in the officer group is determined by an employee's being legally empowered to represent the company in a transaction.

presence of the consultants and the subsequent preparation of organization charts and job descriptions reportedly "shook up a lot of people"—many feared loss of their jobs or, at least, substantial changes in the nature of work and assignments. However, there was little overt reaction among the officer-level employees in terms of turnover and/or other indices of unrest.

Over the years it had been the policy of the company to pay wages that were at least average or a little above the average paid by comparable banking organizations in the area. This, combined with favorable employee relations and the stable and prestigious nature of the work, resulted in a low turnover of personnel. The bulk of employee turnover occurred among the younger employees who filled clerical positions throughout the company's various departments.

Since 1980, the personnel picture at Peoples Trust has been shifting. Several changes have taken place in the top management of the company. By adding several new customer services, the company has altered the very nature of its business. This has resulted in a trend toward "professionalization" of many of the officer-level positions in that these positions now require individuals with higher levels of education and broader abilities. The impact of these changes on current employees has been a matter of concern to several executives in the company, particularly to Mr. John Moore, Manager of the Organization Planning and Personnel Department. Mr. Moore described his picture of the situation to the researcher as follows.[2]

Interview with John Moore, V.P., Organization Planning and Personnel

Our problem here is one of a changing image and along with it the changing of people. As a trust company, we had no other ties with an individual's financial needs . . . we could only talk in terms of death. We wanted to be able to talk in terms of life, we we got active in the investment-advisory business.

The old wealth around here is pretty well locked up, so we wanted to provide services to new and growing organizations and to individuals who are accumulating wealth. Our problem is one of reorientation. We used to provide one service for one customer. We now want to enter new ventures, offer new services, attract new customers. The problem has become one of how to make the change . . . do we have the talent and the people to make the change?

We have a "band" of people (see Exhibits 1 and 2) in our organization . . . in the thirty-five to fifty age group who came in under the old hiring practices and ground rules. Given the new directions in which our company is moving and the changing job requirements, it's clear that, considering their current qualifications and capabilities, these individuals have nowhere to go. Some have been able to accept this; and this acceptance includes watching others move past them. Others have difficulty accepting it . . . a few have left . . . and we haven't discouraged anyone from leaving. For those who can't accept it, there

---

2. Mr. Moore drew from his files a list of ten individuals who he felt were representative of the group whose lack of appropriate experience or qualifications created a road block to their future development and advancement with the company. These individuals are described in Exhibit 1.

Exhibit 1. Peoples Trust Company

Name	Age	Education	Date of Hire	Positions Held
Linda Horn	37	2-year technical institute of business administration	1975	Messenger Clearance clerk Accounting clerk Unit head (working supervisor) Section head (supervisor)
Richard Gaul*	30	2-year junior college program in business administration	1977	Business machines operator Section head (supervisor) Operations officer
Fred James	35	B.A. degree, local university American Institute of Banking	1976	Loan clerk Teller Accounting unit head (working supervisor) Section head (supervisor)
Fran Wilson*	35	1 year at a local university	1981	Methods analyst Operations unit head (working supervisor) Systems programmer Property accounting dept. head
Martin Pfieffer*	32	Prep school	1977	Messenger Accounting clerk Section head (supervisor) Department head
James Klinger	38	B.A. degree from local university	1972	Messenger Accounting clerk Records clerk Unit head (working supervisor) Administrative specialist
Karen Kissler*	35	B.A. degree from local university co-op program	1974	Messenger Real property specialist Assistant estate officer
Charles Ferris	42	2-year jr. college program in business administration American Institute of Banking	1962	Messenger Deposit accounting section head (supervisor) Unit head (working supervisor)
William Jagger	54	High school	1949	Messenger Trust liaison clerk Accounting clerk Bookkeeping section head
Thomas Geoghigan*	42	2-year jr. college program in business administration	1969	Messenger Securities accountant Property custodian Office manager Assistant operations officer

*Officer

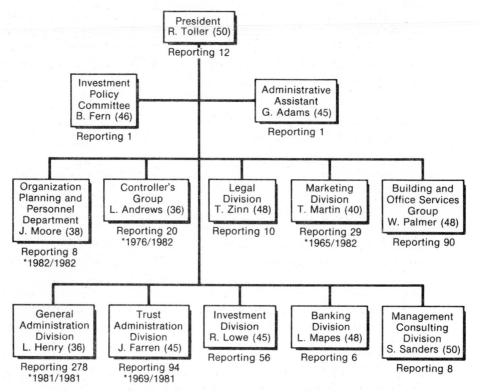

Note: Numbers in parentheses indicate manager's age. These are included for planning purposes only. Numbers below each position indicate number of subordinates.

*Indicates year in which manager joined the Company and year in which he assumed current position. For example, Mr. Larry Andrews joined Peoples Trust Company in 1976, and became Controller in 1982.

Exhibit 2. Peoples Trust Company Organization Chart (June 1983)

is the problem of integrating their career strategy with ours. We've articulated our objectives clearly; now individuals need clarification of their own strategies.

As I see it, change caught up with these individuals. They had on-the-job training in their own areas, but that doesn't help them much to cope with the new demands. New functional areas are being melded on top of old ones. For example, marketing is new; so is electronic data processing. They both require qualities that our existing employee staff didn't have.

To date, we have not approached any of these people in an individual way to discuss their problems with them. Our objectives are to further develop these people, but we'll first have to get the support of the department managers who supervise them.

We want to find ways to further develop personnel of the kind represented by this group through a variety of approaches. I am thinking here not only of formal job training in management development, but also of management techniques that would help individuals identify new kinds of qualifications or possible new standards of performance they must take into consideration in planning their own personal growth.

We also have to find ways to provide more opportunities for minorities and women in the organization, particularly at the officer level. Although Peoples Trust is not a federal contractor, we would like to be seen as and be an affirmative action employer and an organization where everyone has an equal chance for employment and promotion.

We have to change the conditioning of old times throughout the company. A recently hired MBA is now an officer. Years ago that couldn't have happened so rapidly. And not everyone here is in agreement that the appointment I just mentioned *should* have happened the way it did. We have to develop support in our company for the new recruiting image.

There are two things which really concern me most about this whole problem:

1. We have a problem in under-utilization of resources.
2. There is a problem which is presented to the growth and development of the company in having some of the individuals I have been discussing settled into key spots.

The company really bears the responsibility for the current situation as I described it. In addition, what this all means to me is that our personnel function may change considerably over the coming year.

After this interview with Mr. Moore, the researcher talked with other company executives to learn their views of the problems outlined by Mr. Moore. The findings from these interviews are presented below.

Interview with Fred Bellows—Human Resource Planning

Historically we have been conservatively managed . . . you might say "ultra-conservatively." But now we want to change that image. Several years ago there was a revolution in top management. In 1979, Mr. Toller took over and brought in young people, many not from the banking field but from other types of business and consulting organizations. Our employment philosophy may be stated as follows: "We want above-average people . . . for above-average pay . . . and we want to give them a chance to learn and grow and move with the organization." This applies mainly to those in whom we see management-level potential.

They are told in their employment interview that if they don't see opportunity with us, then they should leave. This is in contrast to the old philosophy that this is a secure place to work, that you can stay here by keeping your nose clean, and that you can sit and wait for pot luck to become a trust officer.

Many people are caught in this changing philosophy. A case in the Trust Administration Division is a good example. There we have an employee in a Grade 10 job who has been with the bank eight years. We just hired a new person out of college who we put in that same Grade 10. Now they're both at the same level, but they're entirely different people in terms of education, social background, etc.

Now the Head of our Trust Division bucks this sort of thing. She argues that we don't need all "stars" in the company. Yet, the president wants young, dynamic individuals who can develop and be developed. So I'm trying to get the Trust Division to define: what does the job really require?

We have a number of people with two years of accounting training who have been with the company anywhere from six to nine years. Under our old system they'd be okay, but under the new system they're not. They're not realistic about their future. Our problem is that we're being honest, but few are getting the message.

We bring in a new individual . . . ask others to train that person . . . and then promote that person over their heads. We have people whose jobs we could get done for a lot less money. When, if ever, do we tell them to go elsewhere?

Interview with Larry Andrews—Controller

There is no question but that there has been a complete revolution around here. In the past, we were in business to serve the community; to handle small accounts; to help the small investor who needed investment service. Our motto was "help anyone who needs help." Our employees were geared to this kind of work orientation and felt at home with it. They could easily identify themselves with this sort of approach to doing business. Most people were quite comfortable; their personal goals coincided with the company goal.

But we found that we couldn't make any money conducting this kind of business. So, we've had to extend our services to attract people who have money and can afford our service. Now the company goal has changed. For example, the Trust Department is now concerned with the management of property in general. The "dead man's bank" has become the "live people's service organization." So we've had to create a kind of snob appeal that too many of our people can't idenfity with or don't believe in.

Many problems have emerged from these changes. Before, individuals' knowledge of the details of their jobs was their greatest asset. They worked to develop that knowledge and protected it. Now—and I'm speaking of supervisory jobs—the important factor is to have some familiarity with the work but to be able to work with people; to get others to do the detail. Too many of our people still don't understand this. . . .

The route to the top is no longer clear. Over a five-year period this organization has changed. There have been reorganizations, new functions created, and some realignment of existing functions. Many who felt they had a clear line to something higher in the organization now find that that "something" isn't there anymore.

We've had lots of hiring-in at higher levels. Many old-timers have been bypassed. In some cases, the new, outside hirees came into jobs that never existed before, or were hired into a job that had previously existed, but which is now a "cut" above what it was before. What used to be a top job is now a second or third spot.

What we need now are people who are "professional managers"—by that I mean a supervisor versus a technical specialist. Years ago supervision could be concentrated in a few key individuals . . . but in the past five years we've grown 20 percent to 30 percent and have a management hierarchy. A person used to be able to grow up as a technical specialist and develop managerial skills secondarily.

To a small extent it's a matter of personality too. We have a new president, and what is acceptable to him differs from what was acceptable to his predecessor. There's a new mix of personal favoritism that goes along with the new vogue. Technical specialists are "low need" as far as the company is concerned. I estimate we now have about thirty people in this category in officer-level jobs.

Interview with Tom Martin—Marketing Division Head

There have been many changes over the past six years. Mr. Toller took a look at the entire organization . . . and then hired a consultant to do an organizational study. It was sort of an outside stamp of approval.

His hope was to move some of the dead wood . . . the senior people who were past their peak and didn't represent what the company wanted anymore in its managerial and officer staff. Few of these individuals have the capacity to change, and for others it may already be too late to change. Many had leveled off in their development long before these changes came about, and the changes just made it more apparent. Early retirement has been given to some of those over sixty. Others remained as titular head of their departments, but in essence report to a younger person who is really running the department.

Banking used to be a soft industry . . . you were hired and never fired. If you were a poor performer, you were given a lousy job that you could stay at. No one was ever called in and told to shape up. The pay was so poor it attracted people who wanted to work in a sheltered area, and they were satisfied to try and build a career in that area. So it was a job with low pay, high prestige, and some opportunity.

Our biggest problem is to convince people that they are not technicians anymore, that they are to *supervise* their subordinates and work to develop them. Apparently, for many older individuals, and younger ones too, this is an impossible assignment. They can do the jobs themselves, but having anyone else do it in any other way runs against their grain.

If our rate of personnel growth over the next ten years is as fast as the previous ten years, I'm afraid we can only absorb about 50 percent of our most promising people.

Interview with Jane Farren, Trust Administration Division Head

We have several people for whom there is very little opportunity anymore. We just don't see any potential in these people. There are about fifteen of them who are in their forties and are really not capable of making any independent decisions. We're trying to get them to see other opportunities . . . both inside and outside the company. For example, our Real Estate group was big in the 1960s and 1970s. We're trying to make it important again, and there may be some opportunities in that area.

To give you an idea of the problem we're faced with: One individual is really a personality problem. He's an attorney but he can't get along with others. He wants people to come to him; he focuses on detail too much; and he has great difficulty in telling others what to do and how to do it. He has to do the job all by himself.

Another individual: We gave him a section to supervise but he really hasn't measured up. But, he was the president's pet. I suppose we'll let him continue on . . . he's fifty-seven . . . and then retire him early.

Interview with Mr. L. Henry, General Administration Division

The company has been undergoing basic change. In the past, if people demonstrated technical competence they were promoted, and that was fine while the company was a small, stable group, and everyone knew what the other was thinking. But then, many in the senior group began to retire. With this "changing of the guard" and the growth of the company, many of us have lost communication with our counterparts. Many of us are new in this field, new to this company, and, of course, new to each other. But we recognize this, so half the communication problem is solved. In a sense, we're not constrained by "how it was done before."

My people have reacted to all this change by sitting back and waiting, seeing which way things are going to go, then I guess deciding whether they are going to join you or not. Most of my people are relatively recent employees—as a matter of fact, of the 278 people in my division, only 11 have been with the company more than ten years. Conversion to EDP will really create a lot of changes in my area.

13. Sunday At Al Tech*

Saturday, August 14, 1982, 9 P.M.

George Hayes, Assistant to the President at Star Manufacturing, Inc., was sitting in his motel room in a small city near Chicago with his feet propped up on the bed recalling the events which had prompted his being there. On Thursday, only two days earlier, he had attended a meeting of the top managers at the Star corporate headquarters on the east coast. The day's agenda centered on his analysis of the recent performance of the company's various divisions. One in particular, Al Tech, was receiving an unusual amount of attention that day.

George had the numbers on the table next to him. Sales, net income, and return on investment (ROI) for Al Tech were down from the previous year and below budgeted performance levels. The results were somewhat understandable given the unexpected severity of the current economic downturn and Al Tech's

*Lynda L. Goulet and Peter G. Goulet, Instructor and Associate Professor, respectively, University of Northern Iowa. Reprinted by permission. Copyright © 1983, 1984. All rights reserved. This case describes a hypothetical company based on a composite of several actual experiences in a similar industrial setting.

sensitivities to such conditions. Just when George had felt the meeting was about to adjourn, the president asked him for more details concerning Al Tech's new expansion and equipment acquisition plans. George knew those numbers all too well. He had reviewed them prior to Star's approval of the project. He had even been sent to the equipment manufacturer for a first-hand look at the technology and accompanying manpower and facilities requirements. George recalled that this had been the trip which had caused him to miss the tenth birthday of his twin daughters.

The meeting had continued with George reporting that the building addition at Al Tech was nearing completion and the equipment was scheduled for installation during the month of October. The management group then had briefly discussed Al Tech's forecast for the year beginning in January 1983, the first full year the new equipment would be operational. Several forecasts had been prepared, each based on different assumptions concerning the utilization of the new technology. The most pessimistic forecast—utilizing less than 50 percent of the new capacity and having no new product lines—still resulted in overall profit performance for the division which was better than that from 1981 or from the current year's adjusted projections.

George had also reported that if the most optimistic forecast were attained, Al Tech would become one of the corporation's most profitable divisions. Though marketing new product lines would require development time and the acquisition of experience with the new technology, it was still plausible to expect some sales of new products by the end of the upcoming year.

George's mind wandered. Al Tech had been his pet project for the last four years. He had first heard of the company while attending his ten year college reunion in Illinois over four years ago. George's former fiancee, Julie, who had broken their engagement to marry Ben Brown, introduced him to her husband at the reunion. Ben had just been promoted to Personnel Manager at Al Tech. George recalled, however, that Ben wasn't certain how long he would be able to retain that position as the Carter family, who owned the firm, wished to sell it to settle an estate. Only the Vice-President of Sales, Stuart Carter, was a family member. The President, Russell Wainscott, had been hired several years earlier when the founder of the company retired. Following the founder's death, everyone in the family except Stuart wanted the firm to be sold, for cash rather than for stock in another firm. George remembered the many hours of work and travel time he had invested analyzing this potential acquisition for Star Manufacturing. The work had all come to fruition in late 1978 when Star purchased Al Tech from the Carter family estate.

A door to a nearby room slammed shut. George was jarred back to thoughts of the last few minutes of last Thursday's meeting at Star. At long last Star's President made it clear why Al Tech had been the focus of attention. Russell Wainscott, who had been retained as the General Manager at Al Tech after the acquisition, had been severely injured in a car accident and would be hospitalized for an unknown, though substantial, period of time. George was to assume responsibility for the division as its Acting General Manager until Wainscott was able to assume his duties again.

George slipped into bed early, knowing Sunday would be a very long day. He had made arrangements to spend the day at Al Tech, alone, preparing for his first week as GM. Before going to sleep he felt both apprehension and excitement. Finally he would have the opportunity to get the line management experience he needed to advance his career. However, with line responsibility, especially under these circumstances, comes high visibility. George nervously drifted off to sleep.

Sunday, August 15, 8 A.M.

The keys to the Al Tech office building and the GM's office were in the box at the motel desk when George went to breakfast. A note from Wainscott's secretary, Barbara Curtis, was in a manila envelope with the keys. It read:

> Mr. Hayes:
>
> As you requested in your Friday telephone call, all the managers prepared memos relating any problems under their responsibility which must be resolved in the near future. Five of the memos are in envelopes on Rusty's [Wainscott] desk. Richard Simcox told me he would slip his memo under the office door as he wasn't able to complete it before I left Friday. In addition, I prepared a summary of Rusty's agenda for next week with some explanations of any meetings to the best of my knowledge. Finally there is a stack of mail on the desk. Some of it is left over from before the accident and some arrived since then. I hope this is satisfactory. I'm looking forward to working for you in Rusty's absence and will arrive early Monday morning to help you begin your first week.
>
> (Signed) Barb Curtis

Sunday, August 15, 9 A.M.

When George arrived at the office he found the following items awaiting his attention:

> Memos from managers (Exhibits 1–6)
> Agenda for the week of the sixteenth (Exhibit 7)
> Correspondence (Exhibits 8–17)

Before he began working George scribbled on a piece of paper and added that to the pile on top of his desk (see Exhibit 18).

Place yourself in George Hayes' position. Plan your activities for the week of August 16. What meetings must be held? When? With whom? What decisions must be made? When? Which decisions can be delegated? To whom? A note on Al Tech appears below to provide you with additional background. An organizational chart is also provided as Figure 1.

A Note on Al Tech

Al Tech is a vertically integrated firm which converts aluminum billets (cylindrical ingots of aluminum) into aluminum extrusions which are then converted into finished products. Aluminum extrusions are produced by hydraulic presses which force billets heated to just below the melting point through profile dies of hardened steel. The hot extrusions run out onto long tables for cooling. These extrusions are cut to length, heat treated, and machined through various operations, typically in punch or brake presses, to produce the constituent parts for numerous products. Al Tech makes extrusions for its own lines of windows, storm sash, patio doors, screens, and extension ladders.

The major suppliers for Al Tech are companies which provide the aluminum billets, flat glass, and screen cloth. Al Tech's customers include nearly 500 firms,

---

From: Ben Brown
To: George Hayes
Date: August 13, 1982

George:

Looking forward to working with you for a while—too bad it had to be under these circumstances. Barb passed your message along and I guess there are several issues we need to discuss pretty soon.

1. Sam Howarth, one of our designers, has been suspected of the "appropriation" of minor amounts of company materials for a long time. Two weeks ago, Dick Simcox inadvertently caught him piling some obsolete screens into his car. These screens probably would have been sold for scrap. Dick, Rusty, and I decided to let him take some vacation time until we decided what to do'about it. We'd have fired him on the spot but the truth is he is a good designer and our designers are underpaid and turnover is terrible. Howard has been with the firm for over fifteen years and is responsible for a couple of innovations that have been really profitable. His vacation time will run out at the end of the week so some decision must be reached by the 20th.

2. The new paint process equipment is scheduled for delivery and installation during October. I have placed an ad for a supervisor in that department and I have an application in hand for a good man. He used to supervise a line that painted cabinets for TV sets. The problem is that one of our assembly supervisors wants the job. Dick tried to convince her to stay in assembly but she's being a hard-nose about it. She is not qualified for this job from the standpoint of having run a paint room. She probably could be trained eventually but we don't know how good a job she would ever do. It will also delay us for a long time if we go this route. As I see it all she really wants is the money or the prestige associated with the new position. What she doesn't understand, or won't accept, is that the higher wages for the paint room job reflect the level of skill required. She says she'll cause some trouble if she doesn't get the job this week but none of us knows what she means by "trouble." The final kicker is that this is our only female manager at any level.

3. You probably aren't aware of this, but every year Al Tech has a company party for its employees and their spouses. I have been in charge of the arrangements for the last few years. It's next Saturday at the local Elks club. Some of the people around the office have wondered if it wouldn't be wise to postpone it because of Rusty's accident. My feeling is that it's a bit late to cancel. Besides, it'll be months before Rusty can get back on his feet again. The Carter family started the tradition fifteen years ago and Stuart hates to see it abandoned. Al White thinks it's an awful waste of money but Dick says it's a real morale booster for his workers. I need to know about this no later than Monday afternoon.

4. One final thing, and this is a real winner. Somewhere in Rusty's pile of stuff there should be a copy of a letter from our receptionist. I'll just let you read it for the pure joy of the moment. When you have gotten off the floor let me know and we'll talk about it. By the way, she officially works for me.

EXHIBIT 1

though their major source of revenue derives from about twenty manufacturers of recreational vehicles (RVs) and manufactured housing (MH) and two chains of discount retailers who purchase the ladders for sale under private labels.

The major investment to which Al Tech recently committed itself is a series of machines which electrostatically paint extrusions. The equipment requires a facility with a forty-foot ceiling as the extrusions are painted while suspended vertically. Al Tech's new installation will allow it to paint extrusion lengths among the longest that can be painted in any U.S. facility. Aluminum is very difficult to paint successfully because the paint doesn't adhere to the surface easily. Though painted aluminum also scratches easily, it must still be painted before machining to achieve necessary economies.

There is a great deal of demand for painted aluminum products because painting both colors the surface and prevents the unsightly oxidation of the bare metal characteristic of aluminum. Anodizing also accomplishes these purposes and produces a harder, more durable finish than that achieved with painting. However, the cost of anodizing is so high as to be prohibitive for almost all uses but curtain walls for high-rise office buildings and high-valued decorative products. Painting also offers a greater variety of colors and finish textures than anodizing.

Al Tech built its paint facility for internal use. However, with this facility and its extrusion operation, it felt it could develop demand for high-margin custom-extruded, custom-painted parts for current as well as new markets.

From: Aaron McClosky
To: George Hayes
Date: August 13, 1982

Welcome aboard.

The fellows in engineering have been busy working up some new designs to expand our product lines. Stu Carter, Dick Simcox, and I have been going around for months trying to decide what to do with the extra capacity of the new paint line. We're all in agreement that the window and door lines will go on first. I guess you've got the figures on this, too. There is a lot of demand for white and brown frames on both the RV and MH window lines and the margins are a good deal better than for the unpainted units. However, I believe we'd better develop some new products quickly if we want to get above the low capacity utilization our current products will provide. Dick thinks there's no real problem here because he feels we can land a lot of contract painting jobs. As far as I know Stu hasn't even tried to check out that possibility.

I'm having one of the designers collect some of our more promising designs. She should have them ready for you by Monday. We've been working on the designs for a line of picture frames, some designer curtain rods, and a dynamite set of shower doors. For the last several years there has been talk around the sales office of redesigning our lines for the retail market but we never seem to get anywhere on this. Just when the designers get excited about a new product design, it seems like Stu comes up with a variation on our windows that the mobile home guys just "have to have." By the time that's taken care of the new products get lost in the shuffle. I sure hope that doesn't happen with the paint line ideas.

We really ought to move on this business so my department can develop prototypes by yearend. After that it'll take at least six months to work out the bugs, let the dies, and get into production.

EXHIBIT 2

From: Albert White
To: George Hayes
Date: 8/13/82

Mr. Hayes:

Having just recently corresponded with you at headquarters concerning the latest quarterly report, I am certain you are well aware of our current position. This week I have been reviewing the updated estimates for the fourth quarter. In doing so I have been reminded of a potential problem to which you should be alerted. The details are attached but I have summarized the situation below. [Attachment not shown.]

On July 28, Stuart Carter got an order for 10,000 window units with storms and screens, and 1000 patio doors. [Attachment shows this order to be worth just under $300,000.] The customer, a new one for us, is a large condominium developer with units in five states. The order was to be delivered by November 5. Normally an order of this size would be greatly appreciated. However, these units are all non-standard product for us. Though assembly will not be a problem, the glass will be. For some reason we cannot find any way to cut the glass without a great deal of waste. The upshot of this is that in figuring the costs on this order, given the price Stuart quoted, we would be selling the whole order at about breakeven.

Rusty and I talked about this situation and decided that one solution to this problem might be to try to resell the order using painted extrusions from the new line. We sent Stuart back to the customer and the developer said he would let us know this Wednesday if the order would be changed. By changing to painted windows we were able to quote a price that covered us for the painting and the excess waste and provide a profit. However, there is a catch. The customer is willing to wait a bit longer to give us a chance to operationalize the paint line, as he is in the design stage of the development. However, he wants a penalty clause in the order in case we are late in delivering under the revised order. If for any reason the equipment isn't ready to go on time we will either have to pay a penalty or have the extrusions painted outside. Either way, we would lose about $10,000 on the order if the revised quote is accepted and the paint room isn't ready by November.

EXHIBIT 3

From: Stu Carter
To: George Hayes
Date: August 13

Sorry I won't be in town when you arrive at Al Tech. I've had a big sales trip planned to meet with several of our major window customers in the South. Rusty wanted me to drum up some firm orders for the new painted metal lines since we're going to be going on line soon. He was apparently concerned our customers wouldn't order the more expensive, painted products, given the recession. I told him not to worry, though, as the expensive stuff usually sells OK anyway, especially in the South where the economy isn't as hard hit.

Barb was lucky to catch me before I left. I'll be swinging on back through Cincinnati for the Manufactured Housing Suppliers Show, then home for the big party!

Oh, before I forget, sooner or later you're bound to hear about it. In fact, the lawyer was going to meet with Rusty this week. While I was on the road recently the Groves kid broke into my office. I know he rifled my desk because the drawers were an awful mess. I don't care what he says he was after, he's had it in for me ever since I fired his dad from the sales force a year ago. How did I know his old man, Marv, would end up marrying my secretary! I have a good notion to fire her when I get back. Marv Groves went over my head to McClosky, insisting he could sell more to the chain stores if we had more retail lines. I told Marv to keep his nose out of the design department and when he didn't I finally fired him. Those guys in design would spend all their time on the new stuff instead of helping me out on the window lines. The MH guys are always hot for slick-looking new window designs. Now McClosky is convinced that the new paint line was put in just so his department could have some fun.

Gotta run.

EXHIBIT 4

From: Charles Weber
To: George Hayes
Date: 8/13/82

Mr. Hayes:

Ms. Curtis suggested I prepare a memo to advise you of any problems I may be encountering in Purchasing. I foresee two areas of concern.

First, it will be necessary for me to locate long-term, reliable sources of supply for the paint facility. We have temporary sources for the materials we need for the forecasted window and door production through December. Beyond that we need to be concerned about the demands of any new product lines and/or contract paint work. We also have not accounted for the condominium order, should it require painting.

Second, I have been hearing some rumors that two of our major aluminum suppliers may be cutting back production further. In the last major recession several of the "majors" shut off some potlines [smelting equipment] to artificially tighten supplies so they could raise prices even in a period of slack demand. This strategy worked well last time, so I suspect the rumors may be true. I may know more by the middle of next week. One of our suppliers will have their regional sales manager in the area on the pretext of training a new territory representative. You might wish to join us on the morning of the 18th, should you be available.

The last time billets were in short supply both of our contract suppliers instituted a very restrictive policy before supplying us with metal. For each pound of aluminum we wished to purchase we had to turn in a pound of scrap at the going price. Obviously, we could not keep up such a practice for very long without severe production cutbacks. Otherwise, we would be forced into the spot market to fill our remaining needs. To anticipate this possibility it might be wise to begin stockpiling our scrap. This will hurt our quarterly cash flow, but may help protect our supply of new metal. The next regular scrap pickup is scheduled for Friday the 20th.

Just a reminder, the engineers from the paint equipment company will be here Tuesday. It might be a good time for you to learn more about the new facility firsthand.

If I can be of any additional help, please don't hesitate to ask.

EXHIBIT 5

From: Dick Simcox
To: George Hayes
Date: August 14, 1982

Just before shutdown on Friday I got a phone call from one of our large customers. Apparently Stu had left on his sales trip already, and due to the urgency of the call, his secretary transferred the call to me. Here's the trouble. Our trucks just delivered a shipment of our new hexagonal windows to our biggest MH customer. These babies were right on spec, exceeded federal standards by a mile—the designers did a bang-up job. These are the most expensive windows we make because of the unusual shape. The tooling is incredible and glass-cutting is a real chore. I was real proud of assembly when I inspected these before loading. My supervisor, Judy Mills, did a great job on this. I sure wish she'd get off her horse about this paint job; I need her here. Anyway, the bums wouldn't accept delivery of the order. They told the driver the latch was on the wrong side. What's more like it is that their business is really off and they stopped producing the model that uses the hex windows. The driver's bringing them back this weekend.

What's got me worried is that this was just the first batch. The order was for three times what we shipped. We got a big set of tools and hired and trained a guy just for this product, hoping to get some more customers for it next year. If we could get in touch with Stu we could get him to see the customer at the show this week. The next batch was already started but I cancelled them on Friday night until we find out what gives here. Not filling this order will do some damage to our sales targets for the quarter.

What worries me most is that this could be a trend. If all our customers are hurting now, how are we going to sell the painted stuff? We've been counting on the higher margins there to offset some volume declines in other products. Rusty's been worrying about this, too. He told me just last week. But Stu is convinced there's no problem. Seems to me we ought to be out looking for some contract painting. It'll be a bad Christmas for a lot of our people if we have to cut back in the last quarter.

I can free up an hour or two any time after 10 A.M. Monday if you need me.

ExHIBIT 6

From: Barbara Curtis
To: George Hayes
Date: August 13, 1982

Below is a summary of Rusty's agenda for the week of August 16.

1. Luncheon with Alan Holtman at noon on Monday.

   Mr. Holtman is the attorney retained by Al Tech. The subject of the meeting is the trespass, breaking and entering charge pending against Mitchell Groves, age 16, stepson of Stu Carter's secretary.

   On July 31, the boy was apprehended inside our office building after he set off the silent alarm. He claims to have been looking for proof that his step-mother was having an affair with Stu. They both deny this. When the police searched the boy, they found nothing in his possession belonging to Al Tech. The Groves think the situation can and should be worked out at home, though they want the boy to pay for damages. Stu seems to want to press for prosecution.

2. Tuesday, 11 A.M. to 3 P.M. meet with Janice Schulcraft and Dennis Sanchez.

   These are the engineers from the paint equipment manufacturer. The subject of their visit concerns the finalization of the delivery and installation plans. Rusty had planned a tour of the building addition, now almost completed, lunch, and then a briefing session to include Messers Weber, White, and Simcox.

3. Wednesday, 7:45 A.M.

Rusty had reservations to leave O'Hare for Cincinnati for the MH Suppliers Show, returning Friday after dinner. He was to meet Stu upon his arrival.

4. Saturday, 6 P.M. to midnight, annual party, Elks club

Rusty was to deliver a short speech after dinner.

EXHIBIT 7

Unopened letter dated August 12, 1982:

Dear Mr. Wainscott:

Our office has on file your plans for the construction of an addition to your facility on Eleventh Street, including the remodeling of the south-side entrance. You may be aware of the fact that last Monday, August 9, the City Council approved proposed building code modifications which go into effect immediately.

One section of the revised code may impact on your current construction. This notification is intended to provide you with some warning that, as filed, your new premises may not pass inspection. It is to your benefit to discuss this situation with your architect and your general contractor as soon as possible.

Enclosed is a copy of the changes in the code as approved by the council. [Enclosure not shown.] If my office can help you in interpreting these changes or in answering any other questions, please let me know.

Sincerely,
(Signed) Stanley Lerner, City Engineer

EXHIBIT 8

Manila envelope containing petition:

August 2, 1982

We the undersigned request that the management of Al Tech repair the employees' parking lot. Many of us damaged our tires and suffered wheel alignment problems after last winter from the deep ruts, potholes, and frost heaving problems. We also request that in fall the apples from the trees by the lot be swept up regularly so the lot is not an obstacle course to walk through.

[253 signatures followed]

EXHIBIT 9

Unopened letter dated August 10, postmarked New York:

Dear Mr. Wainscott:

For the past two years you have supplied our chain of stores with your aluminum extension ladders. Let me express to you again how pleased we all are here with the high quality and timely delivery of this product. It continues to be a strong item for us.

In light of recent and expected changes in both demographics and the economic climate, we have redefined our corporate merchandising strategy. It is our intention to provide more variety in home improvement products and hardware. To implement this strategy we are seeking reliable suppliers in such product lines to provide our chain with private label merchandise. We would be interested in talking with you about the possibility of contracting for an exclusive line of windows, doors, and porch enclosures.

Since this may require some rethinking of your firm's priorities, I have decided to approach you directly rather than contacting your sales department. We are very anxious to proceed and I am hopeful we can expand our already cordial business relations further. I am planning to be in Chicago for a regional meeting on the 19th of this month. If you will be available it would be no trouble for me to drive out to your office on the 20th to discuss this in more detail. If you wish to get together at that time please call my office by the 18th.

Sincerely,
(Signed) John Colby
Vice President,
Merchandising

EXHIBIT 10

Letter postmarked August 9, addressed to "Al Teck." Letter was handwritten and is reproduced verbatim below:

To the man who runs things at Al Teck,

I was at your factry a few weeks back to get a job that was in the Want Ads. The boss woodn't hire me. Over the week end I seen my sister inlaw She says I can sue your place cause I am a pertecked class. To be nice I give you one more chance befor I get a loyer.

Marie Grace

EXHIBIT 11

Letter dated July 23, 1982, opened by Wainscott:

Dear Mr. Wainscott:

County General Hospital is vitally concerned with the increasing number of job-related accidents occurring in our community. In an attempt to ameliorate this trend we have added a Safety Consultant to our hospital staff. His job is to suggest specific improvements which can be implemented with minimal expense in offices and factories in our community.

The services of our Safety Consultant will be made available to local businesses under one of two programs: a per-diem consultation or our charitable contribution plan. The per-diem rate is $500. The charitable contribution plan is based on the actual savings accruing to each firm through the reduction in expenses from reduced insurance costs and direct company-borne medical costs. If your company institutes any of the improvements suggested by our Safety Consultant, rather than pay the per-diem expense you may elect to contribute 10 percent of the first year's actual dollar savings to our hospital.

We at County General sincerely believe this program will benefit both the community and the businesses that are so critical to its welfare. Please feel free to make an appointment with me at your earliest convenience so we can confer on this matter.

Respectfully,
(Signed) Michael Franz, Administrator
County General Hospital

EXHIBIT 12

Unsigned, handwritten note, no date, found on the floor near the office door on Sunday morning:

To the new Acting General Manager

Sir, the foremen here at Al Tech got together after quitting time on Friday and talked about the situation since Rusty's accident. We're sure you're a good guy and all or the company wouldn't have sent you. We just want you to know that we think Dick [Simcox] should have gotten the job. It didn't need to go to an outsider.

EXHIBIT 13

Letter dated August 4, 1982, opened by Wainscott, postmarked St. Louis:

Dear Rusty,

It's about that time again. We need to make plans for this year's holiday break. Some of the others want to spend the week after Christmas lolling on the beaches in either southern California or Florida. I'm partial to the Gulf side of Florida because my in-laws are in the area and my kids could spend the week with them. Do you have any preference?

This sure was one heck of a good idea. I don't remember exactly whose it was though—it's been three years now. Doesn't really matter. Since all the divisions are shut down for the holidays anyway and the only thing going on is inventory, we general managers might as well enjoy ourselves. Besides, last year Frank said our gossip about HQ really helped him when it came time to put together the report on closing down his Kirksville plant. Knowing how the guys at HQ felt about things saved him a couple of months time.

Well, give me a call as soon as possible so we can finalize our plans and make reservations. Say hi to your good-looking wife for me.

(Signed) Jonas [Calder, General Manager, Metal Stampings]

EXHIBIT 14

Envelope, hand addressed to Mr. Hayes:

I have been a bookkeeper in the Accounting Department for eight years and heard about your temporary assignment to Al Tech on Friday morning. My parents are retired and vacation in Florida during the winter. Their two-bedroom home is located about a mile from our office at 2132 Elm Street. It's near an elementary school. I called my folks over the lunch hour and they offered to rent the house to you for $250 a month. They are leaving after Labor Day and won't be back until Easter. It's really a good deal as two-bedroom apartments in town are scarce and rent for about $350 a month. Let me know early in the week if you are interested.

Dotty Simmons

EXHIBIT 15

Handwritten note from the Ben Brown, clipped to the letter below, dated August 11:

Rusty,

This is a xerox of a letter I just got today from Joyce Riley, the new receptionist. I don't know what you want to do about this, but we should talk about it on Friday, the 13th (unless you want to meet at the Olympus Club Saturday).

Ben

Dear Mr. Brown

Since you are both my boss and the Personnel Director, I felt it was right to mention a problem I'm having to you. I feel I am being harassed on my job.

When I interviewed for work here I asked if it was all right to moonlight and you said I could use my own time as I wished. The truth was that I had a job then, and still do, working Friday and Saturday nights at the Olympus Club on Sycamore Street. Sooner or later you're bound to hear it so I'll tell you now that I work there as an exotic dancer.

It seems some of the workers who I know work in the factory told a couple of the office people about my moonlighting and several of them came to see me at work. The club was really busy the last couple of weekends. Now rumors are all over the place about me. I know it's true because I overheard some of the workers in the lunchroom talking about drawing straws to see who gets to bring paperwork over to the office from the factory. Some of our office people must even have told customers who call here, because visitors to our office have said a few things to me. I'm not really complaining about what they say to me or how they look at me. I'm used to that. But what happened recently really bothers me.

A woman called here two days ago, wouldn't say who she was, and accused me of all sorts of things with her husband. I finally got over that and then yesterday another woman called and said I was a loose woman who shouldn't be allowed to work in an office where nice husbands worked. She said if I didn't quit my job she'd tell the other wives and get me fired. I enjoy my work but I don't play around with married men and I don't want to give up either job. Can you help me?

(Signed) Joyce Riley

EXHIBIT **16**

Letter dated August 4, 1982, opened by Wainscott:

Dear Mr. Wainscott:

In preparation for the coming year the Board of Education has voiced its continuing support for our Career Day program at Central High School. Your firm's participation last year was appreciated and we hope you will again donate your time and effort to help ensure the success of this year's program.

Career Day is scheduled for Friday, January 7, 1983, from 9 o'clock to 4 o'clock. This year the Board has decided to cancel all classes for the day so the participating firms will have more space for displays and meetings than we had last year.

We need your response by August 20 so we may make the necessary arrangements. Thank you for your cooperation in our efforts.

Sincerely,
(Signed) Robert Wood, Superintendent of Schools

EXHIBIT **17**

Note written to himself by George Hayes when he arrived in the office:

Catch 8:30 P.M. United flight from O'Hare on Friday for our anniversary on Saturday-get present.

EXHIBIT 18

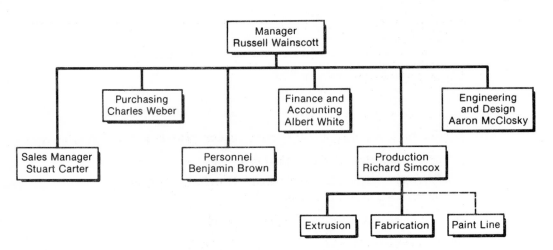

FIGURE 1. Organization Chart—Al Tech Division

Part III

Appraising and Improving Performance

Cases Outline

14. The Engine Plant*

Over the past twenty-five years of its existence, The Engine Plant in Saginaw, Michigan, has been a very profitable company. Although located in an automobile town, The Engine Plant produced gasoline engines for a wide range of customers but not for the automobile companies. Rather it produced gasoline engines for customers who used them in the final assembly of such consumer products as lawn mowers, chain saws, and generators. Sales over the past twenty-five years have increased steadily at a rate of approximately 5 percent annually. In 1985 its sales were $5 million. Recently, however, profit margins have started to erode. Consequently Norma Waters, president of The Engine Plant, is aggressively looking for the possible causes and solutions.

During the past five years the automobile companies and the United Auto Workers have gotten a great deal of press coverage for their worker involvement programs. While the benefits of these programs remain to be determined, thus far there appears to be improved productivity, especially as a consequence of improved quality, lower scrap rates, and reduced absenteeism. An engineer by training, Norma Waters is not entirely convinced that you can get improved profits by human relations gimmicks and "soft" management techniques. Nevertheless, based upon what she has read in the papers about the automobile companies, she is ready to try almost anything. She is even ready to start believing what she has been hearing from her personnel manager for the past two years.

The Personnel Manager

The current personnel manager at The Engine Plant is Lillian Meyers. Meyers is a graduate in business from the University of Michigan. Since she graduated fifteen years ago, she's had a variety of experiences, mostly in the automobile industry. For about five of these years she did personnel work. Since joining The Engine Plant, she has been trying to get Norma Waters to see the value in paying attention to the employees. It was Meyers, in fact, who was largely responsible for bringing the news of the latest human resources developments in the automobile industry to the attention of Ms. Waters.

---

*This case was written by Randall S. Schuler.

Although Meyers is a firm believer in the bottom-line value of more effectively managing human resources, she had to spend most of her first two years getting to know the company and the people, and putting out fires. Recently, however, Meyers has been reviewing the company's performance evaluation system. From what she knows, employees have a mixture of indifferent and negative feelings about it. An informal survey has shown that about half of the supervisors fill the forms out, give about three minutes to each form, and send them to personnel without discussing them with the employees. The rest spend more time completing the forms, but communicate about them only briefly and superficially with their employees. Meyers also found that the forms were rarely retrieved for promotion or pay-raise analyses. Because of this, most supervisors may have felt the evaluation program was a useless ritual. In her previous places of employment, Meyers had seen performance evaluation as a much more useful experience, which included giving positive feedback to employees, improving future employee performance, developing employee capabilities, and providing data for promotion and compensation. Consequently she has recently been telling Norma Waters about the need to take a look at the entire performance appraisal program at The Engine Plant.

The Appraisal Program

The Engine Plant has an evaluation program by which all operating employees and clerical personnel are evaluated semiannually by their supervisors. The form that they have been using is given in Exhibit 1. It has been in use for ten years. The

Exhibit 1. Performance Evaluation Form of The Engine Plant

PERFORMANCE EVALUATION

SUPERVISORS: When you are asked to do so by the personnel department, please complete this form on each of your employees. The supervisor who is responsible for 75 percent or more of an employee's work should complete this form on him or her. Please evaluate each facet of the employee separately.

Quality of Work	Excellent	Above Average	Average	Below Average	Poor	SCORE
Quantity of Work	Poor	Below Average	Average	Above Average	Excellent	
Dependability at Work	Excellent	Above Average	Average	Below Average	Poor	
Initiative at Work	Poor	Below Average	Average	Above Average	Excellent	
Cooperativeness	Excellent	Above Average	Average	Below Average	Poor	
Getting Along with Co-Workers	Poor	Below Average	Average	Above Average	Excellent	

Total _____

Supervisor's Signature_____

Employee Name_____

Employee Number_____

form is scored as follows: excellent = 5, above average = 4, average = 3, below average = 2, and poor = 1. The scores for each question are entered in the right-hand column and are totaled for an overall evaluation score.

The procedures used by the supervisors are as follows: Each supervisor rates each employee on January 1 and June 1. The supervisor discusses the rating with the employee. The supervisor sends the rating to the personnel department. Each rating is placed in the employee's personnel file. If promotions come up, the cumulative ratings are to be considered at the time. The ratings are also supposed to be used when raises are given.

The program was designed about ten years ago by the personnel manager who retired two years ago, Mary Bensko. Since then, however, the ways of doing business and making gas engines at The Engine Plant have substantially changed.

The Challenge

Meyers has not had much experience in designing performance evaluation systems. She feels she should seek *your* advice on what to do. Accordingly she asks you to write a report submitting your evaluation of the strengths and weaknesses of the present appraisal system and to design the entire performance appraisal program (system) that should be in use at The Engine Plant. Based upon her conversations with Norma Waters, Meyers anticipates that the workforce at The Engine Plant will remain nonunion and that it will continue to grow at about one percent annually. In addition to having your help in the development of evaluation systems for the operating employees and the clerical employees, she wants your help in deciding how to evaluate the supervisors and managers.

15. Inner City Community Association: A Challenge in Performance Appraisal*

The Inner City Community Association (ICCA) was founded in 1875 to serve the needs of city dwellers by providing job training and temporary shelter for the homeless. Through the years it evolved into a large nonprofit enterprise offering a variety of important services to its community. Financial support for its programs was provided through government grants and private foundations as well as from fund raising drives in the community.

In 1980, programs provided by the organization included alcohol rehabilitation, shelter for battered spouses, job training programs for youth and the handicapped, as well as daycare for children between the ages of two and six

*Written by Dr. Susan Rawson Zacur, Associate Professor, University of Baltimore, Baltimore, Maryland. Printed with permission.

and health and fitness activities. The first three programs were run out of the headquarters building in a prime downtown location. The daycare and health and fitness activities were provided at both the downtown site and satellite facilities throughout the city.

The organization charts in Exhibits 1–3 help explain how these programs were administered. The ICCA Administrative Organization Chart (Exhibit 1) shows the relationship of the five major agency programs to the central administration functions. Two Associate Executive Directors reported to the Executive Director. These people coordinated and maintained the five major service or program areas. The Executive Director's staff included five Directors responsible for administration of the ICCA as an organization, performing such functions as fund raising, public relations, accounting, building and facility operations, and personnel management.

The Program Organization Charts (Exhibits 2 and 3) show the administrative design of each of the major program areas. Each program was administered by a Director. Other job titles were developed and assigned as appropriate to program needs. The breakdown of agency personnel by job category was as shown in Exhibit 4.

Sandra Day was hired during 1984 to fill the Director of Personnel position. This was a newly created position instituted in response to a felt need to coordinate and streamline agency personnel policies. Until Sandra was hired, personnel policies and directives had been developed on an ad hoc, as-needed basis by the Executive Director and the other Administrative Directors. The result

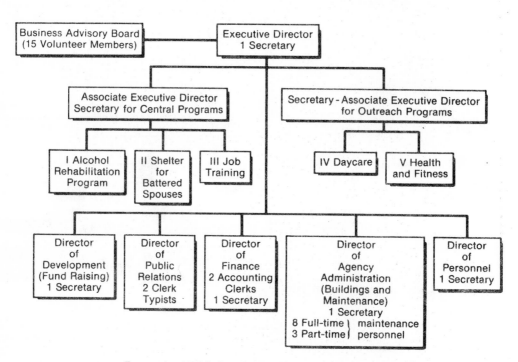

Exhibit 1. ICCA Administrative Organization Chart

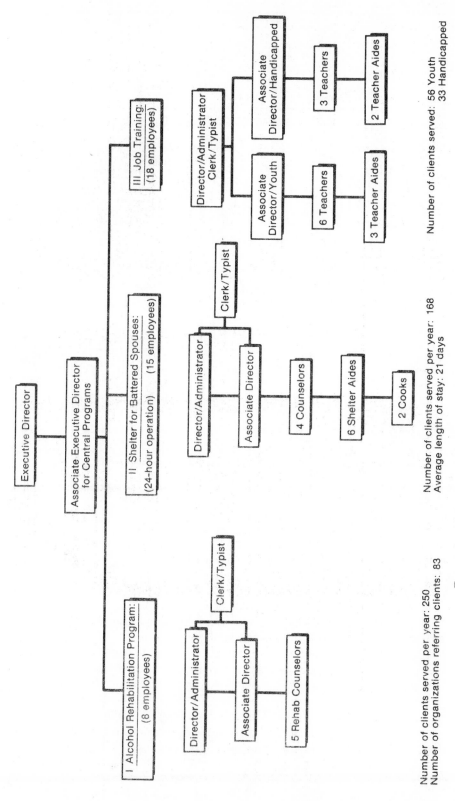

Executive Director

Associate Executive Director
for Central Programs

I Alcohol Rehabilitation Program:
(8 employees)

Director/Administrator

Clerk/Typist

Associate Director

5 Rehab Counselors

Number of clients served per year: 250
Number of organizations referring clients: 83

II Shelter for Battered Spouses:
(24-hour operation)   (15 employees)

Director/Administrator

Clerk/Typist

Associate Director

4 Counselors

6 Shelter Aides

2 Cooks

Number of clients served per year: 168
Average length of stay: 21 days

III Job Training:
(18 employees)

Director/Administrator
Clerk/Typist

Associate
Director/Youth

6 Teachers

3 Teacher Aides

Associate
Director/Handicapped

3 Teachers

2 Teacher Aides

Number of clients served: 56 Youth
33 Handicapped

Exhibit 2. ICCA Program Organization Chart—Central Programs

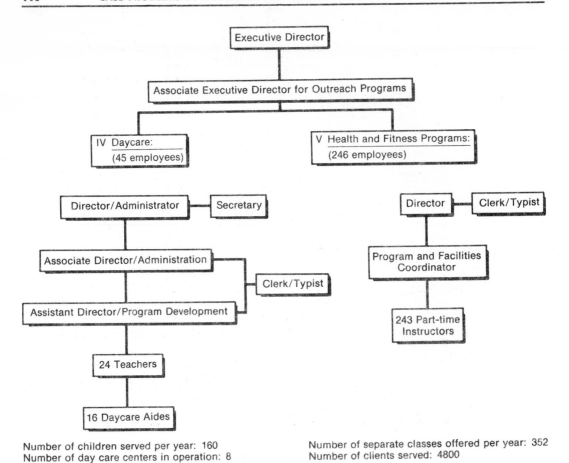

Number of children served per year: 160
Number of day care centers in operation: 8

Number of separate classes offered per year: 352
Number of clients served: 4800

Exhibit 3. ICCA Program Organization Chart—Outreach Programs

was a lack of consistency in policy across organization programs. Further, the policies thus developed appeared to lack appropriate treatment in light of current legal and professional trends in personnel practice. The Directors asked Sandra to tackle the performance appraisal system as her first major move toward professionalizing ICCA's personnel practices.

After doing some research, Sandra uncovered the following pertinent facts. There were two main performance appraisal systems with ICCA. System I was used for professional personnel, teachers, instructors, and counselors. It included a three-step procedure: review of progress on goals for the previous year, feedback on performance in certain behavioral areas, and establishment of goals for the coming year. All this was done by the employee and her or his immediate supervisor once a year. All performance reviews were scheduled in April and May.

System II was designed for paraprofessionals, clerical, maintenance, and other personnel and consisted of a straightforward graphic rating scale. This was completed by the supervisor and discussed with the subordinate on a yearly basis, usually in June.

The forms used in Systems I and II are shown in Exhibits 5 and 6.

EXHIBIT 4

ICCA Employees

	Full-time	Part-time
Professional (Directors, Administrators)	14	0
Paraprofessional (Aides/Coordinators)	28	0
Office or Clerical	17	0
Teachers	33	0
Instructors	0	243
Counselors	9	0
Maintenance	8	3
Other	2	0
	111	246

Total = 357 employees

EXHIBIT 5

PERFORMANCE APPRAISAL SYSTEM I
(FOR PROFESSIONALS, TEACHERS, INSTRUCTORS, AND COUNSELORS)

Name of employee: _____ Date _____

Job Title: _____ Time in Position _____

1. Attach Goal Sheet for prior year.
2. Attach Goal Sheet for the coming year.
3. Employee has shown outstanding job performance in the following areas:

4. a. Please list any areas of difficulty and identifiable causes:

   b. The following plan has been developed with the employee to eradicate the problems:

5. Performance since last appraisal:

   First Appraisal
   Strengthened _____ Unchanged _____ Weakened _____ (check if appropriate) _____

6. Overall assessment of performance (please comment on employee's performance in relation to goals established last year).

7. Employee has indicated interest in further training in the following areas:

   _____

   _____

   _____

8. Employee's comments, if any:

Employee's Signature _____   Supervisor's Signature _____

_____   _____
Date   Date

ICCA GOAL SHEET SYSTEM I

Employee _____ Supervisor _____ Appraisal from _____ Page _____ of _____

Complete during Time 1   to _____

Complete during Time 2 (1 year later)

Major Goal	Objectives	Sup. OK	Results	Appraisal Self	Sup.
I.					
II.					
III.					
IV.					

EXHIBIT 6

ICCA
PERFORMANCE APPRAISAL SYSTEM II
(FOR PARAPROFESSIONALS, CLERICAL, AND MAINTENANCE PERSONNEL)

Rating Guide	Very Satisfactory	Satisfactory	Needs Improvement	Unsatisfactory
	4	3	2	1

Name of Employee: _____

Job Title: _____

FACTORS	RATING	COMMENTS
I. Personal Qualities		
a) Appearance		
b) Manner and voice		
c) Attitude toward work		
d) Relationship to co-workers		
e) Dependability		
f) Attitude toward supervision		
g) Ability to work within agency policies		
II. Job Performance		
a) Knowledge of the job		
b) Skills		
c) Quality of work		
d) Quantity of work		
e) Initiative and resourcefulness		
f) Ability to supervise (if applicable)		

Supervisor's Summary (includes strengths and special skills; also areas where staff member's performance could be improved)

Comments of staff member:

Period covered in this evaluation _____

Signature of staff member evaluated _____

Signature of supervisor _____

Date of Appraisal Interview_____

    Sandy learned that ICCA did not have formal written job descriptions. In an interview with the Executive Director she gained a general idea of the background and responsibilities of major employee categories. Sandy's notes read as follows:

Professional: Master's degree or Bachelor's degree plus experience. Responsibilities include budgeting, program planning and evaluation, supervision.

Paraprofessional: High school plus five years of relevant experience. Assistance work under close supervision.

Office or Clerical: High school plus typing and telephone skills. General clerical duties.

Instructors: No formal education requirement. Demonstrated proficiency in a skill area. Ability to teach a diverse group of students. Instructors specialize in anything from exercise classes to basketmaking.

Counselors: Master's degree of Bachelor's degree in counseling or psychology plus experience. Group and individual therapy sessions with clients.

Teachers: Master's degree or Bachelor's degree in relevant field plus experience. Early childhood development or job training skills as appropriate. Curriculum development and classroom teaching.

Maintenance: No formal education requirement. Demonstrated ability to repair and maintain facilities and equipment.

Interviews with random supervisors revealed problems with Systems I and II. First, employees and supervisors alike had difficulty defining and interpreting some of the terms used on the forms. Further, employees felt that the sytems allowed personal biases and rater errors to affect the accuracy of performance reports.

As presently used, the performance appraisal system was intended for feedback purposes only. Employees were encouraged to work on areas of weakness and strive toward career development, where appropriate, based upon performance appraisal data. The Directors of ICCA expressed an interest in using a revised performance appraisal system as the basis for pay and promotion decisions.

After reviewing the background materials she had obtained, Sandy felt that there were important decisions to be made before she could develop an entirely new performance appraisal system. Some of the issues of concern were:

- the purpose(s) of the appraisal system,
- the understandability of the system to those using it,
- the possible need for separate appraisal systems for various job groupings,
- eliminating bias and rater errors,
- developing a legally defensible system.

She knew that any system she developed would have to address these issues.

16. How Do You Evaluate Your Employee Appraisal Program?*

The Hackney Paper Box Company is having trouble deciding what should be done about its employee evaluation program. Hackney operates forty-seven corrigated box factories located from Maine to California and has a highly centralized corporate personnel department in New York City. Each plant employs about 125 persons.

The union contracts in some Hackney plants allow a junior employee to be promoted over a senior employee if the junior employee has "noticeably" better qualifications for the job. In the South Bend plant a junior employee was promoted to a combiner operator job over an employee with more experience as a combiner first helper and two more years of union seniority. The case went to arbitration. The company correctly contended that the senior employee was not responsible, was lazy, not cooperative, not very bright, and had a horrible attendance record. During the arbitration hearing the union produced copies of all the past employee evaluation forms for Bob Peller, the senior employee. These forms were prepared by his immediate supervisors over the past ten years, the time Peller had been an employee. On a scale of one to five he was rated (4) *above average* or (5) *excellent* in all categories on every evaluation instrument. Bob Peller won the arbitration case, was promoted, and now the company has to have a qualified operator stay with Peller at all times in order to get the job done.

The above-mentioned situation caused Mr. Green, Corporate Vice-President of Personnel, to call a meeting of selected plant personnel managers, the Corporate Compensation Manager, and the Corporate Training and Development Manager. The purpose of the meeting was to decide what was to be done about the existing employee evaluation program.

This meeting produced four suggestions that Mr. Green is considering:

1. Junk the employee evaluation program.
2. Substitute MBO (Management By Objectives) for the present evaluation program.
3. Have the personnel manager at each plant do the evaluation and conduct the evaluation interview that follows evaluation.
4. Leave the program as it is but give every supervisor adequate training in employee evaluation and evaluation interviewing.

The idea to junk the program was advanced by the personnel manager at the South Bend plant. He contended that supervisory personnel were not qualified to evaluate or counsel. He also contended that they would only rate a subordinate high as it was much easier to discuss this kind of rating with the subordinate. In addition to this, if an employee was rated low, the supervisor had to determine and explain to the employee how he or she could improve. This took effort.

*This case was prepared by Professor James C. Hodgetts of the Fogleman College of Business and Economics, Memphis State University, and is intended to be used as a teaching device rather than to show correct or incorrect methods of operations. All names are disguised. Reprinted by permission.

The MBO suggestion was made by a new plant personnel manager who had been transferred to the position from outside the personnel field. He admitted that he didn't know much about MBO but he had heard lots of good things about it.

The suggestion to have the personnel manager do the evaluation and counseling came from a plant personnel manager who had a master's degree in psychology as well as considerable plant experience both as a production supervisor and hourly paid employee. He thought this would work at Hackney as all the plants were small, having approximately 125 employees each.

The suggestion to keep the present evaluation system and train the supervisors in evaluation and evaluation counseling was made by the corporate training and development manager.

Mr. Green is currently trying to decide which suggestion is best or if there is still a better solution.

17. A Big Fish in a Small Pond*

When it rains, it pours. Meet Janet Mirlioni. Janet, a twenty-eight-year-old divorcee, lives with her nine-year-old daughter in the small town of Jackson, Illinois. The odd and part-time jobs she assumed during her two years of layoff left her with a lingering taste of insecurity—a feeling that she stood alone in a crowded and busy world. Nevertheless, she was proud of herself. She passed her first layoff experience.

Now Janet has her job back. During the first meeting with her boss, also the owner of Software General and a retired colonel, he told her that if not for his swift and risky decision to align his business with the growing microcomputer market, they would still be "under." When she asked him about their chances of staying "above" in the new business, he answered, "I think we'll make it this time, but you never know. The market moves so fast, you're never sure if it is night or day. You've got to be up all the time. And that is precisely why I want you with Software."

Janet liked going back to Software General because it paid more than the part-time jobs she had earlier and, most importantly, because she practically ran the business. "What will my position be this time?" she asked. "Exactly as before, the Chief Executive Officer of the place," he answered with a smile. They then agreed he would be responsible for securing new markets for the $500,000 business whereas she would manage the computer operations, handle customer requests, and run the place. Her new salary was $21,000—$500 more than the last salary she made at Software General. This was nine months ago, and she was happy.

---

*A. Magid M. Mazen, Assistant Professor, Department of Managing and Marketing, Illinois State University. Printed with permission.

As they approached the end of the year, Janet noticed that the working atmosphere in Software General had become tense and full of apprehension. These were exactly the same feelings she always had at the end of every year when she ran the Colonel's old business.

One of Janet's good points, however, was knowing her strengths and weaknesses. She liked running the place and the feelings of importance that came with it. But she felt inadequate at times having to deal with the eleven people who reported to her. A few months back, she discussed her feelings with her boss during one of his rare stops: "I know something is missing, but I can't figure it out," she said. His answer was typical and quick: "You're doing a fine job. I don't give a hoot about any of them. If they don't like you, they can leave." Occasionally, during one of his long distance calls, he would ask, "Have any of the troops left yet?" When he heard her negative answer, he would automatically add, "I told you Janet. Jobs are scarce, and it is cold out there."

All this confidence was to make her happy. But she was not. The Colonel wanted everyone's performance to be evaluated secretly, sometime during these last three months. He issued a directive to that effect to all employees. "That will keep them on their toes," he said to Janet. She realized sometime during her experience at Software that being an excellent computer operator did not necessarily mean being an excellent manager. In the new business, with a new crew, she had hoped for a fresh start. But the same apprehensive attitude was haunting the place during the last quarter of the year, just like the first time around. This time, however, she wanted to prevent this atmosphere from spilling over to the next year and becoming commonplace. But she didn't know how.

Everyone at Software knew that Janet was evaluating what they did and said during the last three months, and everybody was unusually tense. She disliked playing God and wished her boss, her subordinates, or preferably both, would be more understanding. But, "the boss believed in his style too much, and the subordinates were overly defensive," she thought. If there was anything about her job that frustrated her it was the discrepancy between her wish to be better and her inability to improve.

That is why she applied for a position with Chips International without hesitation or much thinking. But as the interview data approached, Janet found herself more and more preoccupied with a particular question. "Would you leave a job where you're high on the totem pole to one where you become merely a number?" She preferred to postpone the answer till after the interview.

And He Called Back

A week after the interview Janet received a message to contact Chips International as soon as possible. Something about being wanted made her feel good. The next morning she was there.

They don't waste time at Chips. As she sat down in his office, Chips' local manager, one of the three who interviewed her the week before, said, "Janet, your qualifications and our job requirements do not match. However, this is no reflection on your ability. . . . " Although the line sounded familiar, Janet managed to keep a polite smile on her face. She then asked him, "Is it a company practice to call people in and reject them in person?" He laughed and replied,

"Actually not, but my manager at headquarters has a position that may be for you. They're already through interviewing for the position but I recommended you anyway. Are you interested? If you are, can you be at headquarters tomorrow?" A few seconds of silence elapsed before she told him that she was very surprised and needed some time to think it over. He stood up and said, "Take all the time you want," then walked toward the door adding, "until I get a cup of coffee." Before he left, he turned and asked, "How do you like yours?" "Black," she mumbled.

Chicago, 8:00 A.M. Sharp

What a difference. Chips' building is one of the most prestigious in the city. She was surprised to see that the man who came to receive her in the lobby was one of the three who attended, and did not say a word in, her interview in Jackson; he was the boss with the vacancy. On their way to the fifty-second floor, Janet was shocked to learn that the open position was for a secretary, his secretary. The manager, Mr. Graf, and the elevator were going up; deep inside she was going down, very fast.

Inside Chips

As they took her to a small conference room, Janet convinced herself to have a positive attitude and to go for the experience anyway. Before the interview was over, she was impressed. They managed to make her feel that they knew with minimum or seemingly minimum, certainty what would happen tomorrow, the week after, and next year. Attending the first interview were Mr. Graf, an administrative office manager, and the man who currently held the secretarial position. Later she interviewed with them individually. "All this for a secretarial job?" she asked. "We hire for a career, not for a job," Mr. Graf replied.

They first talked about the link between their company's philosophy and organizational policies. She learned that the company was built on two cornerstones: respect for the employee and excellence of performance. She learned that as business and environment change, policies, plans, and programs may change, but never the cornerstones. She learned that in the company's forty-five years of existence, they had never laid off one employee for one hour. And she learned that the company had pledged positive action to guarantee that all employees had the same chance to succeed.

What impressed her the most, however, was the way they handled performance evaluations, and how it seemed to be the cornerstone for everything else. They first stressed that customer service and respect for the individual were interwoven to create a system. In this system, pay and advancement were based on merit, merit was performance, and performance reflected the employee's worth to the company.

"The appraisal process," Mr. Graf said, "is designed to let you know what is expected of you on the job and how your performance measures up to what is expected. Your job will be clearly defined for you and through periodic feedback, the appraisal process answers, on a continuing basis, questions about how you are doing in your job."

Somehow, every time a question popped up in her mind, their next point provided an answer. One of her unasked questions had a streak of doubt in it, "Do they really do this, or is it only for interviewing consumption?" Their next point was what they called the process. It begins with a performance plan. "To start the process," said the Administrative Assistant, "you and your manager discuss your key responsibilities and write them down. This written document is called your performance plan, and it tells you what is expected of you in your job. If your duties change, you and your manager will discuss those changes and amend written plans accordingly. At any time during the year, either you or your manager may initiate a discussion of your progress under the plan. This is your way of getting regular and prompt feedback on how you are doing."

The Administrative Assistant continued, "At the end of the performance evaluation period, you and your manager will discuss your accomplishments on the job as compared to your performance plan. Your manager will evaluate your performance. This evaluation usually focuses on questions like: How effectively did you carry out your assignments? What strengths were evident? What problems or weaknesses exist? Where can you improve? How can you improve, etc. The results of this evaluation will be recorded and then you'll be asked to sign it. After signing, the completed performance evaluation will be reviewed by your manager's manager. If you have any concerns about the evaluation, you may make comments on the evaluation form and raise the concerns with your manager's manager. This is done within a 'Speak-Up' program that all employees have to attend."

Numerous incidents from Software General flashed into her head, particularly her boss's typical reply to her complaints, "Have any of the troops left yet?"

Mr. Graf then resumed the discussion. "The backbone of Chips' compensation and advancement subsystems is the performance subsystem. At Chips, salary increases and advancement are earned by sustained or improved performance. This means that each individual's performance directly affects the amount of money he or she makes. I, as a manager, review my employees' salaries periodically to ensure they receive increases according to their performance."

The pay subsystem was explained later in detail. They stressed that it aimed at achieving external competitiveness, internal consistency, and merit. "We just explained the merit part of it," said the administrative manager, "and, as you heard, it is based on sustained performance. The internal consistency guarantees that every job is fairly compared to other jobs and is evaluated according to skills and requirements needed to fullfill it. Because excellent performance and training programs can promote and move you around, you can in many cases climb the ladder to better positions. We always promote from within."

"So everything really depends on the performance plan?" she asked. "You got it," quickly and firmly replied Mr. Graf.

Her next item on the itinerary was an individual interview with Mr. Evans, the current holder of the job. He explained many details and personal experiences on the job and in Chicago. She debated whether to ask him a particular question and was finally encouraged by their "Speak-Up" slogan. "Do they really apply what I just heard in the conference room?"

"You bet!" he answered without elaboration.

"What is a performance plan like?" she asked, after a few seconds of hesitation.

"Just like what they explained in the interview," he again answered telegraphically.

She paused to think about another way to rephrase her question without appearing pushy. A few seconds of silence passed before he added, "Would you like to see my performance plan?" She raised her head with a smile and said, "Yes."

"So speak-up," he said. They laughed as he pointed to where his performance plan was, on his desk, under her elbow, apparently ready to be seen (see Exhibit 1).

Exhibit 1. Performance Plan for Bill F. Evans

Responsibilities		Performance Factors and/or Results to Be Achieved	Relative Importance
Secretarial:	1	Review, analyze, and prioritize all incoming/outgoing correspondence with regard to confidentiality, relative importance, and urgency. Gather related data, complete research and administrative details (mailing, copying, logging). Distribute correspondence daily. Review questionable correspondence with management as to relative importance and turnaround.	I
	2	Use the available equipment to enhance turnaround time. Edit, proofread for grammatical and spelling errors prior to submission for management approval.	
	3	Maintain an effective follow-up system to ensure all action items are answered. Review daily activity and document action taken, and results/progress achieved to completion. Seek a determination from management if contents are not clear.	
	4	Prepare replies to correspondence for signature of principals when possible.	
	5	Maintain and update managers' control books and manuals as required.	
	6	Maintain managers' calendars on a no-conflict basis. Remind managers with one-day advance notice of scheduled appointments and meetings. Ensure that managers sign out and that you are aware of their whereabouts at all times.	
	7	Answer telephones for managers. Handle calls in a prompt, courteous, and complete manner. Secure clear, concise information for callers, or refer callers to appropriate individuals. Return calls when managers are not available.	
	8	Meet with your managers at a minimum of twice weekly to ensure maximum communication.	
	9	Serve as lead operator for the Electronic Administrative System. Utilize equipment and all available applications. Complete regular maintenance of systems. Coordinate training for new personnel, serve as focal point for electronic information.	
Branch/Marketing Assistance:	1	Follow to ensure travel advances are cleared within 30 days of return date. Coordinate/handle all travel arrangements for your managers. Ensure all required documentation (such as Petty Cash card, travel authorizations) are complete and properly approved.	

EXHIBIT 1. Performance Plan for Bill F. Evans *(continued)*

	2	Coordinate/handle all meeting requirements for your managers, i.e., room reservations, necessary room setups, travel arrangements.	
	3	Maintain audit-ready status in all of your areas of responsibility.	
Financial:	1	Ensure all invoices/bills are properly coded and sent to cashfund within 24 hours of receipt.	I
	2	Review questionable entries with appropriate manager for documentation and resolution.	
	3	Coordinate operating plan, initial budget spread, and process revisions as required.	
	4	Recap all expense and revenue items monthly, highlighting problem areas. Review with Administrative Manager.	
	5	Track travel expense on a continuing basis—provide monthly reports to all managers concerning activities.	
	6	Track to ensure debit memos are processed in a timely manner.	
	7	Audit daily time card register for expenses versus time cards processed.	

Other Administrative Duties:

1 Serve as copier key operator.   II

2 Timely follow up letters for overdue statements, complete and accurate submission of reports.

3 Maintain portable assets and sign out controls for office equipment. Semiannually ensure new cards are issued and signed.

4 Perform independent checks of general housekeeping, appearance, and cleanliness. Maintain security in all areas of responsibility.

Self Development:

1 Participate in unit meetings/discussions. Offer your ideas/suggestions for improved procedures.   II

2 Handle special assigned projects, etc., as assigned.

3 Become the Branch Administrative expert in the following areas and develop applications:
   - Displaywriter
   - Personal Computer
   - PROFS
   Demonstrate these applications at Branch, Administrative Manager Meeting.

Back up:

Act as primary back up to all secretaries and receptionist. Learn/handle all activities associated with these areas. Ensure audit guidelines are followed.   II

Leadership:

1 Be totally involved in the secretarial operations of the branch. Set an example of excellence, concern, and professionalism.   I

2 Establish and maintain open communications between peers, marketing, and management. Keep management informed of potential problems that may require their involvement.

After Janet read the plan she commented, "This is called a secretarial job?" He answered with a smile, "You can really call it anything you want. They don't call me a secretary around here."

"What do they call you?" she asked. "Bill," he replied quickly, and they laughed again.

Janet looked back in the performance plan and said, "Take this item 7 under secretarial responsibilities. How do they measure whether you answer telephones and handle calls promptly?"

"Easy!" he replied. "When you talk with Mr. Graf, he will explain to you what to expect. I am expected to answer the phone after no more than four rings. Your plan may be different in the beginning." When she asked whether they would check something like this, he confirmed that they would.

A Walk by the Lake

During the interview the day before, Bill mentioned that Mr. Graf was usually in his office about 6:00 A.M. every day! But he did not require that of anybody else. With an idea in mind, she stayed the night in Chicago. In the morning, she took an early refreshing midsummer walk along Lake Shore Drive and thought about all aspects of the move. She then headed for the telephone in Chips' lobby. It was 6:30 A.M. From there she called Mr. Graf:

"Just checking on you."

"There are many unbelievable things around here."

"I've been thinking about yesterday."

"Where are you calling from?"

"The lobby."

"What a dedicated candidate. Come on up."

The Decision

Another decision under pressure. Mr. Graf told Janet that everyone was impressed with her questions yesterday, and that his impressions from the first interview in Jackson were confirmed. Then he hinted: "We think you would be a good fit for the job we have, but it has to be a very quick decision."

Janet looked through his glass door to Bill's empty chair. Then her thoughts traveled 140 miles to Jackson, where the Colonel was examining his troops, giving secret performance directives, and the tension was mounting. Then she stared back at Bill's desk where the performance plan with its duties and responsibilities was still where she left it the day before. She thought for a few more seconds and than asked, "If I accepted right now, what will my starting salary be?" The second she finished, he turned up a desk note and put it in front of her. On it was typed: $16,350.

"That is about $5,000 less than what I make at Software General," she mumbled to herself. "Are the differences between the two job systems worth this difference in salary?"

18. A Leak in the Faculty Lounge*

It was 3:30 in the afternoon when Dr. Bob King made himself a cup of tea and sat in the faculty lounge awaiting the beginning of his Human Resource Management class. Although the topic of the day, performance appraisal, was one of Professor King's favorite subjects, he needed some new examples and exercises to liven up the discussion and drive home the points of the lecture.

Relaxing alone in the lounge, Dr. King noticed that the southeast corner of the ceiling was leaking again. The shapes of the water stains looked so much like natural scenes that they totally absorbed him; he didn't notice that one of his colleagues was in the room talking. "This is about the third or fourth time this leak has been fixed in less than a year," Thelma Wickenhauser repeated.

Dr. King smiled and replied jokingly, "In New York City, Thelma, they would pay someone a fortune to paint an abstract picture like this on the wall." Thelma poured herself a cup of coffee and commented as she left the lounge, "The problem is, we won't have a wall to paint for long if we keep this kind of picture to enjoy." They both laughed as Dr. King mumbled, "Of course, of course."

Eureka! The leak is indeed a symptom of defective performance. What really causes the leak? He remembered seeing the workers fixing it the last time they were there. They seemed seasoned and experienced enough; why then does their performance always leak? Who checks on the workers and accepts the job as complete? What sort of performance feedback and supervision do these workers receive during and after performance? How are they paid—by the hour? job? Do they get paid for defective jobs such as these? Who decides all these issues? He didn't particularly remember seeing any supervisor with the workers; do they evaluate their own performance? Do they evaluate each other's? What actually are the answers that make more sense? Are there any? Professor King was smiling as he headed toward the class thinking about the leak as a relevant subject for performance appraisal discussion.

The class liked the example and enjoyed the several laughs they generated from the abstract pictures on the wall. Five minutes before the end of the session, Randy, nicknamed Mr. Cool by classmates, raised his hand and asked, "How does all this performance appraisa. stuff apply to the class?"

Surprised and wanting to end the class on a positive note, Dr. King glanced at his watch and asked Randy to elaborate a little. "I mean how can we apply all these performance appraisal concepts in evaluating you teachers, in evaluating students' performance, and in motivating all parties involved?" Randy asked.

"Wow, Randy, these are most interesting points," said Dr. King. Randy's neighbor mumbled, "This is what you get for educating people like Randy too much." The class laughed as students started their ritual preparation for taking off. Before they left, Dr. King added an item to their homework. "Please think thoroughly about Randy's questions and come next time prepared to suggest applications of performance appraisal concepts and methods in evaluating the

---

*A. Magid M. Mazen, Assistant Professor, Department of Managing and Marketing, Illinois State University. Printed with permission.

production process that takes place in the class throughout the semester," Dr. King requested.

As Dr. King left the room, he saw some of the students giving Randy an unmistakable look, whereas others rushed to the faculty lounge to see the leak that started all this. He smiled, remember the first law of psychology: People are different.

19.   Lordstown Plant of General Motors*

Introduction

In December 1971, the management of the Lordstown Plant was very much concerned with an unusually high rate of defective Vegas coming off the assembly line. For the previous several weeks, the lot with a capacity of 2,000 cars had been filled with Vegas which were waiting for rework before they could be shipped out to the dealers around the country.

The management was particularly disturbed by the fact that many of the defects were not the kinds of quality deficiency normally expected in an assembly production of automobiles.[1] There was a countless number of Vegas with their windshields broken, upholstery slashed, ignition keys broken, signal levers bent, rear-view mirrors broken, or carburetors clogged with washers. There were cases in which, as the Plant Manager put it, "the whole engine blocks passed by forty men without any work done on them."

Since then, the incident in the Lordstown Plant has been much publicized in news media, drawing public interest. It has also been frequently discussed in the classroom and in the academic circles. While some people viewed the event as "young worker revolt," others reacted to it as a simple "labor problem." Some viewed it as "worker sabotage," and others called it "industrial Woodstock."

This case describes some background and important incidents leading to this much publicized and discussed industrial event.

This case describes some background and important incidents leading to this much publicized and industrial event.

The General Motors Corporation is the nation's largest manufacturer. The company is a leading example among many industrial organizations which have

---

*This case was prepared by Hak-Chong Lee, State University of New York at Albany, and is used here with his permission.

This case was developed for instructional purposes from published sources and interviews with the General Motors Assembly Division officials in Warren, Michigan, and Lordstown, Ohio. The case was read and minor corrections were made by the Public Relations Office of the GMAD. However, the author is solely responsible for the content of the case. The author appreciates the cooperation of General Motors. He also appreciates the suggestions of Professor Anthony Athos of Harvard and Mr. John Grix of General Motors which improved this case.

1. The normal defect rate requiring rework was fluctuating between 1–2 percent at the time.

achieved organizational growth and success through decentralization. The philosophy of decentralization has been one of the most valued traditions in General Motors from the days of Alfred Sloan in the 1930s through Charles Wilson and Harlow Curtice in the 1950s and up to recent years.

Under decentralized management, each of the company's car divisions, Cadillac, Buick, Oldsmobile, Pontiac, and Chevrolet, was given a maximum autonomy in the management of its manufacturing and marketing operations. The assembly operations were no exception, each division managing its own assembly work. The car bodies built by Fisher Body were assembled in various locations under maximum control and coordination between the Fisher Body and each car division.

In the mid-1960s, however, the decentralization in divisional assembly operations was subject to a critical review. At the divisional level, the company was experiencing serious problems of worker absenteeism and increasing cost with declines in quality and productivity. They were reflected in the overall profit margins which were declining from 10 percent to 7 percent in the late 1960s. The autonomy in the divided management in body manufacturing and assembly operations, in separate locations in many cases, became questionable under the declining profit situation.

In light of these developments, General Motors began to consolidate in some instances the divided management of body and chassis assembly operations into a single management under the already existing General Motors Assembly Division (GMAD) in order to better coordinate the two operations. The GMAD was given an overall responsibility to integrate the two operations in these instances and see that the numerous parts and components going into car assembly get to the right places in the right amounts at the right times.[2]

The General Motors Assembly Division (GMAD)

The GMAD was originally established in the mid 1930s, when the company needed an additional assembly plant to meet the increasing demands for Buick, Oldsmobile, and Pontiac automobiles. The demands for these cars were growing so much beyond the available capacity at the time that the company began, for the first time, to build an assembly plant on the west coast which could turn out all three lines of cars rather than an individual line. As this novel approach became successful, similar plants turning out a multiple line of cars were built in seven other locations in the east, south, and midwest. In the 1960s the demand for Chevrolet production also increased, and some Buick-Oldsmobile-Pontiac plants began to assemble Chevrolet products. Accordingly, the name of the division was changed to GMAD in 1965.

In order to improve the quality and productivity, the GMAD increased its control over the operations of body manufacturing and assembly. It reorganized jobs, launched programs to improve efficiency, and reduced the causes of defects

---

2. A typical assembly plant has five major assembly lines—hard trim, soft trim, body, paint, and final—supported by sub-assembly lines which feed to the main lines such components as engines, transmissions, wheels and tires, radiators, gas tanks, front and sheet metal, and scores of other items. The average vehicle on assembly lines has more than 5,500 items with quality checks numbering five million in a typical GMAD assembly plant in a sixteen-hour-a-day operation.

which required repairs and rework. With many positive results attained under the GMAD management, the company extended the single management concept to six more assembly locations in 1968 which had been run by the Fisher Body and Chevrolet Divisions. In 1971, the GM further extended the concept to four additional Chevrolet-Fisher Body assembly facilities, consolidating the separate management under which the body and chassis assembly had been operating. One of these plants was the Lordstown Plant.

The series of consolidation brought to eighteen the number of assembly plants operated by the GMAD. In terms of total production, they were producing about 75 percent of all cars and 67 percent of trucks built by the GM. Also in 1971, one of the plants under the GMAD administration began building certain Cadillac models, thus involving GMAD in production of automobiles for each of the GM's five domestic car divisions as well as trucks for both Chevrolet and GMC Truck and Coach Division.

The Lordstown Complex

The Lordstown complex is located in Trumbull County in Ohio, about fifteen miles west of Youngstown and thirty miles east of Akron. It consists of the Vega assembly plant, the van-truck assembly plant, and Fisher Body metal fabricating plant, occupying about 1,000 acres of land. GMAD, which operates the Vega and van-truck assembly plants, is also located in the Lordstown complex. The three plants are in the heart of the heavy industrial triangle of Youngstown, Akron, and Cleveland. With Youngstown as a center of steel production, Akron the home of rubber industries, and Cleveland as a major center for heavy manufacturing, the Lordstown complex commands a good strategic and logistic location for automobile assembly.

The original assembly plant was built in 1964–1966 to assemble Impalas. But in 1970 it was converted into Vega assembly with extensive arrangements. The van-truck assembly plant was constructed in 1969, and the Fisher Body metal fabricating plant was further added in 1970 to carry out stamping operations to produce sheet metal components used in Vega and van assemblies. In October 1971, the Chevrolet Vega and van-assembly plants and Fisher Body Vega assembly plants which had been operating under separate management were merged into a single jurisdiction of the GMAD.

Workforce at the Lordstown Plant

There are over 11,400 employees working in the Lordstown Plant (as of 1973). Approximately 6,000 people, of whom 5,500 are on hourly payroll, work in the Vega assembly plant. About 2,600 workers, 2,100 of them paid hourly, work in van-truck assembly. As members of the United Auto Workers Union, Local 1112, the workers command good wages and benefits. They start out on the line at about $5.00 an hour, get a 10¢ an hour increase within thirty days, and another 10¢ after ninety days. Benefits come to $2.50 an hour.[3] The supplemental unemployment

---

3. In GM, the average worker on the line earns $12,500 a year with fringe benefits of $3,000.

benefits virtually guarantee the worker's wages throughout the year. If the worker is laid off, he gets more than 90 percent of his wages for fifty-two weeks. He is also eligible for up to six days for holidays, excused absence, or bereavement, and up to four weeks' vacation.

The workforce at the plant is almost entirely made up of local people with 92 percent coming from the immediate area of a twenty-mile radius. Lordstown itself is a small rural town of about 500 residents. A sizable city closest to the plant is Warren, five miles away, which together with Youngstown supplies about two-thirds of the workforce. The majority of the workers (57.5 percent) are married, 7.6 percent are homeowners, and 20.2 percent are buying their homes. Of those who do not own their own homes (72 percent), over one-half are still living with their parents. The rest live in rented houses or apartments.

The workers in the plant are generally young. Although various news media reported the average worker age as twenty-four years old, and in some parts of the plant as twenty-two years, the company records show that the overall average worker age was somewhat above twenty-nine years as of 1971–72. The national average is forty-two. The workforce at Lordstown is the second youngest among GM's twenty-five assembly plants around the country. The fact that the Lordstown plant is the GM's newest assembly plant may partly explain the relatively young work force.

The educational profile of the Lordstown workers indicates that only 22.2 percent have less than a high school education. Nearly two-thirds or 62 percent are high school graduates, and 16 percent are either college graduates or have attended college. Another 26 percent have attended trade school. The average education of 13.2 years makes the Lordstown workers among the best educated in GM's assembly plants.

The Vega Assembly Line

Conceived as a major competitive product against the increasing influx of foreign cars which were being produced at as low as one-fourth the labor rate in this country, the Vega was specifically designed with a maximum production efficiency and economy in mind. From the initial stages of planning, the Vega was designed by a special task team with the most sophisticated techniques, using computers in designing the outer skin of the car and making the tapes that form the dies. Computers were also used to match up parts, measure the stack tolerances, measure safety performance under head-on collision, and make all necessary corrections before the first 1971 model car was ever built. The 2300-cubic-centimeter all-aluminum, 4-cylinder engine, was designed to give gas economy comparable to the foreign imports.

The Vega was also designed with the plant and the people in mind. As the GM's newest plant, the Vega assembly plant was known as the "super plant" with the most modern and sophisticated designs to maximize efficiency. It featured the newest engineering techniques and a variety of new power tools and automatic devices to eliminate much of the heavy lifting and physical labor. The line gave the workers an easier access to the car body, reducing the amount of bending and crawling in and out, as in other plants around the country. The unitized body in large components like pre-fab housing made the assembly easier and lighter with greater body integrity. Most difficult and tedious tasks were eliminated or simplified, on-line variations of the job were minimized, and the most modern tooling and mechanization was used to the highest possible degree of reliability.

It was also the fastest moving assembly line in the industry. The average time per assembly job was thirty-six seconds with a maximum of 100 cars rolling off the assembly line per hour for a daily production of 1,600 cars from two shift operations. The time cycle per job in other assembly plants averaged about fifty-five seconds. Although the high speed of the line did not necessarily imply greater work load or job requirement, it was a part of the GM's attempt to maximize economy in Vega assembly. The fact that the Vega was designed to have 43 percent fewer parts than a full-size car also helped the high-speed line and economy.

Impact of GMAD and Reorganization in the Lordstown Plant

As stated previously, the assembly operations at Lordstown had originally been run by Fisher Body and Chevrolet as two plants. There were two organizations, two plant managers, two unions, and two service organizations. The consolidation of the two organizations into a single operating system under the GMAD in October 1971 required a difficult task of reorganization and dealing with the consequences of manpower reduction such as work slowdown, worker discipline, grievances, etc.

As duplicating units such as production, maintenance, inspection, and personnel were consolidated, there was a problem of selecting the personnel to manage the new organization. There were chief inspectors, personnel directors, and production superintendents as well as production and service workers to be displaced or reassigned. Unions which had been representing their respective plants also had to go through reorganization. Union elections were held to merge the separate union committees at Fisher Body and Chevrolet in a single union bargaining committee. This eliminated one full local union shop committee.

At the same time, GMAD launched an effort to improve production efficiency more in line with that in other assembly plants. It included increasing job efficiency through reorganization and better coordination between the body and chassis assembly, and improving controls over product quality and worker absenteeism. This effort coincided with the plant's early operational stage at the time which required adjustments in line balance and work methods. Like other assembly plants, the Vega assembly plant was going through an initial period of diseconomy caused by suboptimal operations, imbalance in the assembly line, and somewhat redundant workforce. According to management, line adjustment and work changes were a normal process in accelerating the assembly operation to the peak performance the plant had been designed for after the initial break-in and start-up period.

As for job efficiency, the GMAD initiated changes in those work sequences and work methods which were not well coordinated under the divided managements of body and chassis assembly. For example, previous to the GMAD, Fisher Body had been delivering the car body complete with interior trim to the final assembly lines, where oftentimes the workers soiled the front seats as they did further assembly operations. GMAD changed this practice so that the seats were installed as one of the last operations in building the car. Fisher Body also had been delivering the car body with complete panel instrument frame which made it extremely difficult for the assembly workers to reach behind the frame in installing the instrument panels. The GMAD improved the job method so that the box containing the entire instrument panels was installed on the assembly line. Such improvements in job sequences and job methods resulted in savings in time and the number of workers required. Consequently, there were some jobs where the assembly time was cut down and/or the number of workers was reduced.

GMAD also put more strict control over worker absenteeism and the causes for defect work; the reduction in absenteeism was expected to require less relief men, and the improvement in quality and less repair work were to require less repairmen. In implementing these changes, the GMAD instituted a strong policy of dealing with worker slowdowns via strict disciplinary measures including dismissal. It was rumored that the inspectors and foremen passing defective cars would be fired on the spot.

Many workers were laid off as a result of the reorganization and job changes. The union was claiming that as many as 700 workers were laid off. Management, on the other hand, put the layoff figure at 375 to which the union later conceded.[4] Although management claimed that the changes in job sequence and method in some assembly work did not bring a substantial change in the overall speed or pace of the assembly line, the workers perceived the job change as "tightening" the assembly line. The union charged that the GMAD brought a return of an old-fashioned line speedup and a "sweatshop style" of management reminiscent of the 1930s, making the men do more work at the same pay. The workers were blaming the "tightened" assembly line for the drastic increase in quality defects. As one worker commented, "That's the fastest line in the world. We have about forty seconds to do our job. The company adds one more thing and it can kill us. We can't get the stuff done on time and a car goes by. The company then blames us for sabotage and shoddy work."

The number of worker grievances also increased drastically. Before GMAD took over, there were about 100 grievances in the plant. Since then, grievances increased to 5,000, 1,000 of which were related to the charge that too much work had been added to the job. The worker resentment was particularly great in "towveyor" assembly and seat sub-assembly areas. The "towveyor" is the area where engines and transmissions are assembled. Like seat sub-assembly there is a great concentration of workers working together in close proximity. Also, these jobs are typically for beginning assemblers who tend to make the work crew in these areas younger and better educated.

The workers in the plant were particularly resentful of the company's strict policy in implementing the changes. They stated that the tougher the company became, the more they would stiffen their resistance even though other jobs were scarce in the market. One worker said, "In some of the other plants where the GMAD did the same thing, the workers were older and they took this. But I've got twenty-five years ahead of me in this plant." Another worker commented, "I saw a woman running to keep pace with the fast line. I'm not going to run for anybody.

---

4. All of the workers who had been laid off were later reinstated as the plant needed additional workers to perform assembly jobs for optional features to Vega, i.e., vinyl top, etc., which were later introduced. In addition, some workers were put to work at the van-assembly plant.

There ain't anyone in that plant that is going to tell me to run." One foreman said, "The problem with the workers here is not so much that they don't want to work, but that they just don't want to take orders. They don't believe in any kind of authority."

While the workers were resisting management orders, there were some indications that the first-line supervisors had not been adequately trained to perform satisfactory supervisory roles. The average supervisor at the time had less than three years of experience, and 20 percent of the supervisors had less than one year's experience. Typically, they were young, somewhat lacking in knowledge of the provisions of the union contract and other supervisory duties, and less than adequately trained to handle the workers in the threatening and hostile environment which was developing.

Another significant fact was that the strong reactions of the workers were not entirely from the organizational and job changes brought about by the GMAD alone. Management noted that there was a significant amount of worker reactions in the areas where the company hadn't changed anything at all. Management felt that the intense resentment was particularly due to the nature of the workforce in Lordstown. The plant was not only made up of young people, but also the workforce reflected the characteristics of "tough labor" in steel, coal, and rubber industries in the surrounding communities. Many of the workers in fact came from families who made their living working in these industries. Management also noted that the worker resistance had been much greater in the Lordstown Plant than in other plants where similar changes had been made.

A good part of the young workers' resentment also seemed to be related to the unskilled and repetitive nature of the assembly work. One management official admitted that the company was facing a difficult task in getting workers to "take pride" in the product they were assembling. Many of them were benefiting from the company's tuition assistance plan which was supporting their college education in the evening. With this educated background, obviously assembly work was not fulfilling their high work expectations. Also, the job market was tight at the time, and they could neither find any meaningful jobs elsewhere nor, even

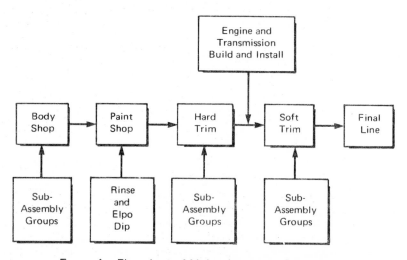

Exhibit 1.   Flowchart of Major Assembly Operations

if found, could they afford to give up the good money and fringe benefits they were earning on their assembly-line jobs. This made them frustrated, according to company officials.

Many industrial engineers were questioning whether the direction of management toward assembly line work could continue. As the jobs became easier, simpler, and repetitive, requiring less physical effort, there were less and less traces of skill and increased monotony. The worker unrest indicated that they not only wanted to go back to the work pace prior to the "speedup" (pre-October pace), but also wanted the company to do something about the boring and meaningless assembly work. One worker commented, "The company has got to do something to change the job so that a guy can take an interest in the job. A guy can't do the same thing eight hours a day year after year. And it's got to be more than the company just saying to a guy, 'Okay, instead of six spots on the weld, you'll do five spots.' "

As the worker resentment mounted, the UAW Local 1112 decided in early January 1972 to consider possible authorization for a strike against the Lordstown Plant in a fight against the job changes. In the meantime, the union and management bargaining teams worked hard on worker grievances; they reduced the number of grievances from 5,000 to a few hundred; management even indicated that it would restore some of the eliminated jobs. However, the bargaining failed to produce accord on the issues of seniority rights and shift preference, which were related to wider issues of job changes and layoff.

A vote was held in early February 1972. Nearly 90 percent of the workers came out to vote, which was the heaviest turnout in the history of the Local. With 97 percent of the votes supporting, the workers went out on strike in early March.

In March 1972, with the strike in effect, the management of the Lordstown Plant was assessing the impact of the GMAD and the resultant strike in the Plant. It was estimated that the work disruption because of the worker resentment and slowdown had already cost the company 12,000 Vegas and 4,000 trucks amounting to $45 million. There had been repeated closedowns of assembly lines since December 1971, because of the worker slowdowns and the cars passing down the line without all necessary operations performed on them. The car lot was full with 2,000 cars waiting for repair work.

There had also been an amazing number of complaints from Chevrolet dealers, 6,000 complaints in November alone, about the quality of the Vegas shipped to them. This was more than the combined complaints from the other assembly plants.

The strike in the Lordstown Plant was expected to affect other plants. The plants at Tonawanda, New York, and Buffalo, New York, were supplying parts for Vega. Despite the costly impact of the worker resistance and the strike, the management felt that the job changes and cost reductions were essential if the Vega were to return a profit to the company. The plant had to be operating at about 90 percent capacity to break even. Not only had the plant with highly automated features cost twice as much as estimated, but also the Vega itself ended up weighing 10 percent more than had been planned.

While the company had to do something to increase the production efficiency in the Lordstown Plant, the management was wondering whether it couldn't have planned and implemented the organizational and job changes differently in view of the costly disruption of the operations and the organizational stress the plant had been experiencing.

20. Traveler Import Cars, Incorporated*

Background

Randy Traveler had been a partner in Capitol Imports, one of the most prosperous foreign car dealerships in greater Columbus, Ohio, selling expensive European automobiles. His wife, Beryl, a holder of an MBA degree from a respected private university, was a consultant specializing in automobile dealerships.

In 1979, Randy and Beryl decided to go into business for themselves. Since between the two of them they had four decades of automobile dealership experience, they elected to acquire their own dealership. With some luck, they obtained a dealership selling a brand of Japanese cars that had become known in the United States for its very high quality. Randy became president and Beryl executive vice-president.

Evolution of the Firm

Stage 1. After obtaining the Japanese dealership, Randy and Beryl decided to locate it approximately two miles from Capitol Imports. The decision was made on the basis of immediate availability of a suitable facility. This location, however, was several miles from a major shopping area of any kind, and the closest automobile dealership was Capitol Imports. Furthermore, the location was approximately three miles from the nearest interchange of a major interstate highway. Nonetheless, the dealership was located on a busy street within easy access to half a dozen upper-middleclass-to-affluent neighborhoods with residents predisposed to purchasing foreign automobiles with a high quality image.

A number of key employees were enticed by Randy and Beryl to leave Capitol Imports and join Traveler Import Cars. Stuart Graham, who was in charge of Finance and Insurance at Capitol Imports, became general manager at Traveler Import Cars. Although Graham is sixty years of age, he lacked any managerial experience prior to assuming the position of general manager at Traveler Import Cars. Before specializing in finance and insurance, Graham was a car salesman. Several mechanics and car salesmen also left Capitol Imports to join Traveler Import Cars. As a rule, the policies and procedures that pertained at Capitol Imports were relied on at Traveler Import Cars, Inc. for the first five years of operations.

No one at Traveler Import Cars was unionized, but the mechanics were given everything that unionized mechanics received at other dealerships in order to remove the incentive to unionize. By everything, it is meant direct compensation, indirect compensation (fringe benefits), and work rules.

Randy and Beryl viewed their dealership as a family. This was in some measure due to the fact that the dealership was part of a Japanese Corporation (which viewed its employees as family), and partly due to the beliefs that Randy and Beryl shared about organizations. Randy and Beryl made every effort to involve subordinates in day-to-day decision-making. As tangible evidence of her commitment to democratic leadership, Beryl decided to introduce a quality circle into Traveler Import Cars, Incorporated. This was done by selecting five non-supervisory employees (one from each part of the organization) to meet once a month with Beryl and Stuart Graham in order to discuss problems, possible solutions, and implementation strategies. No training whatsoever regarding quality circles was provided anyone involved with the so-called "quality circle," and this includes Beryl and Stuart.

Stuart Graham, on the other hand, was a benevolent autocrat, although he tried to create the facade of a democratic leader because he understood well Randy and Beryl's leadership preferences. Most employees agreed with Randy and Beryl that Traveler Import Cars was a family. Furthermore, most employees felt free to voice an opinion on anything to Randy, Beryl, and Graham, or to any other supervisor or manager, for that matter.

Stage 2. As long as the dealership was small everything went well, largely because Randy and Beryl made all key decisions, provided daily direction to supervisors and managers (including the general manager—Stuart Graham, who should have been running the dealership on a day-to-day basis), and resolved problems through face-to-face communications with the involved individuals. As the dealership grew and prospered, it generated enough money for growth. Expanding the dealership rapidly was impractical because of the limited allotment of cars due in large measure to the so-called "voluntary" import quotas by the Japanese car manufacturers. The demand for these cars was so great that cars were even sold from the showroom floor, leaving at times few models for new customers to view.

The first acquisition that Randy and Beryl made was a car leasing company, which they located next to the dealership. Randy elected to spend most of his time building up the car leasing company, leaving the operations of the dealership to Beryl. The second acquisition consisted of another car dealership located approximately ten miles from the original one. The new dealership sold another make of Japanese cars and an expensive European make. The newly acquired dealership was located in the midst of automobile dealerships on a main road, but was housed in inadequate facilities and beset by many problems. Beryl became the chief operating officer of the second dealership as well. Soon after acquiring the second dealership, Randy and Beryl decided to construct new facilities adjacent to the existing ones.

Stage 3. The newly acquired dealership created a great deal of additional work for Beryl, but she understood and accepted that reality because she and Randy knowingly acquired a business that had been plagued by problems prior to acquisition. What bewildered and frustrated Beryl was the fact that the operation of Traveler Import Cars, Inc. took so much of her time as well as physical and psychic energies. After all, it has been five years since she and Randy purchased that dealership. Many key supervisory and managerial personnel now have five years of experience with the dealership, yet the task of running Traveler Import Cars is just as consuming at this time as it was when the dealership was new. Frequently, Beryl would tell one of the managers to do something, but it wouldn't get done. Decisions were reached at management meetings, but they did not get implemented. Programs were initiated, but were frequently permitted to drift and disappear. Important deadlines were being missed with increasing frequency. Mechanics and salesmen were coming to work late and taking excessive lunch breaks with greater frequency. Beryl knew that these problems were not due to insubordination or lack of motivation. Yet, if she did not directly oversee implementation of an important decision, it did not get implemented.

In order to relieve herself of some of the work load, Beryl hired two experienced managers. In order to justify their salaries, however, they spent half of their time at Traveler Import Cars and the other half at the newly acquired dealership. The newly hired managers had good ideas, yet Beryl was working just as hard as ever, and the problems that motivated Beryl to hire two experienced managers remained practically unchanged. In spite of the problems, the dealership grew as rapidly as the increase in the quota of cars that was allotted to the dealership by the manufacturer permitted. In addition, Traveler Import Cars began wholesaling parts to service stations and car repair shops, and started to lease cars in direct competition with the leasing operation managed by Randy. Although an organizational chart did not exist, it would look like Figure 1, if Randy and Beryl bothered to construct one.

About this time, Randy and Beryl's marriage had come undone, and Randy remarried a lady considerably his junior. Even so, Beryl and Randy maintained their business relationship, and were able to work together professionally without visible acrimony. Beryl now had more money than she knew what to do with, and was about to make much more because the newly acquired dealership was being turned around rapidly, largely due to Beryl's considerable talents, the new facility, and the rapidly recovering economy. Yet Beryl no longer wanted to work as hard as she had in the past.

Beryl understood that Stuart Graham lacked the right stuff to be general manager of a car dealership in a metropolitan area, and she approached Randy on the matter. His response was: "Stuart Graham is too valuable of an asset because Traveler Import Cars, Inc. had generated a $500,000 after tax profit last year. He must be doing something right."

Even though Beryl had been a consultant to automobile dealerships for twenty years, she decided nonetheless to retain a consultant. Beryl was fortunate to contact a particularly astute consultant by the name of J. P. Muzak. Her request was that Muzak straighten out the quality circle, which she felt wasn't living up to her expectations. Muzak, however, was reluctant to get involved unless he was permitted to conduct a thorough needs analysis before selecting any kind of intervention strategy. Beryl, after thinking the matter through, assented to Muzak's proposal. The organizational needs analysis relied on confidential structured interviews with all the managers, supervisors, and select non-supervisory personnel. The summary of Muzak's organizational needs analysis follows.

Possible Problem Areas

Goals. Although general goals (such as providing the best customer service possible) exist at the organizational level, many individuals report that what is expected of them, in terms of specific and measurable objectives, isn't clearly

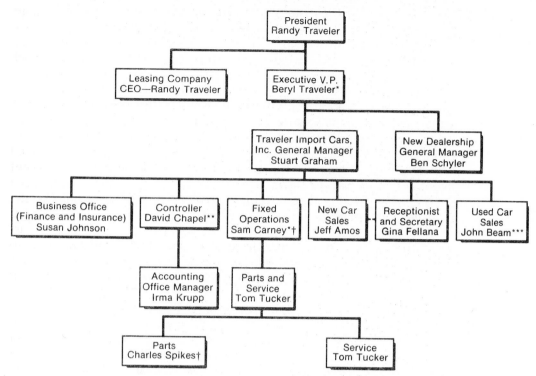

* These individuals spent approximately one-half of their time at Traveler Import Cars and one-half at the new dealership.

** David Chapel is the controller for Traveler Import Cars, the new dealership, and the leasing company. He spends about one-half of his time at Traveler Import Cars and one-half at the new dealership.

*** John Beam frequently is asked by Randy Traveler to assist with matters pertaining to the leasing company.

† Sam Carney owned and operated his own small business prior to joining Traveler Import Cars, Inc. Charles Spikes was a supervisor at a local office of a national automobile parts distributor before coming to work for Traveler Import Cars, Inc.

FIGURE 1. Organizational Chart of Traveler Import Cars, Inc.

defined. It is difficult to make a superior happy if the subordinate isn't sure just what it is that the boss wants.

Also, there does not appear to be a philosophy for setting goals. For example, should goals and objectives be imposed unilaterally by the superior on the subordinate, or should the goals and objectives be set jointly between the superior and subordinate?

Organizational Structure. The organizational structure in a number of instances appears to be confusing. Specifically, a number of individuals appear to be reporting to two or more superiors. Irma Krupp reports to David Chapel and Stuart Graham. Tom Tucker reports to Sam Carney and Stuart Graham. Charles Spikes reports to Tom Tucker, Sam Carney, and Stuart Graham. Susan Johnson seems to work for John Beam and Stuart Graham. John Beam had Susan Johnson's job before he became manager of used cars. David Chapel believes that he reports to the two general managers, to Beryl, and to Randy. Gina Fellana appears to report to everyone.

There is the perception that few managers know what they can do on their own authority and what they must get approved and by whom.

Communications. There appear to be too many meetings and they do not seem to be as productive as they could be. On this point there is a consensus.

A paper flow problem exists in several areas. The Accounting Office at times does not receive properly filled out forms from the Business Office. It appears that Susan Johnson does not have the time to fill out carefully and on a timely basis all the forms and attend to her other finance and insurance duties. The Accounting Office at times does not receive the necessary paper work from New Car Sales. The Parts Department at times doesn't receive on a timely basis the necessary information from New Car Sales.

Some individuals complain that their superiors do not keep them informed. Everything is a secret.

Training and Development. A number of individuals have risen through the ranks into supervisory and managerial positions. Since these individuals have never received formal managerial training, the void must be filled by coaching. In a number of cases, the void has not been filled by coaching, and these persons are learning through trial and error—an expensive and time-consuming way of learning, indeed.

The consensus is that the computer equipment is adequate to the task, but the operators need additional training to realize the potential of the equipment. The mechanics receive the latest training from the manufacturer.

Performance Appraisal. Many people reported that they do not receive a periodic formal appraisal. Thus, their need for performance feedback is frustrated.

Wage and Salary Administration. Numerous individuals have reported that it is the subordinate who has to initiate a wage or salary increase. Most individuals report that they would like to see the superior initiate wage and salary action at least annually. Moreover, a number of individuals are not sure on what basis they are remunerated. The absence of a systematic periodic performance appraisal is responsible, in part, for this perception.

Discipline. In a number of instances, individuals arrive late, take extended lunch breaks, and violate rules with impunity. This creates a demoralizing effect on others.

Control System. The financial control system at the top of the organization appears to be satisfactory. The operational control systems in the rest of the organization are problematic.

Morale. While there is still the feeling that the organization is a family and the best place the employees have ever worked, the feeling is starting to diminish.

Sundry Problems.

1. Quality circle may need restructuring along traditional lines.
2. The time it takes to make decisions should be shortened.

3. The organization has difficulty implementing decisions that have been made.
4. Lack of follow-up presents serious problems.
5. Policies and programs are permitted to drift and disappear (motivator board is an example).
6. Managers may not be delegating enough.
7. New car salesmen do not always turn customers over to the Business Office, resulting in loss of revenue to the dealership.
8. Service desk is crucial and it has been a revolving door.

At a meeting, Muzak presented the findings of his needs analysis to the management team of Traveler Import Cars, Inc., and a discussion ensued regarding each of the possible problem areas. Randy Traveler did not attend since he relegated the operation of the dealership to Beryl. At the end of the discussion, the management team agreed that all the problems uncovered by Muzak were real and, if anything, understated.

Muzak did not present at the meeting his assessment of the potential of the key managers. This he did in a private discussion with Beryl. In summary, Muzak concluded that Stuart Graham was too set in his ways to change. Moreover, he displayed too much emotion publicly, and lacked the respect of his subordinates. Jeff Amos was considered by his subordinates to be a nice guy, but was indecisive, lacked firmness, was manipulated by subordinates, and did not enjoy the respect of his subordinates. Tom Tucker was probably in over his head in his present position. He was only a high school graduate, he was not a mechanic, was unsure of himself, and lacked the confidence of his subordinates. Lastly, he was quite impulsive. His previous experience was as a service desk writer (the person to whom the customer explains the car problems and who writes the work order). All the other managers and supervisors were thought to possess the necessary potential which could be realized through training and experience.

21. Helen's Awkward Problem*

The situation gave her good reason to pause. Helen Lawson had been Supervisor of Metro City Health Department's Suburban Health Center for only two months, yet she reflected that things had been going well.

Helen paused to consider one problem. Unfortunately, her present difficulty threatened to overshadow all the other good things, and Helen was not sure how to avoid trouble.

Dr. Morgan had just left and he had merely added fuel to the fire. He was the staff doctor for a collateral state-funded health project. He had come to plead that Dorothy Wilson be fired. Dorothy, it seems, was the problem. As one of Helen's

*George Cooley, Assistant Dean, and Bruce Evans, Associate Professor of Management, University of Dallas. Printed with permission.

staff nurses and one of only three in the office with a Bachelor's degree in nursing, Dorothy had been with the Suburban Center for three years. Helen had planned to rely heavily upon her, but so far she had not been able to do so.

Helen knew, of course, that she did not have the authority to dismiss Dorothy, since they were all municipal employees. She had trouble convincing Dr. Morgan of this. The doctor was adamant. He had tried previously to have her discharged as his people were unable to work with her. His staff said her attitude conveyed they were intruding in her domain and that she resented them. Dorothy's actions did appear to reflect this attitude.

Dr. Morgan had related several incidents indicating Dorothy was a very weak communicator, and that both her resentment and her inability to communicate resulted in almost no coordination. As coordination in community health services is very important, Dr. Morgan felt it was essential to replace Dorothy with someone more mature who could work effectively with the state agency. Helen had listened. Although she reiterated the limitations on her authority, she promised to look into it further.

Appointments and lunch gave Helen a brief respite from Dr. Morgan's comments. On her return, though, she felt required to quickly carry through on her promise. The first step was to carefully review Dorothy's personnel file. To do so, Helen called for her clerk to bring in the file. In passing she said, "Billie, why don't you go to lunch now? Dorothy will be here to cover the phones." Billie replied excitedly, "Oh no, Mrs. Lawson! I'll just wait for the others to get back. Dorothy can't handle them. I can never make out messages that she leaves after answering the phones."

Helen turned to the file. She had glanced casually at all the personnel files previously, but she had not looked closely to see what they might reveal. Dorothy's job application reflected that she had held eight assorted jobs in the six years preceding her application for this job. Helen wondered what caused these several job changes.

Dorothy's degree work was completed only after coursework from five colleges and universities. Also, Dorothy's excessive tardiness had delayed her attaining full employment stature. Finally, her most recent performance report had been downgraded to "satisfactory" from her previous "excellent" ratings.

Armed with this, Helen decided to meet with Lila Moran, the previous supervisor who had left to take a part-time position closer to her home. At her office, Lila added further information. "I confess I wasn't able to handle Dorothy," she said. "I was afraid of her and did not want to confront her. She could be intimidating. Certainly her ratings were inflated, but I did so only to avoid trouble. Dorothy's work—especially her reports—was often substandard. She often refused to do things, but the others covered for her in the office, so I let it go."

The past two days' input weighed heavily on Helen. Her findings showed that Dorothy's performance was continually unsatisfactory. As a result, Helen felt required to begin and maintain a file on Dorothy's performance. Despite incidents that had been related to her, Helen found no specific deviations committed to writing. The breadth and width of the problem was highlighted by the fact that it took less than two weeks to accumulate several memos in Helen's file. Dorothy's less than satisfactory performance, it seems, was hardly an intermittent occurrence.

One thing Helen noted again and again was that Dorothy consistently failed to leave word with anyone when she left the office. Not only did she fail to sign out, but she failed to even mention when and where she was going. This happened even at peak workload times when the entire staff was needed to handle the work. Dorothy seemed oblivious to these needs and went about tasks that could as easily have been scheduled for slower periods.

Helen also noticed that Dorothy always took two hours for lunch on Fridays. The staff jokingly seemed to know what she was doing, and covered for her often. While Helen never objected to running over on lunch hours, the regularity and anonymity of this bothered her.

In one incident, Dorothy was gone for over an hour one afternoon. When she returned, Helen asked where she had been. "I went to get gas," she said. "I only use this one brand and there is no station on my way home." Helen asked her why she could not go out of her way after work. Rather than answer, Dorothy appeared hurt and just stared. She eventually went off to sulk and was moody for the rest of the day.

Helen next reviewed Dorothy's time sheets and written reports. All employees were required to account for their time on time sheets, and turn in reports on the families for which they were responsible. These reports resulted from periodic visits to the families' homes. Helen noted that Dorothy's sheet reflected consistently longer transportation and visit times than the other staff nurses' sheets. Further, her reports were poorly organized, and provided scant information to justify the time spent. The reports did not reflect why she made the visit, what problems if any were noted, and what actions she planned to take to correct them. Instead she gave a hazy narrative paragraph to show the visit was made.

When Helen asked her about this, Dorothy again seemed hurt, but she also indicated rather hostilely that many of these problems were not her fault. "My district is the most spread out. I also find many families not at home. That's why my transportation time is higher. I can't help that." She also laid much blame on the coordinating agencies. "It's often the agencies' fault. They don't coordinate properly. I can't do it all myself after all." She said further that she often failed to get proper and adequate information because someone else slipped up.

Helen weighed this for a few days and decided to discuss the situation with Betsy Graham—her immediate supervisor at the Health Department—in the hope that she could provide some useful guidance. Betsy began by saying, "Yes, I was aware that Lila was having a personnel difficulty at Suburban, but it never officially got up to me, so I took no action. My main contact with Dorothy came when Lila decided to leave. Dorothy was senior there, and could have taken over your supervisory position, but she expressed no interest in it. She apparently had no desire to move up or accept more responsibility. The job thus remained essentially vacant until you arrived. Everyone pretty much looked after themselves."

Betsy was unable to give Helen any more firsthand information. Nor did she seem to have any concrete advice for Helen. Helen puzzled over the facts as she drove back to the office. She realized there were sufficient facts before her to solve the problem, but what she hadn't been able to do is put them together properly to come to the right conclusion. As she reached the office, she realized something must be done.

22. Retired on the Job: Career Burnout or the Nonmotivated Employee?*

George Benson, the newly appointed manager of Pentarecon Corporation's Production Control and Methods Improvement Division, faced a rather perplexing personnel problem. One of the long-time employees of his division, Harry Norton, wasn't performing his job properly. In questioning subordinates, Benson learned that Norton had not performed any real or substantive work for years. Furthermore, his current job actions were a source of embarrassment to the entire division. "Hangover Harry" Norton was observed to arrive at work approximately forty-five minutes late each morning and proceeded to begin the work day by attempting to recover from the previous evening's outing with his "Scotch friends." Norton's method of recovery appeared to involve (1) reading the paper for about an hour while smoking and drinking coffee; (2) "office hopping" with his coffee cup in order to visit, talk, and interact with his many friends who were employed within the division; (3) a two-hour, three-martini lunch break; and (4) an afternoon nap while secluded back in his office. Benson had expected the employees of his division to resent Norton's behavior and obvious nonperformance. Thus he was quite surprised when he learned that Norton was almost universally liked and considered somewhat of a folk hero among nonsupervisory employees. Therefore, Benson decided to thoroughly investigate Norton's case before taking any type of personnel action.

From company records, Benson learned that Norton had been employed by Pentarecon Corporation for twelve years. He began his employment with the firm as an internal management specialist. The duties of this position involved the development of methods improvements to facilitate both management and manufacturing operations. Initially, Norton was quite successful in this position. His performance appraisals routinely cited him for both his ingenuity and complete understanding of the complex production control systems used by the firm. Norton was credited with the introduction of new work procedures that lessened both worker fatigue and industrial accidents. Additionally, several of his suggestions resulted in substantial improvements in product quality within the manufacturing department. Recognizing this performance excellence, the firm promoted Norton once and issued to him several cash bonuses during his first five years of employment.

During his seventh year of employment, Norton was being considered for a supervisory position within the division. Everyone was surprised when Pentarecon's top management finally decided to fill this supervisory vacancy with another employee from the Research and Development Group. Norton appeared to accept this career setback with some degree of indifference. He still seemed to exhibit his friendly and engaging interpersonal style that had won him many friends within the division. Yet six months later, a project he was assigned to direct seemed to "never get off the ground" because of his failure to exhibit proper levels of leadership and enthusiasm when dealing with other project analysts. Subsequent job assignments also revealed a substantial deterioration in

---

*This case was written by Bill Fitzpatrick. Printed with permission.

performance. Norton's failure to consider a variety of relevant variables in his work assignments resulted in the development of nonusable work methods and production control techniques. Norton's supervisor noted that Harry appeared to be drinking heavily during this period of time and was said to be experiencing marital difficulties. This pattern of poor performance, tardiness, and alcohol abuse continued to the point where Norton's supervisor was afraid to assign him projects of any real significance. Therefore, Harry was either given small, noncritical work assignments or no work at all.

Part IV

Compensating

Cases Outline

- The Piedmont Company
- Elite Software Inc.
- What She Had in Mind
- But Does the Shoe Fit?
- A Day Late and a Dollar Short
- A Permanent Part-Timer

23. The Piedmont Company*

The Piedmont Company, a large midwestern company with sales in excess of $2.5 billion, has experienced increasing difficulty in retaining highly qualified engineering and scientific personnel (technical and professional people) in its Technical Division. Many of those who have left expressed concern that the only way to get ahead in the company was to become a manager in the Technical Division or transfer to a non-technical division such as marketing. They did not feel that adequate recognition was given to the individual *contributor* who preferred to develop his technical or professional expertise to the highest extent. Some of these technical and professional people who quit were managers who stated they were "forced" to accept managerial positions in order to advance their careers. As managers, however, they soon became dissatisfied and/or ineffective, with the net result that the company was losing good technical people and gaining poor managers.

The Piedmont Company is a fairly competitive market which, although dominated by a few large firms, is most troubled by numerous small firms. These small firms have become more numerous and troublesome to Piedmont during the last ten years because of the rapidly changing markets and technology in the manufacture of glass and foam containers. The small firms have been able to meet the changing consumer demand more readily than Piedmont and because some of the recent technological breakthroughs have come from the labs of these small firms. Even more troublesome is that many of the technical and professional people at Piedmont have been leaving for these small firms.

The Technical Director, in reaction to this increasing problem, requested that the Organization Development (OD) Department explore the matter and make recommendations. Although the problem seemed rather urgent, the Technical Director did not impose any time restrictions on the OD Department.

The Organization Chart in Figure 1 represents a typical unit in the Technical Division, with three levels of supervision and three levels of individual contributors. Typically graduate engineers/scientists with limited or no experience were brought in at Piedmont at the entry level—Professional Level I; engineers/scientists with master's degrees came in at PL II; and those with Ph.D.'s

---

*This case was prepared by Ed Schuler and is used here with his permission.

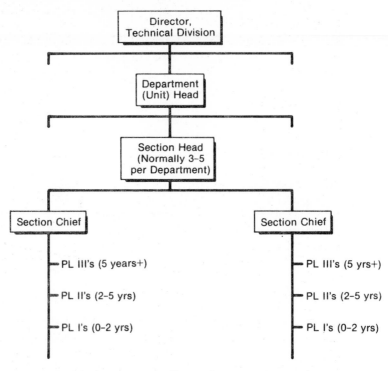

FIGURE 1

without experience started at PL III. The salaries at each level were extremely attractive. The fringer benefits were excellent. The highly competent technical and professional people also advanced rapidly. They tended to reach the maximum salary of the top individual contributor position—PL III—in approximately seven to eight years. However, merit increases were then limited to cost-of-living adjustments. Further promotion required acceptance of a managerial position in the Technical Division or another division of Piedmont. This is where the problems began for many of the technical and professional people at Piedmont.

The cases of Bob Crawford and Jim Baldwin are similar to those of many professionals who left the company during the past three years. After graduating from college with BA's in electrical engineering, Crawford and Baldwin were hired at the PL I level and had progressed rapidly and reached the top non-managerial level (PL III) in four years. Both had developed corporate-wide reputations in their area of expertise and had filed for numerous patents. In addition to this rapid promotion path for both of these people, they had received 10–12 percent annual merit increases since joining the company six years ago. However, at the end of their sixth year they were told they had reached the maximum of their salary range and would be limited to the 3–5 percent annual cost of living increases received by all employees. During the following three years they watched inflation (which during one year was 10 percent) erode their purchasing power. To add insult to injury the salaries of average journeyman professions (PL I) approached their own.

Their Section Chief attempted to justify merit increases beyond the maximum of the salary range based upon their significant contributions, but company policy was very strict on maintaining salaries within range. The company felt it would create too many inequities in the salary structure if it did not maintain a strict policy. The Section Chief had even attempted to rewrite their job descriptions but was told that he was basing the revised descriptions on individual performance rather than on a change in basic duties, another violation of company policy.

Exit Crawford

After ten years with the company Crawford, whose family was now grown, decided to look elsewhere for increased salary potential and job recognition. He was soon hired by a research firm in the same city at a modest increase in salary but with the promise that he could look forward to generous salary increases if things worked out.

Exit Baldwin

Baldwin, on the other hand, decided to remain with Piedmont Company and pursue opportunities at the supervisory level as a Section Chief. Although he preferred to remain as an individual contributor and did not have supervisory aspirations, he knew the next step up would mean a significant increase in salary plus participation in the management incentive plan. Thus, when the next Section Chief opening came up in his area, he applied and got the job. The next two years were frustrating ones as Baldwin found much of his time devoted to training new engineers and general administrative duties. After thirteen years of service, Baldwin left the company "with a yearning to return to 'the Bench'" and joined the same firm that hired Crawford.

The Recommendations

As part of the study by the Organization Development Department, it was found that many large industrial firms like Piedmont were experiencing similar problems in retaining high caliber engineers and scientists. However, the small research and development organizations, often competitors, did not seem to have the same turnover and morale problems. The small companies appeared to have more levels of individual contributor positions in their salary structure which rewarded the outstanding professionals.

After three months of research, the Organization Development Department proposed to the Technical Director and his staff the establishment of two additional levels of professional (and nonmanagerial) positions which would be roughly equivalent to Section Chief and Section Head positions in base salary.

Although the Technical Director's initial reaction was highly favorable, his department heads, section chiefs and section heads—all of whom had MBA's in addition to their undergraduate technical degrees—did not feel individual contributors should be rewarded at the same compensation level as section supervisors. In fact, several threatened to leave if these two additional levels of professional positions were added. Interestingly enough, these section supervisors denied the importance of the turnover and morale problems. Their prime concern appeared to be that most top scientists and engineers might prefer to remain individual contributors if they knew the compensation potential were as great as that of a management position. This, they argued, would deny the company a natural source of future supervisors and managers.

The Section Heads also questioned whether the company should really be competing with the smaller research and development firms which might place more of a premium on pure research.

Although Piedmont's primary emphasis was on applied research, the Technical Director still felt strongly that the company should encourage highly inventive people since the creation of new products and processes was critical to the company's maintaining a competitive edge in the industry. However, because of the strong objections of his key managers, he was reluctant to accept the recommendations of two additional levels.

24.   Elite Software Inc.*

"There goes another one," sighed Frank Gomez as he concluded the exit interview and watched helplessly as another computer programmer left the company for greener pastures and another job. This was the third computer programmer to leave the company this month. Frank works for Elite Software Inc. (ESI), which is presently experiencing a 25 percent annual turnover rate with its computer programmers—considered high even in the computer software industry. Frank, Vice-President of Human Resources at ESI, has observed a pattern from the responses given by the departing programmers. The pattern he detected is that the programmers are generally satisfied with their work and the company policies, but feel that the reward package that ESI offers is not competitive with what is given to employees at other software houses. The firms that attract the programmers tend to be smaller start-ups that offer them a strong incentive pay component of their compensation package.

Frank knows that the salary and benefits given by ESI are more than adequate. ESI subscribes to local, regional, and national salary surveys and has a policy of paying its employees above the median market salary levels. The benefits are comparable to what is offered to employees within the software industry. However, in the area of incentive compensation, ESI is weak. In the exit interviews, the programmers indicated that there was a lack of incentive for them to work the long hours, developing the new products on tight deadlines, when

*David B. Balkin, Assistant Professor of Management, Louisiana State University. Printed by permission.

the company did not seem to recognize their efforts with any form of compensation.

Elite Software Inc. was founded as a software company in 1981 by Ken Mitchell, a marketing genius. Ken and a few executives who started with the company own 60 percent of the company stock. The remaining 40 percent of the stock is owned by public shareholders and by employees who purchase shares under an employee stock ownership plan (ESOP). Under the ESOP employees may purchase shares of ESI stock at a 15 percent reduction in market price.

ESI develops, produces, and markets business applications programs for personal computers. Most of its customers are small businesses who use the programs for record keeping in the financial, manufacturing, marketing, and personnel functions of the business. Its main product, MiniCalc, was one of the first and most successful business applications programs on the market and it was responsible for most of ESI's growth. ESI grew from 40 employees at the end of 1981 to 85 in 1982 to 135 in 1983 to its present 210 employees by the end of 1984. Recently the demand for the MiniCalc has slowly declined as new products that have more powerful features have been introduced to the market. ESI had anticipated the decline of the MiniCalc and the responses of its competitors and is now developing a new, more powerful business applications program, the MaxiCalc, which is designed to replace its predecessor. Unfortunately, due to some unforeseen problems, there has been a delay in bringing MaxiCalc to the market. The turnover of the programmers has resulted in work disruptions and this has contributed to the delay. MaxiCalc is now six months behind its scheduled introduction to the market. Frank is aware that it is critically important for the survival of the company to bring MaxiCalc to market without any further delay.

In response to the problem of programmer turnover and Frank's trouble shooting, a meeting of the ESI Compensation Committee was organized and those present were Ken Mitchell, CEO and President; Frank Gomez, VP Human Resources; Sam Rosen, VP Finance; and Carolyn Jones, Manager of Compensation and Benefits. The purpose of the meeting was to develop a short-term incentive compensation plan for all the employees that would motivate and reinforce employees to design and develop new products at ESI. The pay incentive should also contribute to retaining employees so that there would be far fewer disruptions due to turnover of programmers and other employees.

In preparation for the meeting, Frank and Carolyn interviewed a representative sample of ESI employees to determine their preferences for incentive compensation. ESI has a young workforce with an average age of twenty-eight. Most of the employees prefer to receive direct compensation instead of deferred compensation such as a pension plan (ESI does not yet have a pension plan for employees) or a forced savings account similar to an IRA. Employees at ESI tend to be entrepreneurial and risk takers and prefer to have their money in cash so they can invest it as they choose. The committee decided to develop an incentive compensation program with a short-term (one year or less) cash payout to ESI employees. It was also decided that the incentive pay would have to be connected to some performance criteria.

The committee explored the pros and cons of many possible incentive compensation plans. They were able to narrow their choice down to three possible incentive pay plans. (1) *A profit sharing plan.* Under this scheme, all ESI employees would share a portion of the company's profits. Profits would be reported quarterly and employees would receive a share of the profits distributed as a percentage of their base salary. ESI must meet its quarterly profit goals before the employees are eligible to receive their share of the profits. (2) *A cash bonus.* The cash bonus would be given to employees on a one-time basis contingent upon the successful achievement of certain company objectives. The objectives may be financial (such as profits or revenue targets) or nonfinancial (such as meeting production or research and development objectives.) (3) *Increase the size of the merit pay budget.* It is suggested to raise the size of the merit pay budget so that employee's pay raises are perceived as more meaningful. Currently the merit pay program has a budget of 8 percent of salary expense with a range between 0 and 12 percent salary increases. The average performer will receive an 8 percent annual pay increase under this system. It is proposed to increase the budget so that the average performer will receive a 12 percent pay increase and the outstanding performer may receive as much as a 20 percent increase in salary. ESI will continue to use its performance appraisals as the basis for determining the merit pay increases. The company currently uses a Behavior Anchored Rating Scale (BARS) method of performance appraisal for evaluating its employees.

There was a lack of consensus within the committee as to which of the three proposed incentive pay plans would be most effective to motivate and retain ESI employees. Each program had its positive features and drawbacks. ESI has a fixed budget allocated for next fiscal year to finance one of three incentive pay options. After failing to achieve consensus, Ken Mitchell asked Frank Gomez to study the three incentive pay options and report back to him and the compensation committee in one week with a recommendation.

25. What She Had In Mind*

Ending months of speculation, Bev's employer, National Drug, has just announced a merger with one of the country's leading food and drug chains. That evening, all local personnel from National were scheduled for their first meeting with the regional manager of the acquiring firm. The purpose of the meeting was to introduce the "new and improved" benefit package to be applied to employees of both firms within a month.

"Great, it arrived on time," said Bev, referring to a letter she just received from Steelko Manufacturing, Inc. The letter included the benefits brochure of the company where she interviewed for a pharmacist position a week earlier. It was a slow evening at National Drug, and Bev had filled all the day's prescriptions, so she sat down to read Steelko's brochure. It was a pleasant coincidence that the brochure arrived the same day of the meeting, allowing for a fresh comparison.

*A. Magid M. Mazen, Assistant Professor, Department of Managing and Marketing, Illinois State University. Printed by permission.

Beverly Cox

Bev was twenty-two when she graduated from the University of Illinois School of Pharmacy. She passed the license exam the same year and joined Medicare Drug in a small town near her farming parents. In a year, she received an offer from another pharmacy but Medicare countered it and promoted her to head of their branch office in Peoria, Illinois. In 1977, an independent pharmacist in Peoria convinced Bev to leave Medicare. Soon after she joined his pharmacy, Medicare went out of business. In July of 1978, Bev applied for a position at National Drug and was hired for the job at their firm in Bloomington, Illinois. Two years later, she was promoted to head National's other pharmacy in Bloomington.

A year later, Bev got to know Jerome Cox, a frequent prescription customer, and in another year they married. Jerry is a mechanical engineer who lived through several unlucky experiences. He is a veteran of two wars, Korea and Vietnam; currently he suffers frequent and increasing back pain from an earlier helicopter crash. From his first marriage, Jerry has a seventeen-year-old son, Bob, who lives with him and Bev. During the last four years, Jerry has been laid off twice and is currently out of a job due to economic conditions. Because Jerry's unemployment compensation will be running out soon, Bev decides to fill in for two part-time jobs during her days off. One of these jobs is forty miles north. The family has been discussing the possibility of spinal surgery for Jerry but the cost is formidable given their current economic condition.

Bob is a junior in high school and wants to go to an engineering school when he graduates in a year and a half. Although the family prefers not to leave Bloomington before Bob's graduation, Bev decides to assess each situation separately.

Steelko's Package

Steelko's plant, where Bev interviewed, is located in a university town similar to Bloomington. However, the university is more nationally recognized for its engineering reputation. Jerry is quite familiar with the city and the university because it is his alma mater.

Steelko itself is a heavy manufacturing company with an international reputation in earth-moving equipment and tractor business. Recently, Steelko's local administration decided to have their own in-plant pharmacy so employees and workers could buy their medicine at cheaper rates.

During Bev's interview with Steelko, they told her that their personnel conducted a market analysis for the pharmacist position and the salary they offer for the position will be competitive. When she told them that she now makes $16.65 per hour, they observed that although it is higher than average market they will meet it. What they stressed the most was their benefit package that was recently beefed up by headquarters. They promised to send a copy as soon as it arrived from print.

It was an impressive detailed brochure. Without noticing, Bev thumbed through the booklet to see whether it contained something for dependents. She then read it more carefully from the beginning.

Health Care Coverage

This coverage will help you pay most of the medical, hospital, surgical, and physicians' charges you and your dependents incur during the year. Each benefit year, you pay the first $100 of covered medical expenses per covered person as a deductible. After that, this coverage pays 80 percent of your covered medical expenses for the remainder of the benefit year for that person. You pay the remaining 20 percent of these covered medical expenses, called your "copayment." Your Medical Expense Coverage has a special feature called an excess expense limitation. This feature limits the amount you pay during a benefit year for covered medical expenses. *It does not limit expenses for mental and nervous conditions.* If you or your covered dependents do not have coverage under any other group plans, the most you will need to pay is $700 during a benefit year for you and your covered dependents. Once you have paid $700, this coverage pays all remaining covered medical expenses for the benefit year up to the annual and lifetime maximums. The annual maximum is $500,000 per person. Each person is covered for up to $1,000,000 during their lifetime.

Dental Expense Coverage

Maximum Benefit:
> For orthodontic treatment . . . $650.
> For other covered dental expenses . . . $1,000 per calendar year (orthodontic treatment will not be charged against this maximum).

Vision Expense Coverage

Vision examination . . . once every 24 months.
Lens or lenses for eyeglasses and frames for eyeglasses . . . once every 24 months.
Reasonable and customary charges up to maximum benefits.

Organ Transplant Coverage

Benefits for donation and receipt of an organ.

Medicare Part B Premium Reimbursement

You are reimbursed for your Medicare Part B premium.

Employee Benefits Security Fund

Your account in this Fund offers money to help pay your share of health care expenses. You have an account if you had hospital expense or Comprehensive Medical Expense Coverage for at least one full calendar month in the prior benefit year. If you have comprehensive Medical Expense Coverage on the first day of the benefit year, your Fund account will be credited with $700 *provided you were both at work at least one day in each calendar month and covered for Health Care Coverage* the full prior benefit year. It you had Health Care Coverage, for the full prior benefit year but were not at work at least one day each month, a lower amount will be credited to your Fund account. All of the money credited to your Fund account in any benefit year is available to help pay for qualified medical expenses incurred by you or one of your covered dependents during that benefit year. You will receive any remaining balance in your Fund account as taxable compensation.

Disability Benefits in General

You will be paid Short Term Disability benefits during your total disability for up to twenty-six weeks. Based on your continuous service at the start of your disability absence, the Full Benefit (100 percent of your base weekly salary) will be paid for two to twenty-six weeks. The Partial Benefit (60 percent of your base weekly salary) will be paid for those weeks the Full Benefit is not paid. Extended Term Disability benefits are equal to 60 percent of your base weekly salary. These benefits begin after Short Term Disability benefits end. Payments can continue for a maximum of seventy-eight weeks during your total disability. To be eligible, you must have two or more years of continuous service. Long Term disability benefits range from 50 percent to sixty percent of your base monthly salary, depending on your years of continuous service. To be eligible, you must have three or more years of continuous service.

Retirement

Your Retirement Plan pension will be based on your years of pension service and on your average earnings during your final years of pension service.

Besides paying a pension benefit to you, the Plan may provide a lifetime monthly pension to your spouse following your death, whether you die before or after retirement.

In addition, the Plan may pay benefits to you even if you leave before you are eligible for retirement. For example, if you leave after completing at least ten years of pension service, you have a right to a pension benefit, which can begin as early as age fifty-five.

Steelko pays the entire cost of all the benefits provided under the Rules. You are not required to make any contributions.

Savings Plan

The Savings Plan gives you a convenient and systematic way to save and invest for your future. Like other personal savings and investment accounts, a separate account is set up in the Steelko Savings Plan in your name. Money you save each month is credited to this account.

But there are some big differences from other types of savings open to you. In your Steelko Plan:

> Steelko matches some of your savings with a contribution that is invested solely in Steelko common stock.
>
> You direct the way your savings are invested.
>
> You can transfer money from one type of investment to another . . . "manage" your account to reach your individual goals.
>
> You pay no taxes on Company contributions or on any earnings your account enjoys until you withdraw them.

The full value of your Plan account will be paid to you when you retire. If you have been saving steadily, the value of your account can substantially boost your retirement income. If you leave Steelko *before* you retire, you'll receive the value of your *own savings*—meaning you'll get back what you've saved plus (or minus) any earnings (or losses) on it. You will also get the value of Company contributions that have been in the Plan for three or more full calendar years.

If you die *before* you retire or leave, the full value of your account will be paid to your beneficiary. If you die *after* retirement but before you have received the full value of your account, the beneficiary you've chosen will receive the remaining balance.

Our Savings Plan is primarily designed to help you save for your *long-range* goals; it's an ideal source of retirement income in addition to our Retirement Plan and Social Security. However, you can make withdrawals of your savings while you're still employed by the Company. *All things considered, Steelko's Savings Plan offers you an extraordinary opportunity to expand your savings.*

Stock Ownership

The Steelko Ownership Plan is actually an arrangement between you and an investment firm. The Company's role is to make the regular payroll deductions that Plan participants have authorized. The Company turns these payroll deductions over to the investment firm, which uses them to buy Steelko's common stock. You can ask your investment firm to hold the shares purchased for you in an account set up in your name, or in your and your spouse's name. At your request, you can have a certificate for the shares in your Plan account delivered to you at any time.

You have control over the distribution of stock held in your Stock Ownership Plan account. You can sell your shares or have the certificates transferred to you whenever you want. If you have a joint account, you and your spouse share control of the stock.

Company-Paid Life Insurance

Your insurance goes into effect on the first day you are actively at work with the Company on or after 1984 January 01.

You have Life Insurance equal to $30,000 or one times your annual compensation, whichever is more.

If you die or suffer loss of limbs or eyesight as a result of an accidental injury, you or your beneficiary can receive benefits up to two times your annual compensation. The amount of benefit will depend on your loss.

Travel Accident Policy

This policy pays benefits if your accidental death occurs while you are on a business trip.

Your insurance is $100,000 or 2½ times your annual compensation, if that is more, up to a maximum of $1,500,000.

This insurance also provides these benefits: one half the death benefit for the loss of one hand, foot, or eye and the same amount as the death benefit for the loss of any two of them, if they result from an accident that occurs while you are on a business trip.

Optional Insurance

This Plan allows you to purchase additional Life Insurance. You pay for this additional insurance at group rates.

The amount of your Contributory Life Insurance can be one, two, three, or four times your annual compensation.

Dependent Life Insurance

Steelko also offers a Dependent Life Insurance Plan. You pay for the insurance you elect at group rates that vary according to your age.

You can cover your spouse and each dependent child by electing one of these options:

Option 1
    Spouse $10,000
    Each Dependent Child .... $ 2,000

Option 2
    Spouse $20,000
    Each Dependent Child .... $ 4,000

Your Vacation Benefits in General

Each year you earn from one to four weeks of regular vacation . . . paid time off . . . according to the length of time you've been with Steelko. After you've been with Steelko for one year, you also earn from 1.4 weeks to 3 weeks of additional vacation benefits . . . generally taken in cash . . . also according to your service.

In addition, Steelko observes nine regularly scheduled holidays plus one locally selected holiday for ten paid holidays each year.

Steelko pays the full cost of your regular paid vacation, additional vacation benefits, and holidays.

Holiday Schedule

Steelko recognizes ten paid holidays each year:

New Year's Day
President's Day
Good Friday
Memorial Day
Independence Day
Labor Day
Thanksgiving Day
The day after Thanksgiving
The day before Christmas
Christmas Day

OR

Instead of one of the above holidays, a locally selected holiday.

Ordinarily, your office or plant will be closed on these holidays. If a holiday falls during a week when you are on vacation, you are allowed an added day of vacation. Each year you will be told in advance when the holidays will be.

Bev finished reading Steelko's brochure, attended to some customers, and it was time for the meeting with the regional manager of the acquiring firm. The meeting was at a hotel nearby, and on the way she was deep in thought. If Steelko's salary is competitive, the comparison between the two positions may boil down to comparing their benefit packages. However, National applied a store incentive system that was unmatched by Steelko. At National, every store is given a quota that is based on its performance in recent years. If the store exceeds the quota, the pharmacists may claim extra pay up to $3000 a year. Last year Bev made half that amount.

The meeting started with the regional manager assuring pharmacists that the store incentive system would remain intact. Then he went on to explain the new package. He said, "The package provides employees and their dependents with substantial protection and encourages them to become careful health consumers." The last part of the sentence was apparently included by design. The benefit brochure that he handed out started with a letter from the Executive Vice-President of the firm. In the letter, the VP stated: "Changes have been made in the design of many of our company medical plans to encourage containment of controllable costs and to move toward reasonable uniform treatment of eligible employees throughout our family of companies." Bev noticed that the language of the brochure was more informal than they were used to in National's correspondence. She also noticed that a section on "Health Care Tips" was included.

Benefit Package of the Acquiring Firm

Note: The benefits described in this package are highlighted only. The actual plan documents will govern should there be any questions concerning your benefits.

Health Plan

Our Health Plan pays up to $1,000,000 in lifetime benefits to you, your spouse, and each covered dependent child (up to age twenty-six).

Once your covered medical expenses for one year exceed the annual deductible of $150 per person (or $450 per family), the Plan pays 80 percent of expenses for most covered medical and hospital services, including charges for:

Physician's service
Hospital room and board at semi-private room rate
Hospital services and supplies
In-hospital doctor's visits
Surgery
Maternity
Emergency care.

You will receive a booklet that describes these and other covered services in detail.

Special Incentives

To promote the cost-conscious use of health care services, the Plan offers financial incentives to stay out of the hospital unless medically necessary. The Plan pays 100 percent of covered expenses for these outpatient services, with no deductible required:

Outpatient surgery, including surgeon's fees
Diagnostic testing, including pre-admission tests
Birthing rooms and licensed birthing centers
Home health care.

The claims administrator may also review hospital procedures and treatment prior to your admission to determine appropriateness of care (Pre-admission Review).

Your Maximum Costs

The Plan limits the amount of money you have to pay "out-of-pocket" each year on covered charges. If you have paid $1,000 (for individual coverage) or $2,000 (for family coverage) plus the applicable deductible, the Plan pays 100 percent of remaining eligible expenses for that year.

Coordination of Health Care Benefits

You or a dependent may also be entitled to health benefits from another source that pays part or all of the cost of certain medical expenses. If this is the case, benefits under this Plan may be limited when you receive benefits from other sources.

When there is a claim for an employee, our Plan will pay benefits first. If you have family coverage, when a qualified member of your family has a claim that is covered by another group plan, the other plan may have the primary payment responsibility. We want to make sure that even if they are not primary, your family members still get a total benefit equal to the full benefits covered by the Plan. For this reason, we will pay the difference between the primary Plan's benefits and this Plan's reasonable and customary benefits. In no case will the combined payment be greater than what our Plan would have paid if it had had primary payment responsibility.

To illustrate, let's assume you hae already met your family deductible when your spouse incurs further covered expenses totaling $800.

Total Eligible Expense	$800
Allowable from our Benefit Amount	$640
Minus Payment from Spouse's Plan	$580
Equals Payment from our Health Plan	$ 60

Converting Your Coverage

If you leave the Company, you may convert your coverage to an individual policy if you apply within thirty days. Because you can do so without providing evidence of good health, this may be an important benefit. Also, preexisting conditions would be covered in the conversion policy. Be sure to request a conversion application form when you terminate.

Health Care

These benefits are part of the Health Plan and provide you and your eligible family members with important protection. The benefits described here are covered after you satisfy the deductible.

Well Physical Examination

The Plan pays 80 percent of covered charges toward the cost of a well physical examination, up to a maximum of $100 per exam.

The frequency of routine well physical examinations is limited to:

Once every five years under age forty
Once every two years age forty and over

This benefit is available to employees and all covered dependents who are at least five years old.

Psychiatric Treatment

In-hospital: You are covered at 80 percent for up to a maximum of forty-five days each year, or a lifetime maximum of ninety days.

Outpatient: The Plan pays 80 percent for the first ten visits in a calendar year. The maximum payment for each visit is $70. After ten visits, the Plan pays 50 percent for the rest of the year. The maximum outpatient benefit for a calendar year is $1,500 per person with a lifetime maximum benefit of $7,500.

Substance Abuse (Drug/Alcohol)

Although treatment can be as an inpatient, outpatient, or a combination of both, only one course of treatment per individual's lifetime is allowed. The maximum total lifetime benefit is $11,000.

Inpatient: If you are confined in an approved treatment facility for alcohol or drug abuse, the Plan pays 80 percent for a maximum of one confinement. The maximum lifetime benefit is $8,000 per individual.

Outpatient: After the deductible, the Plan pays 80 percent towards charges for an approved substance abuse program. The maximum lifetime benefit is $3,000.

Vision Care

The Plan pays 80 percent of covered charges. The maximum benefit per calendar year is $100 per person; you are limited to:

One exam per calendar year
One pair of lenses and/or frames in a two-calendar year period unless you
    have a significant prescription change.

Prescription Drug
No deductible required

The Plan provides benefits on an 80 percent copayment basis for the cost of all eligible drugs prescribed by a physician or dentist that are dispensed from a licensed pharmacy. Your cost for each eligible prescription filled is 20 percent of the retail charge. The Plan pays the balance of the retail charge.

If you buy your prescription drug at one of our stores, after showing appropriate identification, you pay only your 20 percent share. However, if your prescription is filled elsewhere, you must pay the full amount and then submit a claim form for reimbursement.

Enrollment

To cover you and your family members for Health Care, return the enrollment card in the back of this folder to your manager or supervisor.

Dental Benefits

Your Health Plan includes separate Dental Benefits that provide some protection against the high cost of dental care. Your benefits emphasize preventive care—and are designed to encourage you to stop problems before they occur.

Deductibles

Before the Dental benefits payments begin to pay for expenses you or your covered family members incur, you must pay an annual deductible of $25 for regular exams and cleanings, and $50 for other services. This $50 deductible is reduced by a deductible already paid during the year for exams and cleaning. However, if the combined deductibles of covered family members reach $100 during the calendar year, no further deductibles will be required on any members for the rest of that year.

Coverage for Routine and Preventive Care

After the $25 annual deductible has been satisfied, the Plan pays 80 percent of the expenses for routine and preventive care, including routine cleaning and maintenance and usual repairs.

Coverage for Other Services

For other dental expenses (except orthodontia), you must first pay the $50 deductible each year for each person covered. The Plan will then pay 50 percent of the expenses for unusual procedures that are generally elective or nonrecurring (such as inlays, crowns, and fixed bridgework).

Maximum Benefit

The Dental Plan provides a $1,500 maximum benefit plan each year for each person covered by the Plan. The Plan also includes a lifetime dental maximum of $7,500 for each person.

Coverage for Orthodontia

The Plan provides for orthodontia with no deductibles. The Plan pays 50 percent of covered orthodontia charges.

The maximum lifetime payment for orthodontia charges is $1,750 per person.

Health Care Tips
"An apple a day keeps the doctor away."

If controlling health care costs were as simple as eating apples, the public would not be spending over $400 billion a year on medical and dental expenses. Nor would the cost of health care have *doubled* every five years.

The spiraling costs of health care have become a national concern. No longer can we expect others to shoulder the entire burden of health care costs for us. We now realize the burden of skyrocketing health care costs must be shared, and we are learning that, as individuals, we can help lessen the burden of excessive medical costs. In the following paragraphs we'll explore ways we can cut expenses—from becoming educated health care consumers to staying healthy.

Alternate Treatment Facilities

Although hospitals can save lives by providing important acute medical care, in less critical situations the need for hospitalization must be considered carefully. Evidence suggests that for many conditions, other treatment facilities covered by your Plan may provide more effective care. For example:

> Skilled Nursing Facilities offer twenty-four-hour nursing care for the patient recovering from a serious illness or injury.
> Home Health Care Services can provide quality medical treatment is a more convenient and economical setting.

Hospice programs may be a more appropriate place for the supportive care of terminally ill patients. Qualified facilities can give the same quality care as hospital inpatient, while protecting your health. Hospice programs provide a coordinated program of inpatient, outpatient, and home care.

Birthing Centers offer quality natal care as an alternative to hospitals.

Outpatient facilities, including surgicenters and doctor's centers, can give the same quality care as hospital inpatient, while reducing the cost of protecting your health.

Auditing Your Hospital Bills

A surprisingly effective way to help control costs is simply to check (audit) your hospital bill. Studies show that it's not unusual for duplicate charges or charges for services and supplies never received to show up on a hospital bill. As the patient, only you will know if services were not performed. Hospitals are usually receptive to reviewing bills as it is good public relations and it helps in maintaining accurate records.

To make your audit easier, record the services you receive each day while you're in the hospital. When you're discharged, ask for an itemized bill. Compare your list and the bill. Then ask your hospital's patient account representative about any charges you don't understand.

Health Habits

You can do more for your health than your doctor can. By defining and applying solid, workable health goals, you can make permanent changes in your life. Lifestyle changes in the areas of exercise, smoking, stress, and eating and drinking habits are long-term commitments that will allow you to live longer, feel better, and have more energy to share with the family and friends. As an added benefit, practicing good health habits is the best way to control medical costs.

Smart Consumer Behavior

We should be cost-conscious about the health care services we use. Of course you will not want to take shortcuts where your health is concerned, but here are some suggestions that may help you receive better care while avoiding unnecessary expenses:

1. When your doctor recommends non-emergency surgery—before you agree to it—get a second opinion on the need for surgery.
2. Insist on a full, understandable explanation of your medical condition and the proposed treatment plan.
3. Use outpatient services whenever you can. Some hospitals have special ambulatory surgical centers for minor walk-in surgery. These can save you the trouble and expenses of overnight hospitalization. Use free standing surgicenters to handle minor surgeries, tests, or other procedures on an outpatient basis.
4. Avoid being admitted to the hospital on Friday or Saturday if your condition is not likely to be dealt with until Monday and if there is no medical reason for you to be hospitalized over the weekend.

5. Many hospitals run a battery of tests simply as a precaution. Some of them may not be necessary. Verify their necessity with your doctor. Also, you may be able to have preadmission tests done on an outpatient basis.
6. Ask for generic drugs. They can often be substituted for brand-name drugs, sometimes at less than half the cost.
7. Review all bills closely. You are not required to pay for any services you did not receive. Check to make sure all charges are accurate. If you have a question about a charge, ask for verification.
8. Shop around. Do not be afraid to discuss fees in advance.
9. Practice preventive medicine. Have regular checkups.

Life Insurance

Life insurance is a key part of your coverage with us. The financial security it provides for your family's future is important. Our Plan also provides your dependents with life insurance coverage.

What It's Worth

Effective January 1, 1985, the benefit amount for our Life Insurance Plan is equal to three times your base yearly salary rounded up to the next full thousand dollars. This benefit is paid for in full by the Company.

For example, if your salary is $25,700, three times this amount is $77,100; rounded up to the nearest thousand your benefit is $78,000.

If you receive a raise, your new benefit amount goes into effect on the date your raise is effective. If for some reason your pay is reduced, your benefit amount will not be reduced as long as you are still a salaried employee.

If your life insurance amount provided by the Company exceeds $50,000, a charge from the IRS imputed income tables will be added to your W-2.

Dependent Coverage

Your dependents are covered under the Plan for the following amounts:

$2,000 for your spouse
$1,000 for each eligible dependent child.

Coverage at Age 65

Once you reach the age of 65 (while actively working), your life insurance coverage is reduced by 35 percent. Coverage for your dependents remains unchanged.

Converting Your Coverage

If you retire or leave the company, you can convert to an individual policy by applying within thirty-one days. Because you can do so without providing evidence of good health, this may be an important benefit. Be sure to request a conversion application form when you terminate.

Enrollment

Be sure to complete the enrollment card in the back of this folder to designate your beneficiary and enroll your dependents.

Your designated beneficiary will receive your life insurance benefit in the event of your death. As your circumstances change, you may wish to update your beneficiary designation.

Completed cards should be returned to your manager or supervisor.

Accidental Death, Dismemberment, and Total Disability Insurance

Accidental Death, Dismemberment, and Total Disability Insurance effective January 1, 1985, is a special kind of benefit that covers you for certain major injuries or death caused by an accident. When you elect this coverage, you can also receive coverage for your dependents.

The Plan covers you for accidents that happen on and off the job, twenty-four hours a day, anywhere in the world—regardless of your health history.

What It's Worth

You can purchase coverage for yourself in $10,000 amounts from $10,000 to $250,000. This is called your Principal Sum.

When you purchase this coverage, you may also elect family coverage. Your family member's Principal Sum is as follows:

Spouse—40 percent of your Principal Sum
Each eligible child—10 percent of your Principal Sum
Spouse with no children—50 percent of your Principal Sum
Eligible children (when there is no spouse)—15 percent of your Principal Sum.

If you or a covered family member becomes totally and permanently disabled due to an accident, the Principal Sum for that person will be paid.

Also, partial or full benefits may be payable if you or a covered family member should become dismembered as a result of an accident. The amount of this benefit will depend upon the extent of the injury.

Enrollment

When enrolling for this coverage, you need to make the following decisions:

Do you need single or family coverage?
What amount of coverage will be required?
Whom will you select as your beneficiary?

You must complete and return the enrollment card in the back of this folder to receive this benefit. Completed cards should be returned to your manager or supervisor.

Employee Stock Ownership Plan

All eligible participants will receive shares of our Company Common Stock through this program. This Plan has been designed to enable you to share in the growth and prosperity of the Company and to provide you with an opportunity to accumulate capital for the future.

Eligibility

You will be eligible to participate in this Plan after completing one year of service (a twelve month period in which you complete at least 1,000 hours). If you do not complete, 1,000 hours during the first twelve months of employment, we will review your hours each calendar year to determine whether you have completed 1,000 hours. When you meet your eligibility requirements, complete 1,000 hours, and are employed as of December 31, you will receive your full share for that year.

Benefits

Each year the Company will make contributions to the Plan. The maximum total company contribution allowed by law is one-half of one percent (0.5%) of the *total* compensation paid to all qualified members. This total contribution will be evenly shared with all qualified members. This means that each of you will receive the same benefit from this Plan, regardless of your actual compensation.

The full value of your account will be paid to you in a lump sum of cash or shares as requested when you retire or if you leave the Company before retirement. You are automatically vested in your account. Your account will primarily be in the Company stock; however, there may also be accumulated dividends and cash waiting to be invested in stock.

If you should die while actively employed, your beneficiary would receive the total value of your account. If you should become permanently and totally disabled, you will receive a lump sum payout of your entire account.

Voting Rights

Participants with allocations will be entitled to direct the manner in which their company stock is voted.

Enrollment

You are automatically enrolled. To designate your beneficiary, you must complete the enrollment card in the back of this folder. Completed cards should be returned to your manager or supervisor.

Monthly Investment Plan

The Company provides each of you with an opportunity to purchase our Company Common Stock through payroll deductions. The purchase of Company stock will be made through an investment firm.

Common Stock will be purchased at market prices. The Company will pay brokerage charges to purchase stock and reinvest dividends from shares in your account. Charges made by the investment firm for the sale of Company Stock or any purchases not made through payroll deductions will not be paid by the Company.

Eligibility

When you reach the age of majority (usually eighteen) in your state of residence, you may participate in this Plan.

Benefits

You may purchase Company Common Stock with a minimum payroll deduction of $1 each week or $4 each month. Your payroll deductions will then be delivered to Merrill Lynch to purchase Company stock at current market rates. Remember, the Company will be paying the brokerage fees for the purchase of your stock. There is no limit to the amount of stock you can purchase through deductions.

Long-Term Disability Plan

As a salaried employee of our Company, you can elect coverage under the Long-Term Disability Plan. The LTD Plan is designed to provide you with a continuing income when a disabling illness or injury prevents you from working. If you do not elect this coverage, you will automatically receive the Short-Term Disability Plan described below.

Plan Coverage

For the first six months of disability, the Company pays you your full salary (less any amounts due you from other sources). After you have been disabled for six months, the Plan provides you with an income equal to 60 percent of your base monthly salary up to a maximum benefit of $5,000 per month. This benefit payment continues for the period of your disability to age sixty-five. If you become disabled after age sixty-two, benefits continue for the number of months specified by the Plan's schedule.

What Is "Total Disability"?

The meaning of total disability changes with the length of time that you're disabled.

For the first twenty-four months, total disability means you're unable to do your regular job. After you've been receiving the usual benefit for twenty-four months, total disability means you can't do any job that you'd normally be suited for by your training and experience.

You cannot receive disability benefits if you're doing any kind of work for pay, unless the work is part of a special rehabilitation program.

Payments from this Plan after the first six months are tax free because you pay the entire premium for your coverage.

Coordination with Other Benefits

Your disability may entitle you to benefits from sources other than the LTD Plan, such as Workers' Compensation or Social Security. These other benefits are considered when determining your LTD benefit. The Plan provides that you will receive a 60 percent disability (up to $5,000) when combining benefits from all sources.

Special Note:

The insurance company requires that you apply for Social Security and appeal any first denial. If you do not follow this procedure, the benefit to which you might be entitled will automatically be subtracted from the Plan's benefit, even if you are not actually receiving Social Security payments.

Your Social Security benefit offset amount is frozen at the level you're eligible for when you're disabled. Any later increases in Social Security benefits except for changes in the number of your dependents will increase the total disability benefit paid to you.

If the total sum of all these other benefits, taken together, is less than your 60 percent guaranteed benefit, then your LTD Plan makes up the difference. And if you have no sources other than LTD, your disability plan provides you with the entire 60 percent guaranteed monthly benefit.

Short-Term Disability Plan

Our Short-Term Disability coverage provides you with a continuing income during short periods when you cannot work. This benefit is only for eligible persons who have not elected the Long-Term Disability Plan.

Plan Coverage

You begin to receive a short-term disability benefit after your regular pay ceases. Your regular pay will continue in full for the week in which you are disabled plus the next full week.

The Plan pays 60 percent of your regular weekly pay up to a maximum of $277 per week. You can receive short-term disability benefits for up to fifty-two weeks. However, you must first submit medical certification of your disability in order to receive benefits. Then you will need to submit continuing verification of your disability.

Benefits from Other Sources

Any disability benefits you receive from Social Security or state disability programs are subtracted from your short-term disability payment.

Any disability that is the result of an injury or illness sustained on the job is not covered under this Plan since these causes of disability are covered by Workers' Compensation.

If you are disabled for more than the fifty-two weeks allowed under this plan, Social Security will continue to pay you a benefit depending on the laws in effect at that time. If you become disabled, check with your local Social Security office to determine whether or not you're eligible for benefits.

When you apply for disability benefits, you will be referred to the proper state agency for necessary vocational rehabilitation service. If you refuse this training without good cause, you will forfeit your disability benefits.

The meeting was longer than Bev expected and she had to call home twice. Driving home, the comparison of the two packages occupied her mind almost totally. She didn't notice she was still thinking about the benefit packages until her husband's sleepy voice came from under the covers as she went to sleep: "Is that you dear?" She answered with the first smile of the day, "Were you expecting someone else?"

26. But Does the Shoe Fit?*

Bob was a little uneasy as he drove into the large parking lot in front of Kiene's Department Store. He always felt funny returning to work after vacation, but more so today, he thought. He had welcomed the break—for him, the shoe department was a tense place to work, and although he and Evonne, the other top salesperson, were on good terms, he and Ryan Clawson, the shoe department's manager, seemed to be at odds. Nothing had actually happened, but there was a certain tension when the two were together. "Ryan should take a break, too," he mused, as he stepped out of his imported sports car and into the store.

As he gazed at the store stretched out before him, Bob felt an excitement that purged his earlier misgivings. Briskly, he entered the door by the personnel office, the one with the big sign: Employees Only. As he made his way down the hall to where the schedules were posted, he thought how little the big department store had changed in the two weeks he had been gone.

"What?" he exclaimed, picking up the schedule. "I can't believe it. They've cut my hours!"

"They cut mine, too," replied a voice from behind.

Upset, Bob whirled around to see Evonne, his fellow salesperson in the shoe department. The anger he had felt subsided, only to be replaced by bewilderment.

"I don't understand, Evonne. Why would they do this to you, to us?"

"I'm not sure either. It was quite a surprise, actually. It happened to me right after I had asked for *more* hours, a few days after you had left on your vacation."

"What did Ryan say about it? He's the department manager, he had to be in on it."

---

*This case was written by Bruce Kiene, MBA, under the direction of Professor Stuart Youngblood, both of Texas A&M University.

"I'm not sure he was, at least not in the beginning. He was almost apologetic when he told me. In fact his exact words were: '*They* decided to hire two new high school kids and that means we have to cut some hours.'"

"What?" Bob was nearly overcome. "We've been here for years. Why, we've been on the district's top selling list nearly every month! Why would they cut our hours to hire two kids who know nothing about selling? Those kids will starve. They will be on commission like us, won't they?"

"Evidently. But maybe that's the key. Ryan had mentioned something about how it was time to 'share the wealth.' Maybe we were too good. I'll tell you one thing, I've been assigned a lot more non-selling duties lately, but mostly I'm bored to death."

There was a silence, finally broken by the sight of Ryan Clawson entering the office thirty feet down the hall.

"Listen, I'd better get to the floor. I'll talk to you later." With a whispered grumble, Bob firmly replaced the schedule in its holder.

"Yeah, later," was the reply.

Ryan Clawson had seen his top salespeople by the scheduling board and suspected problems might be brewing. The "new" commission program was not flawless after all, he thought.

When he returned to his office, Ryan sat at his desk and reflected: "The department has seen the best profits since the recession." He recalled how the department had been when he took over three years ago: no merchandise, no real salespeople——it was a joke! And then the turn-around: he had replaced the deadwood in his department with experienced, hand-picked salespeople, and, at their urgings (and with a lobbying effort to top management), he received the budget necessary to buy a variety of new stock. What a coup! No department in such bad shape had even a slight chance for extra funds, and yet he had done it and it paid off! When the store switched to the new commission program, sales skyrocketed. "Geez, we were sitting pretty," he continued with a fading grin. Who would have thought that his top people were now under scrutiny due to their individual cost factors to the store?

"Are they really that good?" Frank Waters, the force manager, had asked skeptically, "as good as all that?"

"Well, I have bought a lot of contemporary items . . . our selection is much better than in the past," Ryan had replied, hoping to take some of the credit. It was true, he now thought, but he should have simply answered, "Yes, they are that good." He wondered if other retail businesses had the same type of compensation problems, and remembered how innocently this situation had started.

It began with a comment by Sherry, the personnel assistant, in the presence of Ryan and Frank Waters, the force manager. "Wow, that Bob is sure raking it in," she had mentioned, jokingly. The comment, however, had piqued Waters' curiosity. As an explanation, Sherry recounted how Bob's Benefit Wage (his vacation pay) was the same as the department manager's, primarily because of Bob's extensive sales on which his Benefit Wage was based (see Exhibit 1). She further explained how the previous year's total sales were divided by the total hours worked to create the Benefit Wage hourly scale. This hourly scale was then

Exhibit 1. Kiene's Department Store Benefit Wage Worksheet
Shoe Department (Sales Staff)

Name	Total Commission Earned 1986	Total Hours 1986	Benefit Wage Per Hour 1987*
1. Anderson, Sally	$ 4963.56	933	$5.32
2. Bronson, Jim	3560.70	858	4.15
3. Campos, Tom	1372.84	352	3.90 (Removed from Payroll 5/15/86)
4. King, Bob	11544.10	1,850	6.24
5. Parker, Evonne	10588.63	1,733	6.11
6. Seele, Barbara	792.12	167	4.74

*The Benefit Wage is computed from the previous year's productivity and applied to the current year. For example, to calculate the 1987 Benefit Wage, the total commission earned in 1986 is divided by the total hours worked for 1986.

used to budget all the employee's benefits: holiday and vacation pay, as well as disability pay-out schedules.

After this conversation, Waters met with Don Roberts, the store manager, at lunch and exhorted him to do something about the inconsistencies in the pay scale. Roberts said he would look into it, if for no other reason than to avoid being stuck by the force manager's waving fork, thought Ryan with a sigh.

When completed, the study revealed that the veteran salespeople in Ryan's department were indeed well paid. Moreover, they were good workers. In a meeting between Don, Frank, and Ryan it was pointed out to Ryan that the wage and Benefit Wage of his salespeople was nearly twice that of new hires or other salespeople in other departments. And then that question: "Were they really worth two new hires apiece?"

"Damn," muttered Clawson, still at his desk, "even if they weren't, it wasn't their fault. They were just doing their job." He paused, "Or were they?"

Sales had increased, it was true, but with these dramatic increases came other concerns as well. The department never seemed to stay clean: glass was unpolished, stock was not on the shelves, and more. "It's funny", thought Clawson, "the clean-up and maintenance work was given up for individual sales; that's what Bob and Evonne actually gave as their explanation of the situation."

He tried to recall how many times he had heard the phrase "we're too busy selling," and knew that the figure could never be determined, at least not in a single day. Puzzled by the situation, Ryan slowly leaned back in his chair and concluded that he would rather be fishing.

Frank Waters began to hear rumors of discontent among the shoe department's salespeople. But, sure, that was always the case when employees experience a change in the workplace, he rationalized. One thing that didn't need rationalization, however, was his plan for reconciling the wage inconsistencies in "shoes." He was proud to have been the one to locate the problem and implement a solution.

This attitude was apparent in a recent interview with one of the young high school students who applied for, and got, one of two new shoe sales positions. "Your duties will be to: (1) keep the department clean, and I don't have to tell you how important a clean department is to the customer as well as to the many visiting District People, (2) help the customers, wait on them, help them with exchanges and refunds, and, of course, (3) persuade them to buy our shoes. . . . sell!"

"I will be paid on a full commission basis?" asked the young applicant.

"That's correct. You're up against a 'draw,' however. Everything's even at the start of each month. This means you must sell enough to make your base pay, or it's subtracted from future checks. It starts over each month."

"I guess selling is the most important duty of the job, then."

"It's important, but so are those other things I mentioned! You seem to be well prepared. Do you have any other questions?"

"No, sir."

Tweedy Slater, the high school student, was hired, and Sherry, the assistant in personnel and payroll, took her to meet her department manager, Ryan Clawson.

After the first new hire in Ryan Clawson's department was placed, Waters, the author of this new staffing plan, felt somewhat uneasy about it all. It was true, he admitted, the way the commission system was set up was indeed creating problems. The more he thought about it, the more he wondered whether cutting some hours and adding people might *not* be the optimal solution after all. What was it that Clawson had called it? "Flooding the floor?" That was it. Clawson had warned: "Flooding the floor will not bring about the changes we want. Sure, we share the wealth a little bit, but the department will still look unkempt and customers will think they're being attacked by sales-hungry vultures."

Maybe Clawson had a point, continued Waters, but no matter. At least the individual wages of the employees should drop and the Benefit Wage, as well. That should save some money, and with more sales people there's bound to be more time to do the other departmental tasks. It should work.

But what the new high school student said had struck a discordant note in Water's mind. "I guess selling is the most important thing!" she had said. Frank looked at his watch. "Thank goodness!" he exclaimed. "Time for lunch."

27.   A Day Late and a Dollar Short*

The Personnel Committee was having its weekly meeting at Farmers Merchant Bank. In attendance were Rick Talbot, Executive Vice-President—Lending; Harry Lewis, Executive Vice-President—Finance and Administration; and Jennifer Riley, Vice-President—Personnel. The Personnel Committee met on a weekly basis to discuss performance evaluations, proposed salary increases, vacancies, pro-

*Rebecca A. Baysinger, Texas A&M University. Printed with permission.

motions, transfers, and other personnel-related matters. The President and CEO, George Phelps, was supposed to be present at all Committee meetings, but today he was late, as usual.

After fifteen minutes of waiting, Rick, Harry, and Jennifer decided to begin without George. The first item on the agenda was the annual salary review of Donna Jenkins, a clerk in the Automated Banking Department. Jennifer began by reviewing the information on Donna. "This is Donna's first annual salary review and performance evaluation. Her supervisor, Jane Martin, says that Donna is an outstanding performer and has rated her 4 out of a possible 5."

Harry added that he reviewed the evaluation form with Jane, who gave many reasons why she felt such an excellent rating was justified. "And," said Harry, "I've had lots of opportunities to see Donna in action. She's great with the customers, knows her stuff, and has real leadership potential. Jane went on vacation for two weeks in June, left Donna in charge, and had no problems when she got back. In fact," Harry added with a laugh, "Jane said things were neater than they were before she left!"

"Well," said Jennifer, "I fully agree with Jane's evaluation. Donna's the kind of employee we want to keep around for a long time. Donna is currently at $4.00 an hour. Jane is recommending an 18 percent raise, which will bring her hourly rate up to $4.72 an hour. That percentage is a little high—we've been averaging 6–8 percent—but I think that if we're going to keep her, we need to pay her."

"What's the market rate for the position?" asked Rick.

"Oh, it's well within the market range," replied Jennifer. "This puts her in the upper quadrant, but not high enough that she'll max out with her next annual salary review."

Harry interjected, "There's another problem, though. One of Donna's co-workers, Louise Anderson, is making $4.60 an hour, and Louise has only been here for three months."

"How in the heck did that happen?" asked Rick.

Jennifer shifted in her chair uneasily and explained that Louise had worked for the bank three years earlier, but had quit to have a baby. Louise had been one of George Phelps' favorites, so when she requested a position at the Bank three months ago, George agreed to her return and set her hourly rate of pay without consulting anyone. "I might add," continued Jennifer, "that Donna is aware of this situation, but has been willing to overlook it in view of her upcoming salary review."

Rick shook his head wearily and addressed Jennifer. "Didn't George consult you about market rates or comparable rates of pay within the Bank?"

"No, he did not," responded Jennifer. "As you know, George is adamantly opposed to development of a wage and salary administration scheme. And I've gotten no help from the corporate human resources staff either. They don't have any formal scheme, and they say development is at least a year away. In the absence of corporate guidelines, George is reluctant to be in the forefront of compensation policy development."

"Well, it seems clear to me that Donna is a valued employee, and we should reward her for her performance. The 18 percent raise is fine with me," said Rick.

"I agree," said Harry.

"That makes three of us, then. Now let's go on to the next item on the agenda," said Jennifer.

After about forty-five minutes, George walked in and apologized for being late, again. "Had a loan I wanted to work through before tomorrow's loan committee meeting. What have you all been talkin' about?"

"Well, let's see," began Jennifer. "First on the agenda was Donna Jenkins. She's up for her first annual review. Jane Martin has given her an excellent rating and has recommended an 18 percent raise, taking her hourly rate from $4.00 to $4.72. This is within the market range and Rick, Harry, and I are inclined to go along with it."

George exclaimed, "Eighteen percent?! Isn't that a little high? Jane's not using her head!"

"George," pleaded Harry, "Donna is someone we want to keep around here. The woman is a real leader. I would hate to think we lost her to a competitor over a few cents."

"Besides, George," added Rick, "we're dealing with an equity adjustment here, along with a merit increase. She's currently below the market rate. In addition, she knows that Louise Anderson is making $4.60 an hour. She doesn't understand why a less experienced, in fact a brand new, employee is making more than she's making. I'm afraid we'll lose her if we don't give her this increase."

"I understand," replied George, "but 18 percent is out of the question. I got the salary guidelines from corporate headquarters a few days ago. They say we can give only 6 percent for average employees and 8-10 percent for outstanding employees."

"But I'm sure these are just general guidelines, George," Jennifer rebutted. "In a case like Donna's, the combination of an equity *and* a merit increase would probably be acceptable."

"We don't want to set any precedents around here," warned George. "Besides, if she gets an 18 percent raise this time, what's she gonna expect next year? If she's a good employee, which is what I hear you saying, then 10 percent is as high as we can go."

"If that's your final word, George, Jane has requested that she be allowed to present her side of the story before the Committee. Do you have any objections to Jane coming in to address the Committee?" asked Harry.

"No objection," replied George.

Harry then called Jane Martin to come to the meeting. Jane came in and proceeded to explain that Donna was an exceptional employee in many ways and cited examples of her high quality performance in the year since she'd been with the Bank. She concluded by voicing her concern over the inequity between Donna and Louise's pay rates and her fear that Donna would leave if she wasn't given an adequate pay raise.

"Yes, but what you don't understand is that corporate guidelines allow only a 10 percent maximum percentage increase. Now I'm willing to go with a 10 percent increase, but that's all we can do," explained George.

"Well, then I'm afraid we'll lose her," said Jane quietly.

"Do we usually have any problem filling our vacancies, Jennifer?" asked George.

"Well, no, but more often than not we fill our vacancies with inexperienced people, and . . . " Jennifer began.

George interrupted, "There you go. I'm sure she'll be happy with 10 percent. Now if you'll excuse me, I've got a meeting with a big dollar loan customer." George got up and left the room.

"Now how am I going to explain this to Donna? It doesn't make any sense," said Jane.

"You've got to present this in the most positive light possible, and try not to blame it on George," answered Rick.

"You'll just have to emphasize the increase and her excellent performance, and how valuable she is to the Bank, and hope that's enough," added Harry.

28. A Permanent Part-Timer*

Liz Cutler gingerly moved aside the stack of folders blanketing her desk to make room for the cup of coffee that she hoped would give her Monday morning a lift. Liz, the assistant officer for Personnel at Abilene First Bank and Trust, was feeling a bit apprehensive because her boss, Sharon Morris, the vice-president of Personnel, had just begun her two-week vacation and had left Liz in charge. Although Liz has been with the bank for ten months, she still felt that she had yet to learn the ropes.

As Liz prepared to review the bank's computer printout of payroll for the next pay period, the phone rang. It was Jim Brewer, the security guard for the bank (and a night-shift Abilene police officer). Jim was calling Liz to report that he and Gareth Robinson, the Automatic Teller Machine (ATM) service representative, never made it to the jammed ATM at the Culpepper Mall. While waiting for a red light to change, they were rear-ended by an intoxicated driver. Jim arrested the man on the spot and took a complete report. Gareth was a bit upset that their borrowed car (a bank car used by Gareth's boss, Ken Ringleb, the vice-president of Operations) sustained bumper damage and a stuck trunk lid, which meant Gareth couldn't retrieve his briefcase containing, among other things, his ATM tools.

Jim was more concerned for Gareth who, despite refusing medical attention, repeatedly threatened to sue the driver that rear-ended them. Gareth wanted to return to the bank, so Jim advised Liz to send someone to service the recalcitrant ATM.

Liz knew the only person who could substitute for Gareth was his boss, Cheryl Travestead, who was assistant vice-president of Teller Operations. She also knew Cheryl would not be thrilled to leave the bank on a busy Monday morning. Gareth Robinson's position was created by Cheryl's boss, Ken Ringleb, as a means to free up Cheryl's time to handle administrative duties. Gareth was hired as a permanent part-time employee and worked five hours each day. For the remainder of the day Gareth was on call in case an ATM became temperamental.

As a permanent part-time employee, Gareth enjoyed all the benefits of the bank's full-time employees. In addition to the straight-line pay, he received medical, life, and disability insurance coverage at no personal cost. Gareth also

---

*This case was prepared by Stuart A. Youngblood.

received reimbursement for mileage when he used his personal car for on-call visits to service ATMs. As an incentive to maintain a high level of service, Gareth also received a bonus each week for the number of ATMs serviced in addition to emergency calls. All in all, it was a good arrangement for Gareth because it enabled him to pursue course work towards completion of his undergraduate degree in business at nearby Abilene Christian University.

When Gareth arrived back at the bank, Liz arranged for Ken Ringleb and Cheryl Travestead to meet with him in the coffee room to confirm the details of the accident. Liz, Ken, and Cheryl were somewhat concerned that Gareth refused medical attention and encouraged him to seek an emergency room examination at the local hospital. Gareth was still upset that a drunk plowed into them in broad daylight. Ken was becoming agitated because the last thing he wanted was a lawsuit and possibly unfavorable attention directed toward the bank. At their urging, though, Gareth agreed to visit the emergency room.

On Tuesday, Gareth did not report for work, and on Wednesday he called Liz to inquire if she could recommend a local doctor for a second examination. Gareth complained that his "neck didn't feel right." When Liz queried Gareth as to when he thought he could return to work he was evasive. She then asked him to check back with Personnel and let them know his status.

After Liz hung up, she decided to confer with Cheryl and Ken regarding how she should handle the worker's compensation claim for Gareth. Liz couldn't decide whether she should file just his straight-time pay as lost compensation or whether his earned bonus should also be included. At this point she wished that Sharon had not gone on vacation, but she was sure that Ken and Cheryl would know how to handle it.

When Liz posed the question, Cheryl erupted in anger. Understandably, Cheryl was a bit put out because she now had assumed Gareth's work in addition to her already hectic schedule. As far as Cheryl was concerned, Gareth was just malingering, and he should be given an ultimatum to return to work. Cheryl speculated further that Gareth's real motive for staying home was that it was mid-term examination week at Abilene Christian and Gareth was using the accident as an excuse to catch up on his studies. Cheryl disgustedly observed that even if the bank fired Gareth for his antics, he would report to the employment service and drag them through an unemployment compensation claim. Ken sympathized with Cheryl's concerns, but was most worried by Gareth's litigious attitude exhibited upon his return to the bank the day of the accident. Liz could see that the discussion had taken a turn for the worse; what she really wanted was advice on how to file the worker's compensation claim. After redirecting the question, though, Ken and Cheryl were adamant on this point: file for straight-time and not a nickel more.

Twelve days had passed since the accident and Gareth had still not returned to work. Liz, by this time, was exasperated. After checking regularly with Gareth she learned that he had now seen four doctors: the first doctor X-rayed Gareth's neck at the emergency room on the day of the accident; the second doctor was a general practitioner in the community; the third doctor was a physician at the Abilene Christian student health center; and the fourth doctor was an orthopedic specialist whom the health center physician recommended at Gareth's insistence. After repeated prodding by Liz, Gareth committed himself to return to work the upcoming Monday, the two-week anniversary of his accident and the day of return of Sharon Morris, the director of Personnel.

When Sharon arrived, Liz briefed her on the events of the past two weeks. Liz was proud that payroll went out on time with no major errors and that, all in all, the bank functioned quite smoothly in Sharon's absence. When Liz recounted the continuing saga of Gareth's accident, the issue of the worker's compensation claim surfaced. Sharon chided Liz for not handling the claim as she expected. In Sharon's mind it was quite clear that the bonus should have been included in the claim and she instructed Liz to immediately file an amended claim. Feeling like a puppy smacked by a rolled newspaper, Liz proceeded to her office adjacent to Sharon's to complete the amended claim. While working on the claim she noticed Gareth Robinson report to Sharon's office and overheard Sharon say, "Gareth, you'll have to forgive us for botching the worker's compensation claim. You see, Liz was filling in for me during my vacation and, as you know, she is inexperienced in these matters. . . ."

Part
V

Training, Organizational Improvement, and Personnel Research

Cases Outline

- Case Study in Human Resource Development
- Black Diamond Mining Company
- Managerial Systems Ltd.
- Chandler's Restaurant
- The Tailored Management Development Program: A Case of Management Development Design Options
- Kirkridge Mountain Laboratories
- C Company (I) and (II)

29. Case Study in Human Resource Development*

Before his retirement, John Hadley had been President and General Manager of APEX Manufacturing Company, Inc., for fifteen years. Under his direction the company had grown from a small shop to a medium-sized corporation with 1,200 employees (see Exhibit 1).

Over the past eighteen months the profit picture of the company had a slow but continuous slide into the red. Morale and productivity had also followed this slow yet steady downward spiral. While it had been difficult to determine what the exact cause of the trend was, it appeared to have started at the first news of the offer by ARMCO Plastics to buy out 51 percent of the stock of the company. Although ARMCO had said that there would be no change in the status quo at APEX, there seemed to be a steady stream of ARMCO control being exercised over the company. The latest of these perceived changes was the early retirement of Hadley two months ago.

Hadley's successor was Bill Linden, a long-time employee of ARMCO and the General Manager of their Cleveland plant. Upon coming aboard, he had taken little action, which had raised the anxiety level of everyone in the plant. While rumors of sweeping changes were rampant, no concrete actions had thus far been taken. The only actions that could be observed were the constant visits that the new GM was making to all areas of the plant.

On Monday of this week Linden had scheduled a Senior Manager's meeting to discuss the future of the company. This would be the first time that he would enumerate his expectations of the company and its managers. His speech was short and to the point.

> I am sure that you are well aware of the present situation in this company. I have taken the past two months to go around and confirm the problems I feel are causing us to lose our competitive position in the market. The morale of the organization is low and continues to fall. Rumors of massive firings and sweeping changes abound. Our production rate is 80 percent of what it was two years ago and the number of time-loss accidents has doubled in the last fourteen months.

*Neal M. Nadler, The George Washington University. Printed by permission.

EXHIBIT 1.   ARMCO/APEX Manufacturing Present Organizational Chart and
Personnel Assigned

General Manager

Production Manager	Personnel/ Human Resource Manager	Sales/Marketing Manager	Finance Manager	Customer Services Manager
1 Middle Manager	1 Middle Manager	1 Middle Manager	1 Middle Manager	1 Middle Manager
40 Supervisors	3 Supervisors	8 Supervisors	7 Staff	8 Supervisors
761 Staff	7 Staff	76 Staff		280 Staff
802 Total	11 Total	85 Total	8 Total	289 Total

ARMCO/APEX Manufacturing Projected Organizational Chart
and Personnel Assigned 2 Years

General Manager

Production Manager	Personnel/ Human Resource Manager	Sales/Marketing Manager	Finance Manager	Customer Services Manager
1 Middle Manager	1 Middle Manager	1 Middle Manager	1 Middle Manager	1 Middle Manager
5 First Level Managers	3 Supervisors	10 Supervisors	2 Supervisors	4 Supervisors
40 Supervisors 997 Staff	7 Staff	100 Staff	2 Staff	140 Staff
1043 Total	11 Total	111 Total	5 Total	145 Total

I am not here to point fingers and direct blame. I am here to direct this company back to a competitive position in the market and into the profit column of our corporation's balance sheet. In light of that goal, I am recommending a six-point plan that I feel will start us back on the road of recovery.

My six-point plan is as follows:

1. The introduction of new manufacturing technology, which will begin in three months and be in place within the next eighteen months. The new techniques and machines will replace our old outdated processes and will affect approximately 75 percent of our workforce.

2. In concert with my first point, we will be replacing two of our present product lines with updated versions that are presently being developed in the ARMCO R&D department. We are planning to replace our basic model with a version that will give our customers twice the capacity in half the time. The second line will be more expensive but it is virtually maintenance free. Our third line, which has been relatively unprofitable, will be dropped. As you can see, these changes will have a marked effect on our profitability as well as on the present workforce. The changes tentatively projected are these:

An overall increase in our current workforce of 10 percent.
A substantial change in the skill requirement of our present workforce. This

may entail a substantial number of personnel in certain areas being terminated.

A reduction of 50 percent of our customer service personnel.

An increase of 30 percent in the production areas.

Training for all new production personnel as the machinery is state of the art.

The anticipated timing of this action is included in the paperwork on the table in front of you (Exhibit 2).

3. The advent of our improved product line will require an increase of staff in our sales/marketing department. I estimate this will be in the neighborhood of 30 percent. This will afford us the opportunity to recapture our market share and improve to the point where we have a total of 40 percent of the market in the next five years. As you know, our present market position is 25 percent.

4. We need to establish a promote-from-within policy whenever possible. I want this program implemented within four months. This program will ensure not only that we keep our best people but that we think ahead of time about what type of skills our people will need for their next career move.

5. As all of you are well aware, there is a massive problem with low morale in this organization. While we all could make guesses as to the cause, I feel that all it would be is guessing. I therefore want to find out what exactly is causing the problem of low morale and develop recommendations for combating it.

6. We will establish a different performance appraisal system based upon Management By Objectives (MBO). Our present system is all but nonexistent. It is backward looking and in most cases serves as a tool for punishment rather than as a support technique for improved performance. This MBO system should also be tied to the merit pay system that we implemented last year. If this system works well, it should also give us insight into the third point. This system should be implemented and working well within the next twelve months.

Exhibit 2. Implementation of Strategic Plan

Task\Year	1	2	3	4	5
	!	!	!	!	!	!

NEW TECHNOLOGY
Intro   ..3mo.
Hiring   3..............18mo.
Training   3....................24mo.

IMPROVED PRODUCT LINE
Intro   6.............20mo.
Hiring/Sales
Personnel   6.................24mo.
Laying-off
Personnel in
Production/
Cust.Svc.
Departments   6.......................30mo.

PROMOTE-FROM-WITHIN POLICY
Developed..3
Implement 3....................24mo.

MBO SYSTEM
Design   1....6mo.
Implement 5......12mo.

I would like your comments on these recommendations within the next twenty working days. I am also interested in seeing tentative implementation schedules at the same time. If you have any problems or concerns about this program as it is proposed please make an appointment with me before the deadline and let's talk about it. I feel that at this time it would be inappropriate to take questions before each of you has had an opportunity to digest this plan. Please keep foremost in your mind that this is only a plan and if you see changes that need to be made we can discuss them. Please feel free to make an appointment with me at any time and let me emphasize that if you do have problems with this approach, I want to know why as well as what alternatives you are proposing. If there is nothing else, this meeting is concluded.

Jayne Mico, the Director of Human Resources Management, called a meeting of the key people in her department to discuss the matter. Attending the meeting were Robert Armstrong, the Assistant Personnel Manager for OD; Joy Storm, the head of Administration; and Jeff Gilby, the Assistant Personnel Manager and Director of Human Resource Development.

Jayne explained the situation as best she could and asked the meeting attendees to have their inputs ready within the next ten working days. She closed as follows:

You now have all the information that I have. I need not tell you that this project is massive in scope and has many potential pitfalls. My major concern at this point is that it appears that Mr. Linden has not thoroughly thought the program through. Of course it may also be that he is just testing us to see what changes we will recommend to his plan. At any rate, we must give him the best information possible to support any changes we would recommend to the plan.

This is Monday. Give me your recommendations by COB Friday. If there are any areas where you need more information, please let me know.

Jeff Gilby walked back to his office. There were definite problems with the plan, given what he knew about the organization.

Jeff sat back and thought:

I have been with the company for ten years and for the past seven I have been Assistant Personnel Manager and Director for Human Resource Development. This plan may be the most difficult undertaking I have had thus far in my career. The issues as I see them are these:

1. The morale seems to be the key factor to trying to increase productivity but some of the changes that are going to take place are going to affect morale even more adversely than doing nothing. The staff and managers feel that it is only a matter of time before they are replaced by ARMCO personnel and that these technology innovations are just one of a series of changes that will afford them (ARMCO) the opportunity to accomplish that goal. ("These ARMCO people don't care about us like Mr. Hadley did," was a comment he had heard no few number of times.)

2. It is true that over the past few years innovations in our product line have only been cosmetic in nature and the market share that we once held has dwindled to half of what it was. The new technology and updating of our product line are good ideas. Even with their reservations about the new owners most

employees will be in agreement with those needed changes. The other associated issue is demographics; where will we get the people to fill all these new positions?

3. The promote-from-within policy would tend to indicate that APEX was serious about not firing large numbers of people. At the least, it was trying to keep those personnel who were the most productive. However, the changes in technology and major cuts in our customer service department will be psychologically devastating to the plant as a whole. There are a lot of good people who will be let go if this portion of the plan comes to fruition.

4. I have thought for a long time that the implementation of an MBO type of performance appraisal system would be helpful in increasing productivity and improving morale. However, given the general morale problems and some of the other tasks in the plan, now might not be the appropriate timing to implement such a system. The staff might perceive that this appraisal system is just a mechanism for "setting enough unachievable goals to fire us." Even though our other performance appraisal system is basically not working, people at least use it. I wonder if the implementation of this program is the right thing now? But if we have to go forward with it, what would be the best way to implement it given the rest of the plan? Is the timing right? That is a crucial point.

5. Are the aspects of the plan that impact me thoroughly tested? We really have not done a thorough needs assessment to see if the proposed plan is truly what is needed—at least from a Human Resource Development standpoint.

After two days of anguish over this, Jeff decided to seek more information from the Director of the Human Resources Management group. It appeared that everyone was as perplexed as he was. The decision was made to meet the next day and look for the solution jointly. Each member of the group was asked to respond to certain questions for the meeting.

Note: You are Jeff Gilby. Answer these questions as Assistant Personnel Manager and Director for Human Resource Development:

- What implications does the present plan have in your area of responsibility?
- Define all issues surrounding the six-point plan that affect your area of responsibility.
- How would the plan have to be altered to resolve the issues indicated in the above areas?
- Given the work above, develop a new plan with implementation schedules and indicate those areas where potential problems exist.
- Explain the rationale behind your changes.
- Who are the key coordinating constituents within the organization that you need to liaison with for evaluation and feedback on your plan?

30. Black Diamond Mining Company*

Warren Powers sat in his office on the twelfth floor of the National Bank Building in Johnstown, Pennsylvania. As the fresh January snow gently fell on the small city nestled in the Allegheny Mountains, he contemplated the decisions he felt he had to make in the near future. Powers was the president and owner of the Black Diamond Mining Company, a $60,000,000 concern in the bituminous coal industry. While corporate headquarters were located in Johnstown, actual mining operations were conducted near Phillipsburg, Pennsylvania. Warren often traveled to the mine site by helicopter.

Warren Powers was a self-made man. He had become a millionaire by making highly profitable deals in the coal mining industry. He had a reputation as a shrewd manager and a tough bargainer when it came to contracts. He had built his company from the bottom up. In any sense of the word, he was successful. Now he was seeking new challenges and achievements in his life.

As part of his self-education program (The Great Books, executive development seminars at Penn State University, etc.), Warren had become aware of such concepts as Quality of Work Life, socio-technical systems, autonomous work groups, and worker participation in decision-making. The major question facing him was whether to try to implement these concepts, partially or wholly, into his organization. If he decided to proceed, what would be the best course of action? Powers did not consider himself to be a "do-gooder." If he decided to do anything, he still expected a gain of some sort.

The Bituminous Coal Mining Industry

The bituminous coal mining industry in the United States suffered a long decline until recently. Only the severe economic impact on the nation's energy bill caused by the quantum leap in crude petroleum prices as a result of the formation and economic action of the OPEC cartel has halted years of stagnation in the industry. With coal becoming a viable economic alternative to oil, the industry faced a somewhat brighter future.

That future is constrained, however, by the realities of the industry. Coal mining, especially underground mining, is an extremely dangerous occupation. Accident frequency and severity rates are annually among the highest reported for any industry. Furthermore, the product is bulky, dirty, difficult to handle, and creates disposal problems. It has also been blamed for acid rain and other environmental problems. Finally, the steel industry, a major customer, also faced severe problems. Nevertheless, the industry hoped to expand significantly in the 1980s and the 1990s.

About 40–50 percent of the industry is organized by the United Mine Workers of America. At the peak of its power, when John L. Lewis was its president, the UMW

*James B. Thurman, Ph.D., Associate Professor of Business Administration, The George Washington University. Printed by permission.

controlled over 90 percent of the workforce. The decline in the industry, small non-union mines, and the mammouth western strip mines have reduced the UMW to a much weaker organization. The UMW is, however, relatively strong in western Pennsylvania, West Virginia, and Kentucky.

The Black Diamond mine had been unionized in the 1960s, but only after a long and bitter struggle. Labor-management relations in the industry have always been best described as adversarial. Overall, the Black Diamond mine enjoyed an above-average relationship with the UMW local union. Interestingly, Warren Powers also owned a very small, non-union mine located adjacent to the Black Diamond mine. The workers at this mine had consistently rejected UMW organizing efforts. The coal produced at this mine was sold to the Black Diamond Mining Company.

The Black Diamond Mine

The Black Diamond mine is a slope mine, which means that access to the underground coal seam is gained by a sloping tunnel driven from the surface down to the depth of the coal seam, in this case about 225 feet (see Figure 1). Slope mines are used to reach medium depth coal seams. Shaft (elevator) mines are used to reach very deep coal seams. Strip mines are used for coal lying near the surface. The mine had been started in 1965, and is expected to operate for thirty to forty years. It employs 229 men.

The slope tunnel is bilevel. The lower level is used to provide access to the underground for the miners and their equipment; the upper level contains a conveyer belt that transports the raw coal mined underground to the preparation plant located on the surface. There, the coal is separated from rock and other debris, crushed, washed, and stored until it is shipped by rail to the customer.

The Black Diamond mine is a "captive" mine, that is, all its output is bought by a large eastern utility company. The coal is sent by unit-train from the mine to a large electrical generating station where it is used as fuel to make steam that turns huge generators to produce electricity. The Black Diamond mine is one of several mines

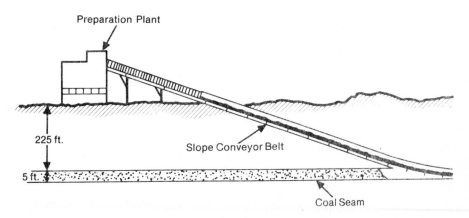

FIGURE 1.   A Simplified Cross-sectional View of the Black Diamond Mine

supplying this eastern utility company. Others are the Tunnelton, Lady Jane, Oneida, and #32 mines.

The workers are drawn from a wide geographical area, with some commuting as far as 100 miles each day. Mining is often a family affair, with brothers or fathers and grandfathers also being miners. The possibility of death is an ever-present but unacknowledged companion to miners, their families, and their communities. The prevailing sentiment is that misfortune will strike someone else.

The workforce shows a bimodal age distribution with many older miners forty-five to sixty years old and many younger miners twenty to thirty years old, but relatively few miners thirty to forty-five years old. Consequently, the educational levels and value systems differ significantly. The older miners remember the difficult struggle to organize and gain job security while the younger miners are interested in today's pay and tomorrow's opportunities. The UMW contract calls for a strict job classification and pay system with promotion largely based on seniority.

The miners face a harsh environment on the job. They must be constantly concerned about poisonous and explosive gases, cave-ins, rockfalls, high-voltage electrical cables, fires, dust, and a multitude of other dangers. Total darkness is only partially penetrated by head lamps on hard hats and equipment. Blindness can easily be simulated by walking sixty feet away and switching off the miner's hard hat lamp. Water may be present in tremendous quantities; the Black Diamond mine pumps over 7,000,000 gallons of acidic water a day from underground.

The average height of the coal seam at this mine is five feet; it varies from three feet to eight feet. The coal seam generally follows the surface contour. The hard hat prevents many painful encounters with the roof. Walking consists of moving in a half-crouch. The actual working area changes daily as mining progresses. An eight-hour shift includes sixty minutes of travel time from the mine surface to the work area and return, thirty minutes for lunch, and six and a half hours of productive time. Primary emphasis is on the amount of coal mined per shaft.

Currently, four production sections are operating, each manned by three crews who rotate through a three-shift-per-day, five-days-per-week schedule. The other employees at the mine perform a variety of ancillary functions necessary for the operation of the mine, but not directly connected to the mining of coal within the production sections. These functions include such tasks as operation and maintenance of the cleaning and preparation plant; water treatment; waste disposal; unit-train coal loading; unloading, storage, and distribution of mine supplies; and development and maintenance of the mine access and haulage ways.

Two maintenance units handle the mine's equipment. The outside maintenance unit handles most maintenance work performed aboveground, while the inside maintenance unit handles most of the maintenance work done on the underground mining equipment. Overlaps in task responsibilities and location of work performance exist, but these are considered necessary for operational flexibility.

The inside maintenance unit is subdivided into two groups of mechanics. One group is composed of the mechanics assigned to the individual production crews, usually one mechanic per crew. The other group is a pool of "floating" mechanics who travel to the production sections as required to handle maintenance problems that are beyond the capabilities of the mechanics assigned to that section.

Figure 2 depicts the organizational structure of the Black Diamond mine.

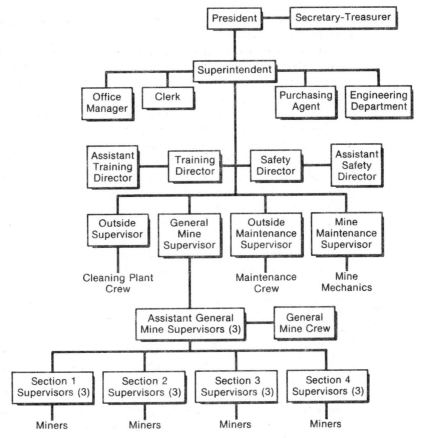

FIGURE 2. Organizational Chart of the Black Diamond Mine

A Production Section

The work of a coal mine production section can be visualized as consisting of all the activities involved in the mining of a seam of coal. A section will operate within the boundaries of an area approximately 840 feet wide by 1,500 feet long with a height equal to that of the coal seam (in this mine, about five feet). Mining operations at this particular mine are conducted using the "room and pillar" method. Continuous mining equipment is used in the production sections. To meet the requirements of accepted mining engineering practice and the legal provisions relating to ventilation, power, water, drainage, and escapeways, five or more entries (an opening in the coal seam twenty feet wide and the height of the coal seam) are driven parallel to each other on sixty-foot centers, initially starting in the middle edge of the section.

As the entries are advanced, twenty-foot-wide "crosscuts" are driven at right angles every sixty feet to connect the entries. The driving of these entries and crosscuts results in forty-foot-square "pillars" of coal being left. This process is known as the advance or "development" phase of mining.

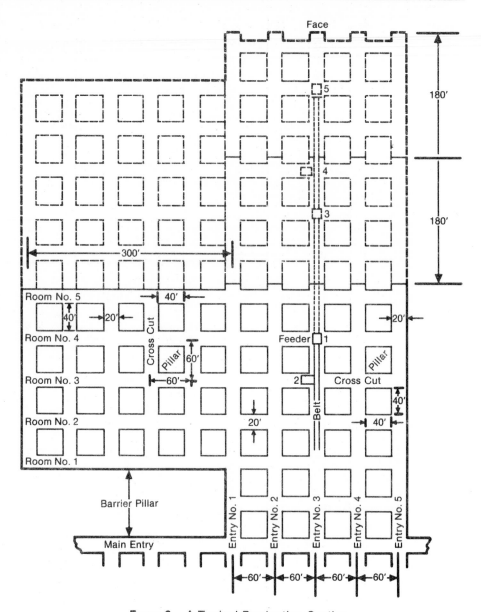

FIGURE 3. A Typical Production Section

As the entries and crosscuts are advanced into the coal seam of the section, panels of five "rooms," also twenty feet wide by five feet high, may be driven on one side of the section if the mine development plan permits. These rooms are also connected by crosscuts. Both rooms and their concomitant crosscuts are driven on sixty-foot centers, again resulting in pillars of coal being left.

When the rooms have reached the outer edge of the section on one side, the pillars of coal in that area are then mined systematically, with the roof falling, or "caving" as the extraction process is carried out. This process prevents excessive pressure from being exerted on the remaining pillars in the section. The extraction of the coal pillars (pulling back or "robbing the pillars") is known as the retreat phase of mining. It is generally hoped that the roof does not fall until the miners have retreated with their equipment behind remaining pillars of coal. As might be imagined, this is the most stressful, nerve-wracking stage of the coal mining process.

After entries have been driven all the way to the end of the section, rooms are driven on the other side. As each panel of rooms is completed, all the coal pillars are extracted as the miners move back out of the section. When a section has been completely mined, the miners and equipment move to a new location and the entire process is repeated. Figure 3 presents a diagram of a typical production section.

All the production sections have one continuous mining machine, two roof bolting machines, two shuttle cars (or four ram cars), a scoop, a tractor for towing supply cars within the section, and a variety of miscellaneous equipment. All the sections have an electric motor-driven feeder that loads the coal from the shuttle cars onto the conveyor belt system that transports the raw coal to the surface cleaning plant. The continous miner, the bolters, the shuttle cars, and the feeder are electrically powered by means of trailing cables, which connect the various pieces of equipment to a centrally located distribution box in the section. Scoops, tractors, and the ram cars are battery powered. Pumps and other miscellaneous equipment are usually connected to the distribution box on an "as needed" basis. The actual model of the equipment used varies from section to section.

The Decisions to Be Made

Warren Powers knew that if he were to implement any changes successfully at the Black Diamond mine, he would need the trust and cooperation of the UMW and its local union, the workers, and the management personnel. Although the task seemed formidable, the payoff could be considerable in terms of increased productivity, increased safety, decreased absenteeism, better labor-management relations, and a higher Quality of Work Life for all concerned.

These thoughts ran through his mind as he watched the snow fall. He might need to call in organizational change and development specialists. Work rules and practices might have to be modified. Many changes would have to occur. All these thoughts were racing through his mind as he tried to decide what, if anything, to do.

31. Managerial Systems Ltd.*

Introduction

It had been a rough week for Managerial Systems Ltd. By Thursday, MSL's president, Ken Long, had received upsetting phone calls from consultants Phil Mercer, Ray Terrell, and Fred Sargent concerning client difficulties. He had also talked at length with Karen Webster about conflicts between her personal and professional lives. Crises always seemed to come in avalanches. Tomorrow's staff meeting promised to last the entire spring day, ruining any plans Ken had for sailing.

Managerial Systems Ltd.

Managerial Systems Ltd. was a behaviorally based consulting organization focused on helping client companies improve the effectiveness of managerial systems through the application of sophisticated behavioral science technologies. (Exhibit 1 briefly explains the basics of behavioral consulting.) MSL consultants worked with client organizations to help define needs and then identify the proper methods for satisfying those needs. (Exhibit 2 lists the types of services provided in the past.) All MSL consultants had at least a master's degree in the behavioral sciences and most had obtained a doctorate in a related field. Many had worked in the behavioral area in either private practice or with institutions prior to joining MSL. (Exhibit 3 is a selected biography of representative consultants' backgrounds.)

MSL incorporated in 1977 when Ken Long, the president, resigned his professorship at a prominent southern business school in order to devote his full time to the company. In the past four years MSL had expanded to ten consultants, two research assistants, and five support staffers. MSL's primary clients had been in the petrochemical industry. However, attempts to implement a strategy of diversification had begun this year.

The diversification into other industries presented something of a problem for MSL. MSL's consulting expertise had been developed and proven in the petrochemical field. But potential clients questioned how well that expertise would translate to their specific types of problems. To help overcome these questions, Ken had decided to concentrate in three areas related to the prior experience of MSL. These included flow process plants, e.g., petrochemical, energy services and equipment companies, and banking. Ken anticipated no major problems transferring techniques from one industry to the others. This was

*This case was written by Molly Batson and Nancy Sherman under the supervision of Associate Professor Jeffrey A. Barach, A.B. Freeman School of Business. This case has been prepared as a basis for class discussion rather than to illustrate effective or ineffective administrative practices. Copyright © 1982 by the School of Business, Tulane University. Reproduced with permission.

Organizational Development (OD) is a process by which behavioral science principles and practices are used in an ongoing organization in a planned and systematic way. It is utilized to attain such goals as developing greater organizational competence while improving the quality of work life and the organization's effectiveness. (Effectiveness refers to setting and attaining appropriate goals in a changing environment.) OD differs from other planned change efforts such as the purchase of new equipment or floating a bond issue to build a new plant, in that the focus includes the motivation, utilization, and integration of human resources within the organization and is focused on total system change.

OD is a vehicle for helping organizations adjust to accelerated technological and social change. OD is not a specific technique, such as sensitivity training, job enrichment, group team-building, or management by objectives. OD may use specific techniques, but only after the relevance and utility of a special technique has been clearly demonstrated by careful diagnosis.

Interventions or techniques can be grouped in ten basic classifications:

- Individual consultation (counseling-coaching) usually involving a change agent in a one-on-one helping interaction with a single client.
- Unstructured group training involving individuals in a group lacking specific task purpose except that of understanding individual or group dynamics.
- Structured group training including management and group development courses structured to change participant attitudes, convey knowledge, or develop skills.
- Process consultation involving small groups or work teams identifying and solving common problems.
- Survey-guided development, involving collection of data about client work-group or organizational functioning and feeding back data to work groups to use in problem solving.
- Job redesign involving altering the tasks, responsibilities, interactions patterns, or the technical and physical environment intrinsic to the work itself.
- Personnel systems involving implementation through traditional personnel functions.
- Management information and financial control systems involving tracking and evaluating employee or work-group performance.
- Organizational design involving a structural change in organizational authority and reporting relationships.
- Integrated approaches including more than one of the methods described above.

EXHIBIT 1. Description of Organizational Development (OD)
Source: Edgar F. Huse. *Organization Development and Change,* 1980.

because MSL tailored each behavioral intervention to a client's particular set of needs.

Ken wanted each consultant to bring in at least one new client by the end of the year. Each consultant was asked to make contacts in new companies and arrange a presentation of MSL's array of services to management. Several of the consultants expressed their feelings of uneasiness in taking on a sales role. They felt they lacked sufficient experience to decide which companies and executives to approach as potential clients. Once they managed to make contact, the consultants were worried about how to make an effective presentation. To alleviate these concerns, Ken had begun training the consultants in sales techniques. The consultants were taught basic sales techniques tailored to MSL's particular marketing needs.

Long felt it was important for MSL's consultants to have divergent backgrounds both academically and professionally. However, he insisted that potential consultants have a fundamental belief in the benefits of a capitalistic society. When hiring consultants he discussed at length how the individual felt

Organizational Development initiation, planning, and execution
Managerial effectiveness training
Supervisory skills training
Organizational team-building
Organizational diagnostic surveys
- Organizational climate
- Employee attitude assessment
- Specific areas of concern
Managerial expectations clarification
- Goal setting
- Organizational dissemination
- Individual superior-subordinate clarifications
Performance feedback enhancement
- Establishing organizational systems
- Expectations setting/feedback skills training
Development of organizational systems
- Progressive discipline
- Managerial communications
- Work system redesign
- Managerial succession system
Employee Assistance Programs
- Individual managerial counseling
- Employee psychological services
- Alcoholic/drug abuse program
- Assisting terminated and retiring employees
Effective planning and implementation of organizational changes
EEO Audit simulation
EEO Assimilation Programs
Research Studies
- Attrition problems
- Employee acceptance/rejection of anticipated change
- EEO-related employee attitudes
- Organization-wide training systems
Workshops on special topics
- Management of stress situations
- Assimilation of new managers
- Problems faced by temporary supervisors
- Successful specific conflict resolution
Facilitating development of overall top management goals

Exhibit 2. Consulting Services Rendered to Clients—1980

about working for major oil companies. If there was a wide gap in the beliefs of MSL and the consultant, Ken would refuse to hire them. He felt the strains of working to improve a system one did not believe in would be detrimental to the consultant's working abilities and effectiveness. Ken encouraged the consultants to come to him to talk about any problems they were having on the job. He felt this minimized the chances of a consultant working him/herself into a corner over an issue.

Ken emphasized the importance of doing a thorough job with a client company. Many times a client company would bring in MSL to solve a specific problem that management had isolated. MSL wanted to gather their own data in order to determine the validity of management's point of view and to find out if there were any additional problems related to the ones indicated. MSL was prepared to walk away from a contract if management refused to allow them to do the necessary research or if management wanted their services for any reason other than to improve working conditions.

Karen Webster,	30, MBA from Tulane University, B.A., psychology, had been with MSL for four years. Prior to joining MSL, Karen worked in a managerial capacity in private business. Her consulting expertise was primarily in management and supervisory development.
Fred Sargent,	55, had been with the firm for three years, joining MSL upon completion of a doctorate in Adult Education. He spent twenty-five years in the Army and rose to the rank of Colonel. During his military career, Fred held many managerial positions, planning and implementing numerous training programs. He also earned an MBA from Syracuse University while in the Army. His Army experience carried over easily in behavioral consulting where Fred focused on development and execution of organizational needs analysis and management training programs.
Ray Terrell,	32, received his Ph.D. in clinical psychology following a master's degree in counseling. He had joined MSL on a part-time basis one and a half years ago while continuing to teach at a local university. Small group facilitation had been Ray's specialty within MSL.
Phil Mercer,	36, had been with MSL on a part-time basis for a year. He continued to teach in the Social Work Department at a local university. His academic credentials included an MSW, an MPH, and a Ph.D. in Human Ecology, a discipline which works against exploitation of the environment. This degree strongly reflected Phil's personal values. He spent many years "throwing rocks at big business from the outside" but had never been a part of that world. He went into consulting to learn more about how big business works and to help improve conditions for people working in the system.

Exhibit 3. Selected Biographies of MSL Consultants

The Dilemmas

Phil Mercer

Phil had just completed a large project on the reasons for the engineer attrition rate for a major oil company. The report and final recommendations would be ready the following week. Phil was quite pleased with the results. He attributed the success of the project to the agreement of management to release the report and the final recommendations to the engineers. The engineers took this as a sign that management was making a serious effort to correct many of the problems they faced at work. Therefore, they cooperated fully and candidly with Phil in the interviewing process.

Phil called Mr. Spencer, the Vice-President of Personnel, Engineering, to inform him of the date the report would be ready. He also inquired about distributing the report to the engineers. Mr. Spencer said the report would not be released as planned. A two-page summary of it would be made available. The recommendations would be omitted.

This upset Phil. He had given his word to the engineers that they would receive copies of the report and the recommendations. He reminded Mr. Spencer of management's promise to release it. All the positive effects of the promised release would be negated and the engineers' attitudes would sour. Phil questioned the wisdom of such a move. Mr. Spencer blamed the change in plans on MSL's failure to stay within the contracted budget. He said there were insufficient funds available to copy the report. Phil was at a loss on what to reply, so he terminated the conversation, promising to call again in the next few days.

Phil reviewed his alternatives. He could try again to convince Mr. Spencer to release the results regardless of the costs involved. He thought this would be fruitless based on the previous conversation. Phil considered going directly to the engineers and giving them the report and the recommendations without management's approval. After all, they had been promised a copy of the report and he could provide it verbally anyway. He also thought about going to someone higher in the company who could countermand Spencer's decision.

Phil called Ken to talk about the situation. Ken suggested that Phil bring up the issue at tomorrow's staff meeting. Before hanging up Ken mentioned that the company had contacted him about another consulting job. He wanted Phil to think about whether or not MSL should accept the job in light of the situation with Mr. Spencer.

Fred Sargent

Hugh Cavanaugh was the Operations Manager of a medium-sized petrochemical refinery located on the Louisiana coast. The refinery was part of a large, well-known energy concern. Cavanaugh was from the traditional school of management ("seat of the pants" or "we've always done it this way"). At sixty-two, his physical condition was excellent, considering his recovery from open-heart surgery two years earlier. Although every other member of the Management Committee supported the Plant Manager's initiation of MSL's organizational development (OD) efforts within the refinery (which included supervisory training, teambuilding, and EEO development work) Cavanaugh thought OD was a waste of time. He reportedly said, "young turks come in and try to change the organization when they don't even understand its history . . . besides, the refinery was maximizing production capacity way before all this new OD rubbish came up." Cavanaugh constantly refuted the OD effort along with other organizational changes. He was against the massive computerization then underway, and blatantly expressed his feelings throughout the refinery. As Operations Manager with thirty-seven years of experience, Hugh was in a potentially powerful position on the Management Committee. As a result, his negative attitude hindered the effectiveness of the Management Committee in the change process.

Dennis Kline, the refinery's young, aggressive Plant Manager, was a strong supporter of OD and realized its potential for improving the refinery's productivity. He had been in his present position for one year and one of his first actions had been to initiate the OD effort with MSL's assistance. This was a good way to revitalize the workforce while improving the bottom line. The OD effort would help him gain the respect of the refinery employees by demonstrating his concern for their working environment. Hugh had been his only obstacle to implementing the OD effort. He had tried to energize Hugh by utilizing him as a leader to work decisions and assume responsibility for part of the OD effort. Kline figured that if Cavanaugh felt ownership of the ideas and participated in them from their inception, he would realize their value and be won over. However,

Cavanaugh refused to get involved in any way and stonewalled all of Kline's efforts over the entire year. Kline had tried everything short of firing Hugh.

Fred Sargent, MSL's senior consultant working with the Management Committee, knew that the members of the committee recognized Hugh's biases against OD, but they really did not have the professional insight and objectivity to see that he had no capability for change. Some of the committee members had blinders on due to their longtime friendship and respect for Hugh. As a result, the whole Management Committee was having a difficult time accepting the realities of the situation. But it was quite obvious to Sargent, based on his past consulting experience, that as long as Cavanaugh was a forceful member of the Management Committee, MSL's OD efforts could never reach their full potential.

Should Fred work with the Management Committee to accept the fact that Hugh would never change, he would be the catalyst for Hugh's encouraged early retirement. This would then allow Sargent to facilitate the OD process. But, if Fred was linked to Hugh's encouraged retirement, he might be labeled as a "hit man," which could inhibit his ability to work with the Management Committee and other members of the refinery organization. They might see Fred's actions as part of a conspiracy to do some housecleaning and thus find working through behavioral dilemmas with him quite threatening. In addition, the loss of Cavanaugh could be detrimental to the refinery's operations. His position as Operations Manager was a subtle link in labor negotiations currently underway as a result of a recent wildcat strike. Cavanaugh was well-respected by his subordinates, and quite effective in the technical aspects of his job which gave him influence on the union negotiations. It was Fred's feeling that Cavanaugh's work was his life and crucial to his survival, both psychologically and financially.

Feeling extremely frustrated, Fred approached George Davenport, Process Division Manager, Management Committee member, and a longtime friend of Hugh Cavanaugh. George was in his early sixties, but, unlike Hugh, had been able to adjust to organizational changes quite well. He was able to see the potential benefits of OD and could look at the situation from a broad perspective.

Fred: George, I'm really concerned about the slow progress of the Management Committee in this recent OD effort concerning EEO and team building. What do you see as the barrier?

George: I seem to be having the same feelings that things are moving rather slowly. If only we could get Hugh on board . . . I think things would take off. I've tried to talk to him about the value of the OD efforts, but I can understand his objections. After all, our past experience with consultants billing themselves as OD experts has not been too good. They cost an arm and a leg and talk in generalities, never touching on our specific problems. However, your company has tailored its efforts to our specific needs. Also, Hugh's knowledge and understanding of company history can't be matched—even by the Plant Manager! He really feels outside consultants aren't qualified to facilitate changes in the organization.

Fred: But, George, everyone else on the committee seems able and ready to accept the OD efforts. Hugh is living in the past. He's dug in his heels and won't budge.

George: Well, I do know he's too valuable not to have on the Management Committee at this point.

Fred Sargent was in a bind and didn't know what to do. If he didn't take any immediate action and chose to buy time, hoping to either change Hugh Cavanaugh or wait for his scheduled retirement, the entire OD effort might be doomed. Cavanaugh would do everything in his power to stop the effort, if not through the Management Committee, then verbally throughout the refinery. Another option for Sargent was to take on the biggest challenge of his career and spend all his time trying to change Hugh Cavanaugh. If he could somehow work it so Cavanaugh received full credit for part of the OD effort and was recognized by corporate headquarters for this accomplishment, he'd have no choice but to go along with the continuation of the effort.

Other options open to Fred included convincing Dennis Kline to "force" Hugh's early retirement with all the usual fanfare; going to corporate headquarters Human Resources Vice-President or the Vice-President of Refining (who were both strong OD supporters) and explaining the situation; going to Hugh directly and asking him to retire; slowly showing the Management Committee in a calculated way that Hugh was damaging the refinery's effectiveness; or creating a scandal in order to get Hugh fired if he refused to retire.

Fred decided that the next step would be to bring his dilemma to MSL's monthly staff meeting for discussion.

Karen Webster

Karen had several problems at work to think about that night. She usually discussed things with her husband, Jack, in order to put things into a better perspective. The weekly staff meeting was coming up and she wanted to be prepared to present her dilemmas as clearly and concisely as possible to the other consultants to get their opinions.

Karen joined MSL at its inception and had been very active in helping the company to reach its current size and in building its good reputation. She was the only woman consultant for several years. MSL did most of its consulting in flow processing plants and many of the plant managers were products of the "Good Ole Boy" syndrome. They had grown up in the back country and had been taught that women stayed at home. There were few, if any, women working in the plants because of the rough nature of the work. Karen found that it was difficult to get the managers to accept her as a professional, knowledgeable consultant. She had to prove herself time and again. She found that she couldn't allow her clients to think of her as a woman first and a consultant second. Her professional reputation had been built with these men through much hard work and continuing efforts to educate them.

After working for MSL for five years, Karen and Jack had decided to begin a family. A lot of thought had gone into this decision. Karen had no plans to stop working after the baby was born. This opened several areas of potential conflict between raising the baby and Karen's career. However, after carefully evaluating the situation, they decided to have a child. As soon as Karen found that she was pregnant, she began planning her projects so any traveling would be completed by the end of her seventh month of pregnancy. Back in December she had confirmed plans for an eight-day team-building session at a plant seventy-five miles away. She planned to commute every other day. This session would be the culmination of almost a year of hard work.

Several days ago the client company had contacted Karen and stated that the session would have to be pushed back. The new dates coincided with the end of the eighth month of her pregnancy. She was very concerned about this change. The thought of having to drive to and from the plant every other day was not pleasant. She also disliked the idea of staying at the plant for the entire week. She knew Jack would be upset if she were gone from home so late in her pregnancy. She would tire more easily and would not be as effective as usual. However, she had made a commitment to the client to complete the team-building process. Karen felt very strongly about fulfilling her obligations to MSL and to her career.

Karen considered her options. On some projects it would be possible to bring in another consultant to complete the training. However, this was not the case with team-building. Team-building's purpose was to improve the effectiveness and performance of people who work together closely on a regular basis. Because of the difficulty and time necessary to build a close, trusting relationship between the consultant and the group, it would be impossible for another consultant to take over. She could also go back to the client company and try to convince management to allow the original dates to stand. She could refuse to do the training now and try to complete it after she returned to work.

As Karen talked with Jack she voiced these possibilities and wondered how the other consultants would react to her situation. She was worried about the impact cancellation would have on her career and professional reputation. There was even a possibility that MSL would lose the client if she cancelled. How would her decision affect Ken's decisions to hire other women consultants? Karen wanted to get some feedback from the other consultants at the staff meeting before making her decision.

Ray Terrell

Back at MSL's New Orleans office on the morning of the monthly staff meeting, Ray Terrell's mind began to wander. Only twenty-four hours ago he had been in Dallas, Texas, in the midst of a tension-filled Management Committee meeting and a potentially explosive discussion with Bill Matthews, Vice-President of Refining—Southwest Region for a major energy concern. Ray had decided that this was an issue to be discussed by the entire MSL professional staff, as it had serious implications for MSL's future. He began to jot down notes in preparation for the meeting. . . .

During the first quarter of this year, Ray had become involved in an OD effort at one of the company's Southwest Region refineries located in Corpus Christi, Texas. Terrell, representing MSL, spent approximately three weeks in the data-gathering phase of the OD process, which included employee-consultant inter-, views in all refinery divisions. According to MSL's standard practice, prior to conducting the employee interviews, Ray had assured the employees that any information obtained during the interviews would be kept confidential. The Management Committee was aware of this practice but had no explicit confidentiality agreement with MSL. MSL had no formalized written statement on the subject of confidentiality in their signed contracts due to their philosophy of tailoring each OD effort to the particular client. It was strongly believed by all MSL consultants that their current practice was in the best interest of the client organization, the individual, and the consulting firm. This was based on the premise that a consulting organization's ability to collect accurate data about individuals and corporations was critical to successful performance. Effective data-gathering depended on trust that the information would not be used to the possible detriment of the individual unless clearly indicated up front.

Upon completion of the data-gathering phase, Ray compiled his results into a written document and presented it to the refinery's Management Committee which included Bill Matthews as an Ex Officio member. The report emphasized a heavy concern for race relations as expressed by black wage earners in particular. Ray had stated, in a broad general sense, that blacks felt mistreated given their seniority and the jobs they got in relation to other refinery workers with similar seniority. He supported this racial concern by stating that blacks felt they were not receiving as adequate career counseling and development as white workers were (both in technical areas and otherwise) so that blacks could compete for higher level positions. Ray's report concluded with recommended action steps which specified supervisory training in EEO awareness and counseling skills as the first steps. In addition, Ray would undertake an intensive study and revamping of the company's employee training program and practices.

Following Ray's presentation, Plant Manager Ron Gallagher called for a discussion. The EEO issue was of great concern to the entire committee, given an impending Department of Labor audit within a few months. Negative audit results could cause significant delay in the expected promotions of Ron (to a headquarters divisional V-P position) and Bill Matthews (to President of the corporation's small Chemical Division) at the end of the year. It was obvious to Ray that he had hit one of the company's most vulnerable spots. This meant that chances for successful implementation of his recommendations were even greater than he had expected. As a result, MSL could probably count on at least six months of steady billing. This would definitely please Ken.

The Management Committee discussion did not seem to be accomplishing anything. It was apparent the members were quite uncomfortable with the topic of EEO in addition to being defensive of their own subdivisions' non-discriminatory posture. Finally Bill Matthews spoke. He congratulated Ray on his effective presentation, reiterated his deep concern for the findings, and stated that he was all for immediate action. However, it would be essential for the Management Committee to find out exactly who had expressed these concerns so that steps could be taken to rectify their situation right away. After all, Ray and MSL were working for management. Of course, his major concern was for the employees, but there was the upcoming audit to consider, since EEO charges or possible lawsuits could easily result in a prolonged audit and bad publicity. Once the situation was under control, the problem as a whole could be tackled.

When Matthews finished there was an awkward silence in the room. Ron Gallagher made an attempt to neutralize the situation by acknowledging the refinery's potential racial problem and admitting that blacks never came to any of the refinery's social gatherings.

Terrell could not believe that Matthews had the nerve to ask for identification of his information sources in front of the entire Management Committee! He was even more enraged that no one had objected to the request. Terrell did not know how to respond. As a management consultant he did have a responsibility to management, but had Matthews overstepped the professional boundary? This company was currently MSL's largest client, having produced the majority of projects and billing days throughout MSL's short history. If this situation got out of control, there was the possibility that the relationship would be severed. This could be devastating to MSL since their diversification strategy targets for this quarter had not been realized. At this point MSL was relying heavily on its current clients to produce further projects in other areas of their organizations. This vertical penetration marketing strategy had worked very well with almost no specific sales effort on the part of MSL consultants and now seemed crucial to the firm's immediate survival.

Since all refinery divisions were represented on the Management Committee would Ray be putting MSL's immediate financial future on the line if he did not divulge his information sources? Additionally, if Gallagher and Matthews did get those promotions into the upper echelons of the company, would he be jeopardizing MSL's future with the entire corporation and MSL's reputation in the industry? Finally, one of his goals as an MSL consultant was to improve organizational effectiveness. If he gave the Management Committee the information Matthews wanted, he could be the catalyst needed for the refinery to address the racial concerns affecting the organization's effectiveness.

Ray's mind raced through his confused thoughts. Matthews would be expecting an answer. Ray decided to hold his tongue for the moment and told the Management Committee he'd be in touch with them at their meeting next week.

The Staff Meeting

Ken opened the staff meeting with a brief discussion of the various projects in progress. He then asked the consultants if they had any problems they wanted to discuss. Four hands shot up and Karen, Phil, Ray, and Fred then presented the problems confronting them. Once the initial recitals had been made, Ken recommended a fifteen-minute coffee break so everyone could digest the problems they had just heard about. He asked the group to think about possible courses of action for each situation, the pros and cons of each, and what their final recommendations would be.

32.   Chandler's Restaurant*

In discussing the kitchen as a status system, we have only incidentally taken account of the fact that the kitchen is part of a communication and supply system, which operates to get the food from the range onto the customer's table. Looking at it this way will bring to light other problems.

Where the restaurant is small and the kitchen is on the same floor as the dining room, waitresses are in direct contact with cooks. This does not eliminate

---

*This case was prepared by William Foote Whyte and is reprinted here by permission of the author.

friction, but at least everybody is in a position to know what everybody else is doing, and the problems of communication and coordination are relatively simple.

When the restuarant is large, there are more people whose activities must be coordinated, and when the restaurant operates on several floors, the coordination must be accomplished through people who are not generally in face-to-face contact with each other. These factions add tremendously to the difficulty of achieving smooth coordination.

The cooks feel that they work under pressure—and under a pressure whose origins they cannot see or anticipate.

As one of them said,

> It's mostly the uncertainty of the job that gets me down, I think. I mean, you never know how much work you're going to have to do. You never know in advance if you're going to have to make more. I think that's what a lot of 'em don't like around here. That uncertainty is hard on your nerves.

For a cook, the ideal situation is one in which she always has a sufficient supply of food prepared ahead so that she is never asked for something she does not have on hand. As one of them said, "You have to keep ahead or you get all excited and upset."

Life would be simpler for the cook if she were free to prepare just as much food as she wanted to, but the large and efficiently operated restaurant plans production on the basis of very careful estimates of the volume of business to be expected. Low food costs depend in part upon minimizing waste or leftover food. This means that production must be scheduled so as to run only a little ahead of customer demand. The cook therefore works within a narrow margin of error. She can't get far ahead, and that means that on extra-busy days she is certain sometimes to lose her lead or even to drop behind.

When the cook drops behind, all the pressures from customer to waitress to service pantry to runner descend upon her, for no one between her and the customer can do this job unless she produces the goods. From this point of view, timing and coordination are key problems of the organization. Proper timing and good coordination must be achieved in human relations or else efficiency is dissipated in personal frictions.

While these statements apply to every step in the process of production and service, let us look here at the first steps—the relations of cooks to kitchen runners to the service pantry.

When the restaurant operates on different floors, the relations must be carried on in part through mechanical means of communication. There are three common channels of this nature, and all have their drawbacks. Use of a public address system adds considerably to the noise of the kitchen and service pantries. The teleautograph (in which orders written on the machine on one floor are automatically recorded on the kitchen machine) is quiet but sometimes unintelligible. Orders written in a hurry and in abbreviated form are sometimes misinterpreted so that sliced ham arrives when sliced toms (tomatoes) were ordered. Besides, neither of those channels operates easily for two-way communication. It is difficult to carry on a conversation over the public address system, and, while kitchen runners can write their replies to orders on the teleautograph, this hardly makes for full and free expression. The telephone provides two-way communication, but most kitchens are so noisy that it is difficult to hear phone conversations. And then in some restaurants there is only one telephone circuit for the whole house, so that when kitchen and pantry runners are using it, no one else can put in a call.

The problems that come up with such communication systems can best be illustrated by looking at a particular restaurant, Chandler's where teleautograph and phone were used.

A kitchen supervisor was in charge of Chandler's kitchen, and pantry supervisors were in charge of each pantry, under her general supervision. There was also an assistant supervisor working in the kitchen.

The supplying function was carried on in the kitchen by two or three runners (depending upon the employment situation) and by a runner on each of the service-pantry floors. Food was sent up by automatic elevator.

The kitchen runners were supposed to pick up their orders from storage bins, iceboxes, or direct from the cooks. When the order was in preparation, the cook or salad girl was supposed to say how long it would be before it was ready, and the runner would relay this information by teleautograph to the service pantries. When the cooking or salad making had not been begun, the runner had no authority to tell the cook to hurry the order. Before each meal, the cook was given an open order (a minimum and maximum amount) on each item by the kitchen supervisor. She worked steadily until she had produced the minimum, and, from then on, she gauged her production according to the demands that came to her from the runner. That is, if the item was going out fast, she would keep producing as fast as she could until she had produced the maximum. Beyond this point she could not go without authorization from her supervisor. Ideally, the supervisor and cook would confer before the maximum had been reached in order to see whether it was necessary to set a new figure, but this did not always happen.

While the runner could not order the cook to go beyond her maximum, his demands did directly influence her behavior up to that point. He originated action for her.

That was at the base of his troubles. Among kitchen employees, as we have seen, the cooks have the highest status. In Chandler's, runners had a low status, just above potwashers and sweepers. The jobs were filled by inexperienced employees, women or men who, if they performed well, were advanced to something of higher status. Their wages were considerably lower than the cooks', and the cooks also had a great advantage in seniority. In this particular case, the age difference was important too. The runners were a young man, a teen-aged boy, and a young girl, while the cooks were middle-aged women.

The runners would have been in a more secure position if they had been in close touch with a supervisor, but here the communication was sporadic and ineffective. The supervisor was inclined to let the runners fend for themselves.

When the runners put pressure on them, the cooks were inclined to react so as to put the runners in their place. For example, we observed incidents like this one. One runner (Ruth) asked another to get some salmon salad from the salad girl. The second runner found that the salad girl had no more on hand.

"They want me to get some of that salmon salad," he said. "Couldn't you make it, please?"

"Who told you that?" she asked.

"Ruth did."

"You can tell Ruth that I don't take no orders from her. I have a boss, and I don't take orders from nobody else. You can just tell her that."

Now it may have been that the salad girl had made her maximum and could not go on without authorization from her supervisor, but the runner had no way of knowing that this was the case. He put his request to her politely, and she could have responded in kind by saying she was sorry that she could not make more without consulting the supervisor. Instead she responded aggressively, as if she felt a need to make it clear that no mere runner was going to originate action for her.

Even when they complied with the runner's requests, the cooks sometimes behaved so as to make it appear as if it were really they who originated the action. They always liked to make it clear that they had authority over the foods after they had been prepared, and that they could determine what should be done with them. While this was a general reaction, the salad girl was most explicit in such cases.

A runner went to look for some boiled eggs. The salad girl was not present at the moment, so he could not ask her, but after he had got the eggs from the icebox, he saw that she was back at her station. He showed her the pan of eggs, asking, "What about that?"

"I don't like that," she said belligerently. "You have no business taking them eggs out of the icebox without asking."

"Well, I'm asking you now."

"I have to know how much there is. That's why I want you to tell me. . . . Go on, you might as well take them now that you have them."

On other occasions when he asked her for salad, she would say, "Why don't you people look in the icebox once in a while?"

In such a case, whatever the runner did was wrong. The salad girl's behavior was irrational, of course, but it did serve a function for her. Behaving in this way, she was able to originate action for the runner instead of being in the inferior position of responding to his actions.

The runners also had difficulty in getting information out of the cooks. When there was a demand from the service pantries, and the food could not be sent up immediately, the runners were always supposed to give an estimate as to when they could furnish the item. This information they were expected to get from the cooks. The cooks sometimes flatly refused to give a time and were generally reluctant to make an estimate. When they did give a time, they nearly always ran considerably beyond it.

Incidentally, time seems to be used as a weapon in the restaurant. It is well known that customers feel and complain that they wait for a table or for service far longer than they actually do. Waitresses, as we observed them, estimated their waiting time on orders as much as 50 to 100 percent more than the actual time. While they were not conscious of what they were doing, they could express impatience with the service-pantry girls more eloquently by saying, "I've been waiting twenty minutes for that order," than by giving the time as ten minutes. In the front the house, time is used to put pressure on people. In the back of the house, the cooks try to use time to take pressure off themselves. They say that an item will be done "right away," which does not tell when it will be done but announces that they have the situation well in hand and that nobody should bother them about it. Giving a short time tends to have the same effect. It reassures the runner, who reassures the service pantries. When the time runs out, the pantry runners begin again to demand action, but it may take a few minutes before the pressure gets back to the cooks, and by that time the item may really be ready for delivery. Furthermore, the cooks' refusal to give a time turns the pressure back on runners and other parts of the house—a result that they are not able to accomplish in any other way.

In the case of some of the inexperienced cooks, it may be that they simply did not know how to estimate cooking time, but that would hardly explain the persistent failure of all the cooks to cooperate with the runners in this matter.

The management was quite aware of this problem but had no real solution to offer. One of the pantry supervisors instructed a kitchen runner in this way:

> "You have to give us a time on everything that is going to be delayed. That is the only way we can keep things going upstairs. On our blackboards we list all our foods and how long it will take to get them, and most of the time we have to list them 'indefinite.' That shouldn't be. We should always have a definite time, so the waitress can tell the guest how long he will have to wait for his order. We can't tell the guest we're out of a certain food item on the menu and that we don't know how long it will take to replace it. They'll ask what kind of a restaurant we're running."
>
> The runner thought that over and then went on to question the supervisor. "But sometimes we can't get that information from the cooks. . . . They won't tell us, or maybe they don't know."
>
> "Then you should always ask the food-production manager. She'll tell you, or she'll get the cook to tell you."
>
> "But the cooks would think we had squealed."
>
> "No, they wouldn't. And if they did, all right, it's the only way they'll ever learn. They've got to learn that, because we must always have a time on all delayed foods."
>
> "Yes, surely we couldn't tell on them if they refused to give the information."
>
> "Yes, you could. You have to. They'll have to learn it somehow."

The efficiency of this system depended upon building up a cooperative relationship between cooks and runners. For runners to try to get action by appealing to the boss to put pressure on the cooks is hardly the way to build up such a relationship. It is clear that, considering their low status in relation to the cooks, runners are not in a position to take the lead in smoothing out human-relations difficulties.

Some of the runner's problems arise out of failure to achieve efficient coordination and communication between floors. For example, on one occasion one of the upstairs floors put in a rush order for a pan of rice. With some difficulty, the kitchen runner was able to fill the order. Then, fifteen minutes later, the pan came back to the kitchen again, still almost full, but apparently no more was needed for the meal. The cooks gathered around the elevator to give vent to their feelings. This proved, they said, that the rice had not been needed after all. Those people upstairs just didn't know what they were doing. After the meal was over, the kitchen runner went up to check with the pantry runner. The pantry man explained, "I ran out of creole, and there wasn't going to be any more, so I had no use for any more rice."

This was a perfectly reasonable explanation, but it did not reach the cooks. As a rule, the cooks had little idea of what was going on upstairs. Sometimes there would be an urgent call for some food item along toward the end of the mealtime, and it would be supplied only after a considerable delay. By the time it reached the service pantries, there would no longer be a demand for it, and the supply would shortly be back. This would always upset the cooks. They would then stand around and vow that next time they would not take it seriously when the upstairs people were clamoring for action.

"In the service pantries," one of the cooks said, "they just don't care how much they ask for. That guy, Joe [pantry runner], just hoards the stuff up there. He can't always be out of it like he claims. He just hoards it."

A kitchen runner made this comment:

> Joe will order something and right away he'll order it again. He just keeps calling for more. Once or twice I went upstairs, and I saw he had plenty of stuff up there. He just hoards it up there, and he has to send a lot of stuff downstairs. He wastes a lot of stuff. After I caught on to the way he works, I just made it a rule when he called for stuff and the first floor was calling for stuff at the same time, I divided it between them.

On the other hand, when Joe was rushed and found that he was not getting quick action on his orders, his tendency was to make his orders larger, repeat the orders before any supply had come up, and mark all his orders *rush*. When this did not bring results he would call the kitchen on the phone. If all else failed, he would sometimes run down into the kitchen himself to see if he could snatch what he needed.

This kind of behavior built up confusion and resentment in the kitchen. When orders were repeated, the kitchen runners could not tell whether additional supply was needed or whether the pantry runners were just getting impatient. When everything was marked rush, there was no way of telling how badly anybody needed anything. But most serious of all was the reaction when the pantry runner invaded the kitchen.

One of them told us of such an incident:

> One of the cooks got mad at me the other day. I went down there to get this item, and boy, did she get mad at me for coming down there. But I got to do *something!* The waitresses and the pantry girls keep on yelling at me to get it for them. Well, I finally got it, or somehow it got sent upstairs. Boy, she was sure mad at me, though.

Apparently the cooks resented the presence of any upstairs supply man in the kitchen, but they were particularly incensed against Joe, the runner they all suspected of hoarding food.

One of them made this comment:

> That guy would try to come down in the kitchen and tell us what to do. But not me. No sir. He came down here one day and tried to tell me what to do. He said to me, "We're going to be very busy today." I just looked at him. "Yeah?" I said, "Who are you? Go on upstairs. Go on. Mind your own business." Can you beat that! "We're going to be very busy today!" He never came down and told *me* anything again. "Who are you?" I asked him. That's all I had to say to him.

Here the runner's remark did not have any effect upon the work of the cook, but the implication was that he was in a superior position, and she reacted strongly against him for that reason. None of the cooks enjoy having the kitchen runners originate action for them, but, since it occurs regularly, they make some adjustment to it. They are not accustomed to any sort of relationship with the pantry runners, so when they come down to add to the pressure and confusion of the kitchen, the cooks feel free to slap them down.

It was not only the pantry runners who invaded the kitchen. The pantry supervisors spent a good deal of time and energy running up and down. When an upstairs supervisor comes after supplies, the kitchen reaction is the same as that to the pantry runners—except that the supervisor cannot be slapped down. Instead, the employees gripe to each other.

As one kitchen runner said,

> I wish she would quit that. I wonder what she thinks she's doing, running down here and picking up things we're waiting for. Now like just a minute ago, did you see that? She went off with peaches and plums, and we'd never have known about it if I hadn't seen her. Now couldn't she have just stepped over here and told us? . . . She sure gets mad a lot, doesn't she? She's always griping. I mean, she's probably a nice person, but she's hard to get along with at work—she sure is!

There were other pantry supervisors whose presence in the kitchen did not cause such a disturbance. The workers would say that so-and-so was really all right. Nevertheless, whenever a pantry supervisor dashed into the kitchen for supplies, it was a sign to everybody that something was wrong—that somebody was worried—and thus it added to the tension in the atmosphere and disturbed the human relations of the regular supply system—such as they were.

In this situation, the kitchen runner was the man in the middle. One of the service-pantry girls we interviewed put it this way:

> Oh, we certainly are busy up here. We don't stop even for a moment. I think this is the busiest place around here. It's bad when we can't get those foods, though. We get delayed by those supply people downstairs all the time. I could shoot those runners. We can be just as busy up here—but down there it's always slow motion. It seems like they just don't care at all. They always take all the time in the world.

On the other hand, the cooks blamed the inefficiency of the runners for many of their troubles. They felt that the runners were constantly sending up duplicate orders just through failure to consult each other on the progress of their work. Actually, according to our observation, this happened very rarely, but whenever a runner was caught in the act, this was taken as proof that duplication was common practice. The failure of the runners to coordinate their work efficiently did annoy the cooks in another way, as they were sometimes asked for the same order within a few seconds by two different runners. However, while this added to the nervous tension, it did not directly affect the flow of supplies.

Such were the problems of supply in one restaurant where we were able to give them close attention. However, as it stands, this account is likely to give a false impression. The reader may picture the restaurant as a series of armed camps, each one in constant battle with its neighbor. He may also get the impression that food reaches customers only intermittently and after long delays.

To us it seemed that the restaurant was doing a remarkable job of production and service, and yet, in view of the frictions we observed, it is only natural to ask whether it would not be possible to organize the human relations so as to make for better teamwork and greater efficiency.

According to one point of view, no basic improvement is possible because "you can't change human nature."

But is it all just personalities and personal inefficiency? What has been the situation in other restaurants of this type (operating on several floors) and in other periods of time?

Unfortunately we have no studies for other time periods, but we do have the testimony of several supervisors who have had previous experience in restaurants facing similar problems, and who have shown themselves, in the course of our study, to be shrewd observers of behavior in their own organizations. Their story is that the friction and incoordination we observed were not simply a war-time phenomenon. While increased business and inexperienced help made the problem much more acute, the friction came at the same places in the organization—between the categories of people—that it used to. The job of the kitchen runner, apparently, has always been a "hot spot" in such an organization.

This, then, is not primarily a personality problem. It is a problem in human relations. When the organization operates so as to stimulate conflict between people holding certain positions within it, then we can expect trouble.

33. The Tailored Management Development Program: A Case of Management Development Design Options*

The midwestern university business school was certainly no stranger to management development programs. Its management development division already conducted hundreds of seminars each year dealing with a full spectrum of business and management topics. But this request was different. Parker Hannifin Corporation, a diversified Fortune 500 manufacturer, had asked the university to

---

*Donald F. Parker, Dean, College of Commerce and Industry, University of Wyoming. Printed by permission.

design a management development program tailored specifically to the needs of the firm's five hundred plus line and staff managers whose duties ranged from plant department head to corporate vice-president.

Although they had sent managers to a variety of development programs over the years, especially in marketing and finance, Parker Hannifin's last attempt at a general management development program had lapsed more than ten years earlier. The desire of top management to exert renewed effort in this area came about because of two principal factors. The first was growth: extensive diversification through acquisition into three relatively disparate business lines; expansion to more than fifty divisions having over 20,000 employees; and extensive U.S. and offshore geographic dispersion. Almost equally important was the intense pressure being felt from foreign competition, especially from the Japanese.

The Vice-Chairman of the corporation and the Personnel Vice-President were very straightforward. They were contacting a number of management consultants and universities to determine whether these organizations would be interested in their project. If so, the Company would want to know the approach each would employ. Neither specific program designs nor curriculum topics had been decided upon, they said, but Parker Hannifin had definitely decided that they wanted a program designed exclusively for their own managers.

Two meetings followed during which interested professors outlined their thoughts and suggested possible approaches. Following these discussions, the Company suspended discussions with other organizations and decided to ask the professors from one of the universities to prepare a program design proposal. They also stressed that the Firm would like to inauguarate the new program as soon as possible.

Planning and Data Collection

Three professors agreed to develop the program proposal. They began immediately to plan a needs analysis that would provide data for the program design. Reasoning that a tailored development program should have at its base both the principles of learning and training and the goals and values of Parker Hannifin, the design team concluded that the first step should be a thorough assessment of the strategy, goals, management practices, and culture of the Firm. The C.E.O. agreed not only to allow this diagnosis, but also to bear its expense.

The professors devoted the next two months to visiting the Corporation's three principal offices to conduct extensive interviews with the C.E.O. and thirty-five members of top management. This effort produced a wealth of information about the history and goals of the organization, and a distinct "feel" for its culture and values. One unexpected dividend was an extensive collection of Company anecdotes that would prove to be invaluable as classroom examples of Parker Hannifin values and practices.

The interviews, supplemented by frequent discussions with the company's two contacts, helped the three professors to clarify top management's somewhat ambiguous goals for the program. By the end of the interview phase, it had been agreed that the program should provide its participants with the following:

1. Broader understanding of management theory and practice.
2. Greater familiarity with the disparate facets of the Corporation's operations, and its desired culture and values.
3. Greater insight into their own behavior for the purpose of helping each one to improve his or her own managerial performance.

Having learned a great deal about Parker Hannifin and about top management's aspirations for the program, the designers turned to an assessment of the attitudes and perceptions of the prospective trainees. They developed a comprehensive mailed questionnaire to be completed by the 500 managers who would ultimately receive the training. This survey was designed to accomplish four objectives:

1. To validate preliminary diagnoses formed during the interview phase.
2. To determine managers' attitudes about the Corporation, their jobs, and the management processes of the Company.
3. To ascertain managers' perceptions about their own training needs and those of their superiors, peers, and subordinates.
4. To serve as a baseline for future assessments of change following implementation of the proposed program.

The questionnaires were mailed from and returned to the university, thus maintaining the confidentiality of each manager's response. Almost 80 percent of the surveys were quickly completed and returned. Their data were analyzed as rapidly as possible, yielding a wealth of additional information about corporate goals, practices, culture, and weaknesses. Also provided were extensive data indicating what prospective trainees thought about their own and other managers' shortcomings and developmental needs.

Designing the Program

The professors now began the final design, while also holding frequent discussions with the two corporate action officers. Consequently, many questions and issues were dealt with even before the proposal was complete. The proposal was presented to the C.E.O., top management, and representatives of the three sectors of the Corporation. The designers described specific goals and objectives the program should achieve and presented an outline of the proposed curriculum. Also included were recommendations pertaining to class size, composition, and scheduling. Almost six months had elapsed since Parker Hannifin's representatives first contacted the university.

Early Agreement.. The design proposal meeting resulted in quick agreement on several issues: each class would have thirty participants; there would be maximum heterogeneity of participants in terms of rank, job function, and geographical location; classes would take place at the university where participants could live together in a former fraternity house dedicated exclusively to their use, thus assuring maximum interchange of experiences and ideas during both working and non-working hours; an intensive working schedule would be employed with classes ordinarily lasting from 8:00 A.M. to 10:00 P.M. except for lunch and dinner breaks; a trial class consisting of senior managers from all major segments of Parker Hannifin would be convened within three months.

Program Design. The approved program layout called for two five and one-half day weeks. The first week would be devoted to individual manager effectiveness, with broader issues such as strategy formulation and implementation being dealt with during week two. The design and topics included in the original proposal are shown in Figures 1, 2, and 3.

PRIOR TO FIRST WEEK

Pre-Program Survey:
Information From Senior Management, Self, Boss, Subordinates

WEEK ONE
(Focus on Individual Management)

	Sunday	Monday	Tuesday	Wednesday	Thursday	Friday
Morning						
Afternoon						
Evening						

BETWEEN WEEKS
(Focus on Observation, Application, and Self-Evaluation)

Action Project: Based On First Week's Learning

WEEK TWO
(Focus on Strategic Issues and Self in Relation to Corporate View)

	Sunday	Monday	Tuesday	Wednesday	Thursday	Friday
Morning						
Afternoon						
Evening						

FIGURE 1. Course Content

WEEK ONE

	Sunday	Monday	Tuesday	Wednesday	Thursday	Friday
Morning		Organization Simulation	Organization Simulation	Leadership	Communication	Action Planning
Afternoon	Welcome and Introduction	Organization Simulation	Organization Simulation: Debriefing	Motivation and Goal Setting	Self-Management Action Planning	Effective Application
Evening	Pre-brief For Organization Simulation	Key Issue Presentation	Leadership and Motivation Case	Integrating Case	Fun and Games	

FIGURE 2

In order to capitalize on the results of longer term exposure to the learning environment and to relate the material covered to the manager's own jobs, the design split the program into two Sunday-through-Friday segments to be held four to five months apart. During the intervening months each manager would carry out an action plan. This plan would be devised and reviewed with classmates and faculty during the first week, and then carried out during the months between weeks one and two. The purpose of this project would be to improve some deficiency in each manager's own performance or that of his or her organization. In order to take maximum advantage of the knowledge and expertise of the participants, as well as to engender intragroup relationships, members would also be encouraged to act as informal consultants for each other's projects.

Another important feature of the approved program was a process to collect data from each participant's superior, peers, and subordinates, prepare a participant-specific computer summary of the data, and feed it back to each person at appropriate points in the program. Data were collected with respect to each participant's behavior in the following areas: strategic management; motivating subordinates; leadership; communications; self management; and

WEEK TWO

	Sunday	Monday	Tuesday	Wednesday	Thursday	Friday
Morning		Strategic Management	Productivity (Work Design)	Human Resource Management	Case Completion Debriefing	Action Planning
Afternoon	Introduction Share Action Plan Results	Strategic Management	Productivity (Quality Circles)	HRM (Continued)	Implementation of Managerial Skills	Program Wrap-up and Participant Recognition
Evening	Action Plan Results (Continued)	Strategic Management	Key Issue Presentation	HRM Strategy and Design (Case)	Awards Night	

FIGURE 3

human resource management. When motivation was discussed, for example, each participant would receive a packet of information summarizing his or her superior's, peers', and subordinates' responses to questions about the individual's ability to motivate others. Also contained in the packet would be the participant's own response to the same questions.

These data would be collected in the weeks immediately preceding each new class, with all aspects of the process being handled by the faculty or other university personnel so that no person in the Company would know how a participant had been rated by co-workers, nor would any participant know how individual co-workers had evaluated him or her.

A final decision made at the design presentation was for the course designers to research and prepare Company-specific cases to be used in the program. Case topics would be chosen jointly with management for the purpose of describing actual Parker Hannifin experiences, both successful and unsuccessful, to add realism to case study exercises that would be an integral part of the curriculum.

Faculty Selection and Preparation. Because the designers believed that the success of the program would depend heavily upon the faculty's familiarity with the Corporation and participants' trust of the faculty, they decided that a maximum amount of the teaching and all personal counseling should be carried out by a small number of core instructors. In addition to teaching a large number of the program modules, at least one core faculty member would always be present while the program was in session, and all would join the participants during meals and social hours. The professors who best fitted the criteria for core faculty were the three who had designed the program. Accordingly, they were asked to serve as the core faculty. One of the three also agreed to serve as program coordinator and principal liaison with the Corporation.

With a relatively short time remaining until the first class would convene, the core faculty completed their own presentations, selected other professors to cover topics outside their areas of competence, and supervised the completion of other required details of the program.

Program Delivery

The first class convened in October, with the second week in February. The initial offering experienced two forms of growing pains, one expected and the other unexpected. As expected, participant critiques showed that the usefulness of some training modules was not apparent to the participants; in others, the organization or presentation simply had not worked well. For example, many participants did not agree that a management game was worthwhile. These problems were worked out without significant difficulty; there was a good deal of give and take between the faculty and company liaison, who by now had come to know each other very well.

The principal source of unexpected difficulty was the resistance of managers to suggestions of company shortcomings, even when the suggestions were supported by data from the recent manager survey. In addition to complicating the instructor's job, this reaction, typically by the most senior participants, noticeably intimidated all but the few most vocal managers, especially those who were new to the Company or who held relatively junior positions. In such instances, the faculty had to be extremely careful to avoid the emergence of an "us and them" relationship between faculty and students.

Two other unexpected occurrences deserve mention. First, because the program was new and represented a significant commitment on the part of Parker Hannifin, top management and the faculty had agreed that there should be relatively frequent visits by top management to demonstrate the importance of the program. Thus, during the initial class, there were relatively frequent visits by top management, including the President. The faculty quickly discovered, however, that the presence of such officials significantly restrained open discussion. Thereafter, visits by top management had to be scheduled more judiciously.

A second unexpected occurrence was immediate evidence indicating that the performance feedback from superiors, peers, and subordinates was both novel and very unsettling for many participants. It was the first time that most had ever received completely unadorned information showing what others actually thought about their behavior and performance. Recognizing the potentially harmful effect of such information without explanation and counseling, the faculty quickly redesigned the first week to afford each participant a private session with one of the core faculty in which the information could be explained and the participant could come to accept its implications.

Despite the expected and unexpected problems encountered in the inaugural class, surveys prepared by both the university and the Company after the first offering indicated that almost all the participants considered the program to be very valuable and recommended that it be continued. Accordingly, Company officials decided to enter into a formal arrangement with the university to continue the program and to expand it to two classes the following year.

Epilogue

The management development program is now in its third year. The corporate officers who supervised its design and early revisions continue to be its overseers. Two of the three university professors who developed the program have moved to other universities, but the third is still involved. Other professors have moved into the core faculty positions, and gradual improvements continue to be made, although the basic design is essentially unchanged.

Parker Hannifin has seriously discussed a further expansion, but this has not yet occurred. Although the program is generally regarded as being worthwhile by the Firm's representatives, they have been noticeably disappointed by the university's seeming inability or unwillingness to retain a stable faculty. Nevertheless, all indications are that the Firm plans to continue the program, and the relationship continues to be moderately profitable for the university.

34. Kirkridge Mountain Laboratories*

Howard Alan Amer was a physically imposing person: six feet eight inches tall, two hundred ninety pounds, and a shaved head. Howard was independently wealthy. While getting his BBA and MBA degrees at Golden State University he parlayed the money he earned from running the Xerox concession on campus into a multi-million dollar estate by shrewd investment in the stock market as well as by capitalizing a number of small high-technology businesses. In 1978, on his forty-fourth birthday, wealthy, successful and in good health, Howard became severely depressed.

After fifteen months of psychotherapy Howard concluded that the cause of his depression was that he felt that he had not contributed anything to the betterment of mankind. He felt guilty because all of his efforts had been for his own personal gain and benefit. In November 1979 he applied for and got the job of Director of the Kirkridge Mountain Laboratories (The Mount, as it was referred to by employees) at Cooper University. Cooper was a large university which engaged in widespread research. The Kirkridge Mountain Laboratories were involved in research primarily in electronics and geophysics.

In his position as Director of the Laboratories Howard felt that he could fulfill his need to contribute to humanity by using his business and administrative experience. The laboratory had been running in the red for four years. Howard was encouraged to use his skills to turn around the organization's sluggish financial performance.

Previous to this, administrative and budget activities were the responsibility of the individual division or department heads, who were Ph.D. scientists and professors with no formal business or management experience. The research establishment was formally organized by discipline, which meant that people were functionally grouped by skills or knowledge. This didn't entirely correspond with academic disciplines (mechanical, electrical, chemical engineering), but rather was treated as an area of specialization.

The Board of Trustees felt that there was a need for "professional managers" to run the research laboratories. "Business principles needed to be applied, especially to those labs losing money." Each of the laboratories on campus was reorganized, and Howard was hired to manage Kirkridge Mountain Labs. Kirkridge was reorganized into a project system in which the basic administrative structure of the laboratory was contingent upon the task or project for which there was a technical program and a plan for achieving a goal of a technical nature. The basic departments or divisions, which were clustered administratively by specialties, were not eliminated, but primary functional administrative focus changed to a project system.

Howard fully agreed with the structural reorganization of Kirkridge from a system organized solely by disciplines to one that was organically defined by project. "In a highly scientific and research oriented organization, good creative

*Martin R. Moser, Ph.D., Assistant Professor of Management, Clark University's Graduate School of Management, Worcester, Massachusetts.

relationships and good personal relationships between scientists are extremely important. The project system encourages the growth of these relationships by lessening the chances of interdepartmental rivalries and competition through focusing on task objectives. It encourages the growth of a team spirit." Howard made a very strong impression during his job interview.

Howard's recent experiences in group pyschotherapy at the Center for the Whole Being sensitized him to the importance of "interpersonal relationships." He had always been a loner, rarely working closely with other people. He now felt that he had missed many opportunities for professional as well as personal growth because of his "fears of letting anybody get too close" to him.

Howard instituted weekly divisional and project staff meetings over which he presided or, as some observed, reigned by his dominant physical presence. The purpose of these meetings was twofold: to take care of administrative business as well as to develop interpersonal relationships through the use of group process exercises such as role playing, feedback, simulation games, etc. Howard also required division and project heads to meet individually with each of their staff people for one hour each week.

In February Howard met with Rebecca Youngblood, his boss, and the President of Cooper University. Dr. Youngblood came to Cooper in 1957 for her first job as a librarian after completing her Masters degree in Library Science. In 1964 she was appointed Director of the University Library. From 1968–1970 she took a leave of absence to complete her Doctorate in Educational Administration. In 1975, when she became administrative assistant to the President of the University, she left a library which had become one of the most prestigious and well-run university libraries in the country. Dr. Youngblood was appointed President of Cooper University in January 1979. Dr. Youngblood was fifty-one years old, single, and deeply devoted to her career in higher education. Her goal was to turn Cooper into one of the country's top teaching and research institutions. It was her direct influence which stimulated the reorganization of the research laboratories. "I've heard through the grapevine that you have made some very interesting changes at the Mount. I'd like to hear your thinking about the changes you are implementing and the long and short range goals you have in mind for the laboratory."

This was the first time Howard met with the President alone. He had spoken to her twice during his interview process and had heard the usual scuttlebutt from other employees. She was regarded as a competent, no-nonsense, but fair manager. "I'm attempting to remold the basic structures of the laboratory. It had not been managed as it should have been in the past. An R&D facility needs to be managed differently than a manufacturing organization. Kirkbridge had been managed as if it were a manufacturing concern. I'm attempting to develop new patterns and styles of communications which I believe are necessary for this type of environment. In the short run there won't be too much change in terms of productivity and output. In fact, I'm expecting a substantial decline. Behavioral habits and established routines of communicating are hard to change. But by building a new foundation, based on communication patterns necessary for an organization like Kirkridge, we will develop the basis of a sound and creative research organization."

Dr. Youngblood listened attentively to Howard's comments. "In other words, what you are saying is that you are implementing behavioral changes and that it will take some time to develop. Further, you are claiming that these new patterns of communications will increase the efficiency and effectiveness of Kirkridge in the long run. What is your projected time frame before we can see the results of remolding?"

Howard quickly responded, "The place will settle down in less than a year. At that point there will be a gradual but steady increase in output and efficiency.

Dr. Youngblood nodded her head and looked directly at Howard. "I'm relying on your expertise as a business manager to carry out your plans. That's the reason we hired you. Feel free to contact me if you feel you need to. You will be working autonomously and I will not intervene or undermine your activities unless I believe that you are not doing your job effectively."

By late summer a number of people had left Kirkridge, including two department heads, Harold Orlow and Richard Runko. Some expressed that their main reason for leaving were the newly imposed meeting requirements and the emphasis on interpersonal relations at the laboratories. "It invades our privacy," they stated. Orlow wrote a ten-page letter to Youngblood which was critical of the reorganization and Amer's management abilities. He sent each of the members of the University's Board of Trustees a copy of the letter. Four Board members called President Youngblood in regard to the letter. The President defended Howard's tactics.

Howard perceived the turnover at the lab as a positive sign. "People left Kirkridge because they wouldn't change their communications patterns and were unwilling to adapt to the new structure." He felt that his plans for the laboratory were going well.

Howard received a telephone call from President Youngblood. "I wanted to let you know that I have received a number of calls from concerned Board members. Harold Orlow wrote each Board member a very critical letter about you and your management tactics. I defended you in my conversations with them, but I want to let you know I am becoming a bit concerned. I have to meet with them at the beginning of December and I'm not sure of what I will be able to do if they demand some assurances about your plans."

Howard was annoyed. "First of all why wasn't I given a copy of Orlow's letter? Secondly, I told you what you should expect at our meeting in February and you told me that you had confidence in me and that you would leave me alone. I am concerned at your subtle pressure tactic of calling me without preparing me. Send me a copy of the damn letter and then we can talk." He hung up the receiver without waiting for an answer, put on his coat and went home.

The next day some members of the administrative staff of Kirkridge came to Dr. Youngblood's office. Stewart Evans, the Personnel Officer at the lab, spoke first, "I apologize for coming unannounced to your office, Dr. Youngblood, but we didn't want to take a chance of Howard finding out that we were going to meet with you. The reason we are here is to tell you our perceptions of what is happening at the Mount. We feel that we are not being listened to by Howard. He has his own ideas about how to do things and does not accept any feedback from us. We would like you to know what some of us are thinking."

Peter Bourne, head of the Physics Division, spoke next. "I think that the basic problem with Kirkridge is that it does not have the minimum number of people necessary for a Research and Development Laboratory. R&D is a very complex activity. In most cases the development of new products or processes requires a wide diversity of talents and knowledge. An R&D laboratory like the Mount needs to have a minimum size of about one thousand people if we are to compete effectively with major labs like Lincoln, Battelle, and the like. We're now operating with less than six hundred employees. We need to increase our numbers until we reach the minimum number of people needed to effectively operate a faculty such as ours. I don't believe that the change in structure will have any significant impact on our effectiveness as a research organization. In fact, as a result of the changes, we have already lost a number of very good people."

Ira Romoff, Electrical Engineering Department Head, added the following, "I go along with Peter's analysis that our organization does not have enough people in order to effectively carry out the tasks that we are involved in. An R&D organization needs diversity but there is an alternative to hiring four hundred new people. We can develop outside consulting support. By doing this we can still involve the additional people we need, but we don't have to add the additional expense of hiring four hundred full-time employees. Overall, we can involve enough consultants in our activities to get the kind of diversity we are looking for, and also save a lot of money by not having to provide the support and fringe services full-time people would require. The restructuring that is going on now is treating the symptom and not the real problem."

Henry Miller, Department Head of the Psychology Division, was next to speak. "My point of view is in close alignment with Howard's. I don't think increasing our size deals with the real problem. The issue is not that we need to increase the diversity and talents of the organization. We already have a wide range of diversity and talent. What we need to do is to continue to work on techniques and devices for improving our internal communications. We already have the talent, but we don't know how to effectively communicate with one another. The problem of keeping current within our own disciplines, not to mention interdisciplinary sharing, is acute in our organization. I think Howard is hitting the nail right square on the head with what he is doing. Increasing our size or bringing in outside people will only make things worse. Changing communication patterns is the first step and we are attempting to make it."

Just at that point Dr. Youngblood's telephone rang. It was Bob Alberti, Dr. Youngblood's secretary. "Howard Amer called and asked if he could talk to you. I told him that you were already meeting with some of his staff members. He said he would be right over. He sounded a little angry."

35. C Company (I)*

Assignment

After reading the following problem, develop a list of interview questions that will be useful in conducting an assessment of company practices.

Problem

You are a team of management consultants hired to assess the current management practices in the corporate offices and the Research and Development Division of a large, heavy equipment Manufacturing Company. The product line of the company is limited to industrial motors such as those used in overhead cranes, heavy moving equipment, road building equipment, and motors to power large trucks. The company designs and makes both gas and diesel engines. Approximately 200 professional and/or managerial employees are located in the corporate offices, and 200 in the R & D division. You plan to interview a select sample of 50 to 75 employees at various levels in the organization, from eleven departments. The sample will be selected with the aid of the Personnel Vice-President and is intended to include employees at various age levels, with various years of tenure with the company, and with various perspectives and educational backgrounds.

Specifically, the management is interested in having you develop questions which, when asked, could render answers to the following questions:

1. How should the company corporate offices and R & D divisions be organized, i.e., should it have a classical, organic, a mix of two, or some other kind of structure?
2. What are the kinds of policies and practices that will
   - most likely motivate employees?
   - most likely attract and retain employees?
   - most likely develop employee ability to improve job performance?
3. What style of leadership should the company be attempting to select and develop for the management of its corporate offices and R & D Divisions?

Group Discussion Assignment

Since this is a planning session for the consulting team, the problem is to develop a list of interview questions that will be used to guide team members in the investigation.

*This case was prepared by Robert J. House, University of Toronto, and John R. Rizzo, Western Michigan University, and is used here with their permission.

Assumptions

You are to assume there is no universal "best way" to manage, and that the organizational structure, leader style, and motivational strategy of the company will depend on what you find in the interviews. Assume that after conducting the interviews you will have another planning meeting to develop recommendations for the company management. The problem before you is to develop the key questions to be answered in the investigation.

C Company (II)

Problem

After reading the following interview findings, prepare notes to answer the following questions:

1. What are the appropriate organizational structures and leadership style for this company?
2. How should the company go about making the necessary changes?

Discuss this question thoroughly and be prepared to defend your position to the class.

Assumption

Assume that as a result of your investigation your team has been able to agree on the following description of the client company.

Interview Findings

The following description of the company is based on actual interviews with seventy-five members of a large heavy equipment manufacturing company. The interviewees included nine vice-presidents of the corporation and sixty-six others who the personnel vice-president selected on the basis of criteria suggested by the consultant. The personnel vice-president was requested to select persons in all divisions who (a) represented a wide variety of experience, perspective, age, and training, and (b) would be willing to give frank opinions concerning their perceptions of the organizational climate, the leadership styles of superiors, their satisfactions and dissatisfactions, and any problems they were experiencing in carrying out their responsibilities. Of the seventy-five interviewees approximately forty were in supervisory or managerial positions. The remainder were in engineering or corporate staff groups such as finance, marketing research, or personnel. The interviewees were generally very cooperative and willing to share their perceptions and feelings in the interviews. Approximately twelve interviewees appeared to be unwilling to share feelings, and restricted their comments to descriptive rather than evaluative statements. The results of the interviews are reported here.

In general, the interviews revealed an organization seeking to excel and grow, offering its members opportunity and challenge in the endeavor. Yet many employees were experiencing a marked degree of frustration, tension, and stress.

More specifically, interviewees described an organization highly motivated toward the maintenance of a large share of a growing and increasingly competitive market. Within this framework, there existed opportunity for individual success and contribution. It was reported that higher management dealt with problems openly and fairly, and treated recommendations from below with thoroughness and objectivity. The interviewees' statements also suggested that the firm appeared remarkably free of political maneuvering.

However, the organization was not without significant problems. The manner in which the foregoing attributes manifested themselves created substantial personal and organizational strains. For example, there was an emphasis on short-run productivity and activity designed to meet day-to-day problems. The emphasis on the immediate was perceived to occur at the expense of long-range projects and of creative efforts designed to both prevent the day-to-day "firefighting" and to enable continued growth and market penetration. Communication often consisted of ambiguous changing and inconsistent directions frequently coming from different sources several levels above one's immediate superior. Cases of alleged unwarranted or unexplained change, incompatible goals, and the like, were frequently reported. Cases of exasperation and cross-pressure on individuals seemed commonplace. Downward communication was highly work-oriented and impersonal. The rationale and intent of directions often went unexplained and frequently took the form of requests for information or productivity which required individuals to work toward seemingly uncoordinated, short-run efforts. Upward communication consisted of progress reports, responses to inquiries, and requests for approval. The latter was viewed duplicative, delaying, and representative of failure to delegate. Many signatures were required for approval of expenditures budgeted earlier. There was a lack of philosophy, policy, or stable objectives to guide work. Minor reorganizations were almost commonplace, and major reorganizations were not uncommon. These conditions prevented the development of cooperative and coordinative team efforts.

At the individual level, there existed little in the way of orientation upon employment or systematic training and development efforts. New employees had to rely on their own sensitivities to obtain a "feel" for both company needs and the definition of an acceptable contribution. High rewards for outstanding performances were promised to individuals early in their careers, but to attain them a visible and outstanding contribution was expected within the first two years of employment.

One form of evidence that the firm sought exceptional individual achievement existed in its recruitment practices. Approximately eight years prior to the time of the study, the company recruited a number of top students from prominent midwestern graduate business schools. Four years later, the recruiting effort was redirected to prominent Ivy League and California schools. In many cases these new employees were given upper-middle management and staff positions of considerable responsibility, or placed as assistants to key top officers. Several assistants became vice-presidents of the firm. This recruiting practice resulted in frustration and resentment among those already in the firm, for newly recruited groups filled positions and assumed responsibilities which might have served as rewards for others. Consequently, longer tenured employees perceived the reward system as emphasizing educational credentials rather than service and experience. This contributed to turnover in the "forgotten" groups. There were also frequent incidents of new top recruits leaving due to lack of receptivity to their ideas, or having to fill unchallenging positions.

The foregoing was coupled with a narrow-based reward system consisting primarily of economic (pay, bonus) and status (promotion) recognitions.

This situation was exacerbated by several other related conditions. The criteria used to evaluate performance were perceived as ambiguous, and sometimes inconsistent. And peer competition (though not malicious) was reported as very high. Appraisal took place behind closed doors, and feed-back on performance usually occurred after the reward had been determined and approved at levels far above the immediate superior. Although the members of top management were generally viewed as sincere in their intent, and dealt with *operational* problems openly, *personnel* decisions were dealt with secretly and management was viewed as "past and blame oriented," seeking to find who was responsible for errors rather than treating errors as learning experiences to be avoided in the future.

Hence, individuals were surrounded with cues of success and failure, sensed the importance of achievement in an aggressive and energetic firm, yet were left ambiguous regarding evaluation in a blame-oriented climate. Supportiveness, coaching, feedback, and mutual confidence necessary for cooperative team efforts were lacking. These conditions created a great deal of uncertainty, tension, and strain for many individuals. They constitute, basically, a stress climate. In summary, the characteristics of the organization suggested by the interviews were:

- Aggressive, achievement-oriented firm
- Well-intended, sincere top management
- Open, fair receptivity and resolution of problems
- Low political and malicious behavior, open discussion
- Emphasis on short-run productivity and innovation
- Downward task-oriented communication
- Changing, conflicting, or ambiguous directives
- Lack of clear policies or philosophy
- Individual motivation to achieve and succeed
- Ambiguous criteria used in personnel decisions
- Blame orientation
- Low feedback, coaching, team efforts
- Limited base of rewards
- Uncertainty, tension, stress

Technological Environmental Description

Having described the internal structural and interpersonal characteristics of the organization, we now turn to the primary technology and the external environment of the organization.

The company designs, assembles, and markets its own products, the major product being a heavy industrial capital goods item that is assembled in the main domestic plant from parts manufactured there, in other plants, or by suppliers. Annual sales of the company had increased over the last five years from $175,000,000 to $330,000,000. At the time of the interviews the company employed 14,500 employees.

The industry in which the company operates is one in which technological advancements are infrequent. There have been no fundamentally new products introduced in the industry in the last ten years. However, the existing products and manufacturing processes of the industry change continually as a result of product and process modification. Such change is change in degree rather than kind, however, reflecting incremental advances in technology rather than major breakthroughs into fundamentally new products. Competition, increasing in the industry, is based primarily on cost reduction, marketing service, improvement in existing product capabilities, increases in product life, and ability to meet customer demands for delivery and customization of fixtures.

Products are produced in response to customer orders in lots ranging from a few to several thousand. The major components of the product are almost always standard parts but even these are numberous. Furthermore, each order has a different combination of fixtures, and occasionally minor parts will be manufactured specifically to meet customer requirements. Hence, although an assembly line exists, it must be highly responsive in meeting varied orders.

Although the firm varied the basic product greatly, there seemed to exist marked opportunity to systematization and standardization of production and assembly. Evidence for this lies in the fact that there existed in the firm strong differences of opinion regarding standardization versus responsiveness to all customer demands for modifications. Many felt that much more was possible in the way of standardization and reduction in order variances, while others felt that responsiveness and a job-shop operation were major strengths of the firm.

Description of Task Structures

The tasks of the majority of the employees were semi-structured since they were almost all engaged in somewhat repetitive, analytic work (such as product engineering, personnel, marketing, and financial analysis).

Immediate superiors neither completely lacked position power nor had the complete power over the career welfare of their subordinates. The employees in the organization units studied were all classified as professional or managerial employees, and the majority of them possessed educational credentials or technical skills that are in high demand in American industry. Consequently, dependence on either their immediate supervisors or the company for career welfare and employment security was minimal.

Part VI

Career Development

Cases Outline

36. Career Management—The Case of Len White *

Len White's Career

Len White is a vice-president and head of the New Services Development Unit (NSDU) at Metrobank. He has been in his current position for two years, with Metrobank for eight years, and out of college for seventeen years. Reflecting on his career, Len feels that things have progressed well. He earns $80,000 plus bonuses each year, has a budget of $1.3 million, and has the ear of several top managers. Yet the promotion he is interested in—to senior vice-president—still seems out of reach. He is unsure of what he must accomplish to attain his goal.

Len describes his high school and college years as very active. In high school he was involved in many social activities. He participated in sports and ran for student association president but lost. In college he joined a fraternity and played interfraternity sports, but failed to make the two college varsity teams he wanted. Women moved in and out of Len's life until he met Jan in his senior year. They married two years later.

After receiving his undergraduate degree in liberal arts, Len entered an MBA program at a major state university. He majored in marketing and sought employment in companies with good prospects for expansion. Using the University's MBA placement services, Len interviewed with several firms in the consumer package goods industry. He received job offers from two firms and decided to go with CPH, which was the sixth largest in the industry. Len commented on this decision: "I felt CPH would give me the best training and career advancement opportunities. The company had a formalized career ladder for product managers (i.e., the manager responsible for all marketing, sales, and production aspects of a product), paid well, and was prestigious. If you made it in CPH, you could go anywhere in the industry."

*Stephen A. Stumpf and Thomas P. Mullen, New York University Schools of Business, adapted from Stephen A. Stumpf and Manuel London, *Managing Careers,* © 1982, Addison-Wesley, Reading, Ma., pp. 15–27. Reprinted with permission. We appreciate the cooperation of the individuals and organizations involved in the case. All names are disguised.

Len's simple but clear idea of his short-term goal was to become a product manager. His first job was as an assistant product manager on a new bar soap. This position involved substantial numerical analysis of market and competitive information by product, package size, geographical region, type of distributor, etc., and was the first step in the product manager career path. Assuming acceptable performance in a "number crunching" role, he would be promoted to associate product manager within two years. A second promotion to product manager normally occurred two to three years later. His responsibility would increase with each promotion so that promotion to product manager would give him primary control over a single product. This included product pricing, distribution, packaging, market segmentation, advertising, and product promotion. Since one's budget and product were part of a group of related products, his decisions as a product manager would have to fit the product group manager's strategy.

Although Len felt that his early career goals were clear, he reported that initially he knew relatively little about what an assistant product manager actually did. The stereotype Len had was that a product manager would manage a product, develop it by making changes, and coordinate the efforts of subordinates. Hence Len's first few years, although interesting and developmental, did not meet the expectations he had formed as an MBA.

Establishing Himself at CPH

During his first five years, Len's career was managed primarily by CPH; he was seldom consulted on job changes or career interests. After nine months, Len was moved to another product (a fabric softener) within the same product group but under a different product manager. While CPH referred to the move as a developmental rotation, Len was not sure how to interpret it at first: "Was I being transferred because I was good and needed elsewhere, because I needed additional development not available in my current position, or because my immediate superior did not want me any more?" The skills CPH was trying to develop in Len by the transfer were not made clear.

After a two-month adjustment to his new work associates and the duties of the new position, Len reported that analyzing fabric softener data was really no different from working on a bar soap. The fabric softener was somewhat more interesting to Len, given the recent changes in the fabric softener market. More judgments had to be made based on less information, and he was involved in some of those judgments. Len's family situation had also changed—he was the father of a seven-pound newborn boy.

The Advancement Years

During his second year at CPH Len was promoted to associate product manager on the fabric softener. He was transferred ten months later to a new clothes washing detergent, and moved back after a year to a fabric softener as a product manager. While each move was somewhat disruptive to Len's social relationships at work, he met several people, whom he worked with indirectly during this period, who would subsequently affect other career moves. The most notable of these was a superior, Pete Fallon. "I really enjoyed and learned from Pete. He was one of those people who was always getting involved with new things."

After being in the product manager position for a year, Len examined the aspects of various jobs that he liked and disliked. "I liked the feelings of success, the exhilaration of being promoted and accepted, and the career opportunities CPH seemed to offer." However, several concerns were growing: "Did I want to proceed into management which would involve more attention to financial data, accounting reports, and interpersonal relationships, or should I stay with my marketing specialty? How should I proceed from here—just work hard, conform to CPH, innovate, find and nurture political support, and/or be an outstanding contributor?" A third issue related to managing his family relationships in light of the long hours devoted to CPH. He and Jan were expecting another child.

By the end of his third year as a product manager Len realized that the managerial career path was not right for him. He still wanted the higher salary, power, and prestige associated with managing, but not the day-to-day worries, interruptions, coordination hassles, meetings, and continual firefighting. Working on new products was more exciting, seemed to involve less general management, and was more marketing-oriented than working with established products. He felt technically competent in marketing and enjoyed exercising his expertise in new products. Since Len had previously worked with the current group manager for new products, Pete Fallon, it was easy to approach Pete with his career concerns. Several months later when Pete was transferred, he recommended Len as his replacement Len was subsequently offered the position of group manager for new products. "It was one of the happiest times of my life. My career seemed to be going in a direction that felt good; I enjoyed going to work. My family was settled into a new home. My son was five; my daughter was four months old and she was finally sleeping through the night."

Len's job over the next three years included another promotion to senior group manager for new laundry and cleaning products. His most notable project was developing and analyzing the plans for a new plant to manufacture two new products. The plant would cost $20,000,000 to build, involve hiring 2,000 workers, and be the sole producer of two new products as well as have the flexibility to produce several existing products.

Quite unexpectedly, Len was approached by an executive search firm regarding a position in a smaller competing firm (Cleanit) that would involve the strategic redirection and expansion of its household cleaner line. Len's name was given to the executive search firm by an ex-associate at CPH who was now with Cleanit. "With relatively little investigation of the position, I decided to take it. The salary was better, the challenge was clear and entirely marketing related, and after eleven years with CPH I was beginning to feel the need for change." While the position had potential, the rest of Cleanit was not yet ready for strategic redirection or innovative ideas. When an opportunity at Metrobank presented itself eight months later, Len made another career move.

New Roles at Metrobank

Metrobank had been actively recruiting senior product managers from the consumer package goods firms to meet its goal of becoming a national consumer bank. Metrobank's goals required rapid expansion, new banking services, and greater market penetration. It was looking for an experienced and successful senior product manager to start as a vice-president.

"I probably would not have changed firms so easily during this period if it had involved relocation. But it did not. Besides, I missed working for one of the top firms in the industry. Smaller firms didn't have the resources I needed to do new product development. Since I was only thirty-six, I felt I could risk another move, especially one that promised opportunities for growth and advancement."

The move to Metrobank was a major one in that the organization, its environment, and its products (actually services) were very different from the organizations, environment, and products in the consumer package goods industry. Yet Len agreed with Metrobank that his marketing and new product development expertise would transfer to banking. Having been disappointed with his brief tenure at Cleanit, Len interviewed with four Metrobank executives.

"It was the discussion with Metrobank's president that convinced me. Metrobank was one of the top twenty commercial banks in the U.S. It was embarking on a statewide expansion program that could ultimately double its size, and I had an opportunity to be in the middle of it. I would also be doing the kind of work I wanted to do—new product development and marketing."

During Len's first year at Metrobank he was involved in a new retail banking expansion program; he was learning about marketing financial services by being in the field and talking to branch bank presidents, officers, and consumers. About the middle of the year the legal/regulatory environment changed to permit statewide branch offices. The project quickly moved into the "brick and mortar" stage with twenty-three branches being opened throughout the state during the next few years.

By the end of his first year with Metrobank, an even bigger challenge was presented: the use of minicomputer machines to supplement bank tellers. Len became the lead marketing manager on a task force that might revolutionize branch banking. However, there were technical and marketing challenges that could result in millions of dollars of losses rather than a successful new approach to branch banking: "Could we get consumers to use the machines?" Len organized and implemented marketing research which subsequently suggested that consumers would use machines under certain favorable conditions such as low risk of robbery, provision of receipt, easy access and use, and "idiot-proof" transactions. Once it was reasonably clear that consumers would accept the technological change, it was necessary to get senior management's approval.

Len gave several presentations on the project to senior management (John Snow) and business unit managers in the Retail Banking Unit. After several months of discussion, presentation, financial analysis, and market research, the go-ahead was given: (1) to invest $16 million in bank machines, (2) to redesign branches to permit 24-hour access to machines, and (3) to heavily advertise the new service system.

After more than two years of task force development, the new systems were installed in over 100 branch banks. Len moved into the role of market strategy development specialist for the Retail Banking Unit, Consumer Banking Group (CBG), of Metrobank. After six months Len's role was changed as part of a major reorganization. Len subsequently became Head of Marketing, CBG.

During the development of the machine banking system, Len first met John Snow, head of CBG. When CBG was reorganized, Len began to report directly to Snow at Snow's request. Over the next three years, Metrobank continued its efforts to become a national consumer bank by offering banking services via direct mail (e.g., card products such as VISA and MasterCard, traveler's checks, etc.). Federal regulations prevented branch banking across state lines, hence efforts to become a national bank lacked the physical presence offered by a branch banking system. Len's role as head of group marketing was to provide marketing guidance to the various businesses within CBG on their development of new services.

After three years of working with the CBG businesses with some notable new services successes and failures, Len White suggested to John Snow that "the business units (e.g., Retail Banking, Card Products, Traveler's Checks) just don't know how to develop and integrate new services into their businesses. They are consumed with day-to-day operations; new services get second shift. What is needed is a new services development unit to help institutionalize the new services development process and pass along expertise."

After hearing such suggestions several times, John Snow created the New Services Development Unit (NSDU) as a temporary unit with an expected life of two or three years to get new services developed and implemented throughout CBG. John Snow commented on his decision to create such a unit: "We have been trying to develop new products for several years with only moderate success. Len knew more about new product development than any of the business unit managers or other staff members. The time was right to create a task force to improve our hit record with new products. I might have acted on Len's suggestion earlier except that Len has not always worked effectively with the business unit managers in his role on CBG staff. Sometimes his marketing expertise is perceived to get in the way of running a business. Len does not have 'bottom line' responsibility whereas the business unit managers do. Since it is difficult to determine the cost effectiveness of marketing methods and activities, ideas get suggested that are not easy to evaluate. When a business unit manager rejects marketing ideas or, more typically, stalls action on them, Len has been known to show his frustration. Hence, this new position should give Len some autonomy to get the job done."

During his first two years as head of NSDU, Len and his staff of fourteen banking professionals and six clerical assistants developed four new services. Two were implemented, and two were placed on hold by senior management pending a change in the legal/regulatory environment. Four other new services had been conceptualized and looked favorable based on initial qualitative research on marketability. The NSDU was doing well. However, the latest reorganization of Metrobank and CBG resulted in two layers of management now separating Len from John Snow. John Snow had been promoted and a new layer of management had been created. (See Figure 1.)

The success of NSDU and the Metrobank reorganization stimulated Len's thoughts regarding his career. "Where do I want to go from here? Have I leveled off at age forty-four? Am I beginning to stagnate? Should I redirect my efforts to teaching others and pass my expertise on to my subordinates? What can a staff person do to continue to progress in a line-oriented organization?"

APPENDIX

Metrobank as an Employer

Two years prior to Len's employment at Metrobank, the bank began to design and implement a human resource planning and career development system which would provide: (1) a personnel data base to identify and categorize top talent,

(2) a management information system to make use of the data base in filling critical jobs, and (3) a career development program to ensure that the careers of the most talented individuals were being managed effectively.

The need for a personnel inventory, allocation process, and career development program stemmed from rapid growth and market expansion into additional consumer banking services. Managerial jobs at many levels were being created due to the expansion, and there was insufficient talent within the organization to fill the newly created positions. This lack of available talent from within heightened the need for future human resource planning. Dozens of management trainees were hired, many with MBA degrees from top-ranking universities. While the management trainees progressed rapidly to the junior officer level, there was still a gap in managerial talent in middle management.

Len White was hired at the time Metrobank was hiring many middle level managers from outside the banking industry. Based on an analysis of current and future needs, top management identified two areas of expertise that were needed but not currently available within the banking industry: marketing managers and operations managers. The former were recruited from major consumer package goods firms, the latter from manufacturing organizations such as Ford and General Motors.

Metrobank followed the strategy of hiring highly skilled middle managers to reduce their training costs and shorten the amount of time required for a new hire to become effective. The underlying assumption was that it would be more efficient to transfer marketing or operations management skills to banking than to train bankers in marketing or operations management. Given this strategy, it was necessary to develop the new hire's knowledge of banking.

New middle managers and college hires were typically assigned to several projects and rotated through several positions in their first few years to provide developmental experiences. However, the dramatic growth of Metrobank made adhering to historic career paths difficult. The results of this unilateral organizational career management with little regard for individual career plans did not become clear for several years. Many individuals were progressing rapidly; middle management was viewed as effective, and Metrobank was rated as one of the best managed corporations in the United States by *Dun's Review*. While some managers were highly committed to Metrobank, others were not and quietly waited for an opportunity to leave. Turnover among recent college hires was higher than the industry average. This increased the costs of recruitment and selection, and lowered productivity at the junior officer level.

The group within Metrobank of which Len's unit was a member had not begun to utilize the human resource planning and career development systems to any noticeable extent. The pressure of rapid expansion, both geographically and through new product development, had put significant pressure on the group. As a result, any new systems, while recognized as important and useful, were considered too time consuming to investigate fully or implement at this time.

Historically, Metrobank had encouraged an informal but strong mentor/ sponsor approach to career planning. It was felt that the better young managers would be identified and coached by more experienced managers while the mediocre and poor managers were treated with benign neglect.

While CBG adhered to this informal policy, several formal human resource functions were also part of the group. CBG, with 200 officer personnel and 2,000 exempt and non-exempt workers, had its own Personnel Office. This office was divided into two departments around functional activities. The two departments are presented below:

Hiring	Evaluation and Development
• recruiting	• compensation and benefits
• compensation	• training and development
• job analysis	• Equal Employment Opportunity (EEO)/ Affirmative Action Planning (AAP)
	• performance appraisal

The Hiring Department was the larger of the two and focused primarily on recruiting high potential individuals for entry level and middle management positions. At the entry level they recruited primarily from the top twenty business schools. Upper management believed that you "get what you pay for" and the average starting salary for new recruits was in the upper 20 percent for the industry. A similar policy was used for filling the middle ranks of management during the group's rapid expansion. CBG paid what was necessary to hire the right people to meet their needs.

Job analysis was used primarily by the Hiring Department for middle level positions. Management believed that intelligent new recruits could be molded to particular jobs and the Metrobank culture. As a result, job analysis was not typically used for entry level positions.

The Evaluation and Development Department was considered largely administrative in function. In the compensation area, line managers were given a pool of money three months prior to the annual performance appraisal period from which they drew salary increases for those within their unit. Guidelines for this process were distributed to unit managers but no policy for adhering to the guidelines was enforced.

Training and development was managed internally by a small staff of professionals who worked with the business units to identify programs that were needed. Primary emphasis was on targeting this effort to meet the specific, immediate needs of CBG. Outside consultants were used frequently to augment the internal staff for both designing and implementing these training activities. Programs developed by consultants were owned by Metrobank and considered proprietary.

More generally, the training and development area was expected to pay its own way and therefore needed to generate sufficient cash flow to cover expenses. As a result, each unit sending managers to a program was charged for this service. Rates were comparable to those charged by outside organizations such as the American Management Association (AMA), and managers were free to select between internal training or training at AMA-type institutions.

EEO/AAP activities were largely routine and were administered consistent with Metrobank's corporate-wide Fair Employment Policy. This policy incorporated all existing legislation in this area within a Metrobank-wide Position and Guidelines Statement which was widely distributed throughout the bank. Any major personnel problems or labor disputes were referred to the Metrobank legal department. The centralization of this particular function was done to ensure that the public image of Metrobank was protected.

Performance appraisals were done by each of the units within CBG on an annual basis. Performance appraisal forms—distributed by the Evaluation and Development Department and used by most managers—were frequently modified and augmented by individual units. Organization charts and job descriptions were used with much difficulty because of frequent reorganizations. As one manager said, "Organizational charts are useless. I get a new one at each performance appraisal."

Evaluation of performance was based primarily on one's ability to achieve unit objectives. With the decentralized, profit-center orientation managers were expected to show results within six to nine months. Financial objectives for each unit were identified annually and performance was evaluated against these objectives on a quarterly basis. Judgments by upper management about new managers within a division were made quickly; once formulated they were difficult to change. For cost centers, such as the New Product Development Unit managed by Len White, performance evaluations were judged on the response NSDU received from line managers. Frequently, the careers of cost center managers were made or broken by the evaluations of the line managers who interacted with center.

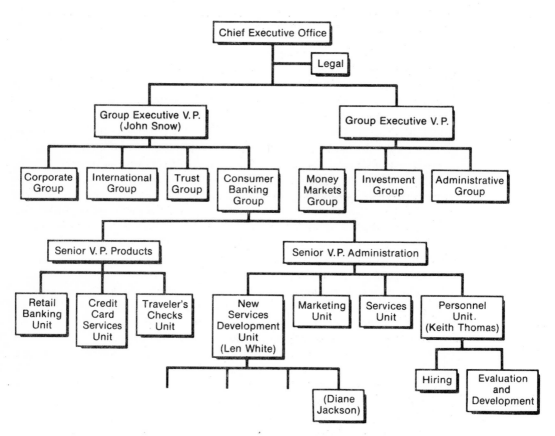

FIGURE 1. Metrobank

Managers throughout Metrobank with unsatisfactory performance were generally not fired. A lateral transfer to a less important area was usually arranged. However, the culture was such that lower performing managers frequently left on their own accord. Metrobank was considered an upwardly mobile company and internal competition was heated. As one executive in the Personnel Office noted, "Managers who do not move up quickly realize the opportunities within the bank were very limited." As a result, many managers leave Metrobank each year.

Metrobank recently estimated the cost of management trainee turnover to range from $20,000 to $100,000 *per person* depending on the type of position and amount of formal in-house training required. Given the turnover of high-potential individuals whom Metrobank had hoped not to lose, the cost of replacing management trainees was several million dollars per year.

37. Career Management—The Case of Diane Jackson*

Diane Jackson's Career

After receiving an undergraduate degree in mathematics, Diane Jackson started work at Metrobank in computer services. She left after one year to get her MBA. She worked as a summer intern the following year in a different Metrobank group. By the time she completed her MBA, she had developed an interest in marketing and received several job offers. She chose Metrobank because she was familiar with the company and felt that Metrobank offered the combination of financial analysis, computer applications, and marketing that she wanted. Her first post-MBA year with the bank involved financial analysis work within the Consumer Banking Group (CBG). She was given an opportunity to work on the minicomputer banking machine task force when the machines were first considered for in-branch use. The assignment "sounded like fun" so she took it. This was Diane's first contact with Len White.

Diane worked on the banking machine task force for nearly two years and was promoted to assistant vice-president in the process. Since it was a task force, it was to be disbanded upon the successful implementation of the systems and services. This meant that task force members needed to find positions in other CBG business units. In her task force work, she developed contacts with officers in the Credit Card Services Unit and they subsequently offered her a position. She was also offered an opportunity to manage a branch within the Retail Banking Unit

*Thomas P. Mullen and Stephen A. Stumpf, New York University Schools of Business, adapted from Stephen A. Stumpf and Manuel London, *Managing Careers,* © 1982, Addison-Wesley, Reading, Ma., pp. 65–80. Reprinted with permission. All names are disguised.

which she turned down. "I didn't want to manage a branch, or even a group of branches. I figured Retail Banking was probably the way to progress quickly in Metrobank, but I didn't want that job." The position Diane accepted involved new services development work for Credit Card Services (e.g., VISA, MasterCard). Diane again crossed paths with Len White while working in this department. Now Len was head of CBG marketing.

Diane worked in Credit Card Services for six months before being transferred to the newly created New Services Development Unit (NSDU) headed by Len White. She reported to Len through an intermediate superior who was in charge of two new service concepts. Diane's responsibilities were to develop the service concept, prepare a test market plan, and coordinate marketing efforts with the customer services and systems managers. The NSDU's goal was the quick development of new services which would be handed off to the relevant business units within CBG.

The service concept Diane worked on for a year was one of the NSDU's two implemented successes. The service provided consumers with higher interest on savings than the usual passbook rate. Diane's performance was rewarded by her assuming responsibility for one of the four new service concepts NSDU had defined, but had yet to market. Diane indicated that she felt good about her new role, but really would like to be promoted to the vice-president rank by year's end. This desire was made more salient by unsolicited interest on the part of another organization. She interviewed with a large electrical and appliance manufacturer's credit business for a position as head of new services development. The offer would be a promotion and included a 25 percent increase in salary and "the promise of a line job in eighteen months." "But I didn't want a line job in eighteen months. I like new services development work and want to progress in management along a staff route. I might like to run a business someday, but not by working my way up from the production floor through line positions."

Diane's Discussion with Len

She decided to talk with Len White about her career and met with him several days later. Beginning the conversation, Diane asked Len if she could use him as a sounding board for some career concerns she had. She briefly described her career up until this point including her decision to join the minicomputer task force and her subsequent decisions to join Credit Card Services and then Len's unit, NSDU. She said she was satisfied with her career up until this point but was concerned as to where it was going. Throughout this time she felt that the responsibility for her career development was almost entirely her own. While the bank offered many challenging opportunities and the compensation was high by industry standards, she was not sure if her career had a direction, and even if it did, she was not sure there was a viable career path at Metrobank.

Shortly after she completed her MBA, Diane said she had decided on a three-year career path along a staff functional line that would focus on marketing computer-related services. She also decided she would be an Assistant Vice-President before she turned thirty and was very satisfied when she was promoted at the age of twenty-eight.

More recently however, she had seen many of her associates leaving—some because they were not doing a good job, but others because of the pressure and ambiguous opportunities. "I'm very competitive and I like the pressure, it motivates me. But the fact that I'm not interested in a line job means that there is no standard career path for me to progress along. This makes me think my career opportunities at Metrobank may be limited."

Len responded that her career advancement thus far had not been as haphazard as she might think. In fact she had been identified early in the informal employee tracking system as a high performer. He said one of Metrobank's corporate policies was to challenge new management trainees with special assignments. While the task force position was not part of a formal career development plan, it was considered developmental by CBG management. The offer made to her to manage a branch was also part of CBG's informal career development plan for her. Her decision to turn that offer down shifted future development efforts to her. While the move to the Credit Card Unit was viewed by Diane as continued development, CBG had temporarily abdicated its career management role. Len said that he took up this responsibility again in his offer to Diane to join NSDU and that he subsequently designed a role for her further development in marketing new services.

Despite Diane's concerns, Len knew it was possible to advance in Metrobank to a VP level in a staff role, but was not optimistic about a promotion to senior vice-president. Len indicated that he interacted with a number of high-level people like John Snow and knew a lot about Metrobank. Yet he felt the bank was so decentralized that it was hard to know what career information was really relevant to Diane.

After further discussion and reiteration of these main points, Diane thanked Len for his time and left. She was not sure she felt any better after the conversation and wondered whether Len "had the power to get things to really happen for her."

For Len, the conversation highlighted his concern over Diane's career. "What is the best career pattern for good people like Diane? She has the ability to be a top level manager in Metrobank, but chooses not to take the conventional route of becoming a line manager in a branch bank. Her next promotion to vice-president would reward her high performance and possibly attract other good people into New Services Development. However, it may be difficult for her to move into a line unit as a VP without previous line experience, and without line experience her career path may be blocked. Yet, she has been with Metrobank almost five years, has done an outstanding job, and deserves the promotion."

Personnel's Concerns with Diane

Keith Thomas, the Personnel Director for CBG, had many of the same concerns about Diane that Len did. He had followed Diane's career since she joined CBG as a financial analyst. He had placed her name onto the employee tracking system when she joined the minicomputer task force and had been part of the approval process for her promotion to assistant vice-president.

At the time of her promotion Keith had talked with Diane about moving into a line function at a branch and Diane said she would consider it. After she turned down the move to become a branch manager, Keith had not reviewed her situation again until recently. Len White had contacted him about considering her for promotion to vice-president. Keith had been noncommital at the time Len mentioned it to him and was feeling less favorable about it as he thought about the implications of such a promotion. In his mind, CBG wanted to encourage their better junior people to get line experience. If Diane was unwilling to do that, he wondered if CBG was the place for her. If CBG was not the place for her, should he contact Corporate Personnel to explore alternative solutions? Since Metrobank was decentralized, this was not as easy or even as appropriate as it might first appear. Each of the seven groups of Metrobank had their own personnel office and transferring between groups was not that common. Another concern was the effect that an internal transfer would have on individuals in situations similar to Diane's. Branch management was not always that popular with many of the bright, young junior managers yet those were exactly the people that CBG wanted out in the branches. How many of these professionals who were currently deciding about a branch manager position would opt for an internal transfer to another group if it became available?

Keith knew he had to sort out his ideas on this pretty quickly. Diane Jackson had called his office earlier that day to ask for an appointment.

38. The Buzzy Company Downturn Case*

The Challenge

During his regular weekly staff meeting, Mr. I. M. Topman, President of the Buzzy Company, expressed his serious concern over the report he had just received. "I have indications that there is not enough *enthusiasm* prevalent throughout the Buzzy plant," he stated emphatically. "We are not going to tolerate such an attitude," President Topman continued. "Buzzy people are always enthusiastic, and you, the staff members, are going to help me straighten this out!"

Most of the staff members realized that the recent business slowdown had necessitated a sizable reduction in workforce, causing many key people to personally question their own job security. To avoid the stigma of being laid off, many employees often actively sought and accepted positions in other companies. Those who remained were becoming conscious of protecting their job status. Established informal communication networks were being broken as a result of people leaving. Coupled with the fact that sales were down significantly from the previous year, many staff members wondered when they could expect Buzzy's employee and financial recovery.

---

*Bruce Evans and Hugh L. French, Jr. Printed by permission.

Mr. Topman told his staff that this trend had to be reversed. Somehow, they would have to bring about a management renewal to ensure the successful achievement of their newly established company objectives. The President charged each member of his staff to carefully consider methods for overcoming their present dilemma.

Business Situation

Financially, the Buzzy Company had operated profitably over the years with about 80 percent of the business defense oriented. However, in 1969, changes in the defense market coupled with an altered economic environment began to reverse the trend. By 1972 consumer sales were up to 70 percent of total. Since 1978, however, an unexpected decrease in sales caused considerable alarm throughout the organization. In an effort to remain profitable in the face of declining sales, the company management found it necessary to make corresponding and significant reductions in force. In addition, wages became essentially frozen.

As viewed from top management levels, the business prospects for the future, by contrast, looked encouraging. In anticipation of improved business prospects, Mr. Topman re-directed its business objectives toward those opportunities which would most likely yield the highest return on investment.

Recognition of Problem

Mr. Topman and his immediate advisors recognized that the achievement of their newly established business objectives would require the support of an effective management organization to execute their carefully formulated plans. Unfortunately, the uncertainty that shrouded the general workforce was not seen by Mr. Topman as a major obstacle to achievement of company goals. This problem was the surprisingly sticky subject which generated considerable discussion at the next few weekly staff meetings. Many staff members thought that there was an insidious decay of personal motivation eating away at the vital elements of the organization. It finally became obvious to everyone that unless the current trends were reversed, the company would be faced with the prospect of replacing key individuals.

Because of the mounting concern expressed frequently by the members of his staff, Mr. I. M. Topman appointed a special task force to investigate the problem, to evaluate various alternative solutions, and to make appropriate recommendations. The task force consisted of the Director of Industrial Relations, Mr. O. K. Peoples; the Executive Assistant to the President, Mr. U. R. Helper; the Director of Research and Development, Dr. R. N. Dees; the Vice-President of Finance, Mr. A. C. Counter; and the Director of Business Planning, Mr. C. N. Future. The make-up of the group was intended to represent a broad spectrum of company interests and talents.

Following the appointment of the task force, a series of meetings was held to accomplish their assigned task. It was decided that interviews with selected employees should be conducted to gather data relating to the problem. A reputable consultant firm was retained to assist in the investigation.

It was agreed that the survey data obtained from interviews throughout the company revealed at best an incomplete picture of the real problems facing the company. This was attributed to the fact that in this setting of uncertainty, people were reluctant to speak freely about their real concerns. As a consequence, the use of qualified interviewers from outside the company organization was seen by the task force as a mechanism for obtaining the data necessary for an intelligent definition of the problem.

Accordingly, the services of a reputable consulting firm, Need to Know Corporation, were obtained for the purposes of conducting confidential interviews, analyzing the data, and identifying pertinent problem areas. The results of this activity as summarized by Need to Know revealed that " . . . the central problem was communication throughout your organization—upward, downward, and laterally." This opinion expressed by the outside consultants was, of course, confirmed by the earlier reluctance of people to discuss their concern freely with company interviewers.

In addition, Need To Know interviews with many in management positions indicated a widespread desire to improve their management skills. For example, many managers indicated they would like to learn how to make better use of time in the execution of their assigned job.

Based on the findings of the consultants and their own independent investigations, the task force came to the conclusion that a management development program, specifically designed to address the identified problems and needs of the Buzzy organization, could contribute greatly toward the achievement of company objectives. Toward this end, the group then considered alternative methods of implementing such a program.

Consideration of Alternative Solutions

Three alternative approaches to implement the recommended management development program were considered by the task force. Identified as Plans A, B, and C, they are described briefly as follows:

Plan A—Existing In-House Talent

Adoption of this approach would involve the identification of individuals presently within the company who possess the unique talents required to implement such a program. The task force members agreed that the qualifications of the selected person (or persons) would have to include:

- An advance degree with at least a minor in education and/or psychology,
- Previous related experience in the field of management development.
- A keen appreciation of the unique problems and their relation to the company.

Once selected, the individual(s) would become thoroughly familiar with the problems, investigate appropriate management training objectives directed toward the specific needs, and administer the resulting management development program.

Plan B—Hiring of a Professional Management Training Director

If this approach were recommended by the task force and adopted by the company, a lengthy sequence of activities and events would occur beginning with the preparation of a fairly comprehensive description of the job to be performed, not only in terms of the immediate problems at hand, but also the longer range requirements associated with continuing management development training. Having established such a job description, the company would then advertise for prospective applicants. The qualifications and salary requirements would be carefully screened and the best qualified would be selected. Following his employment, the new Management Training Director would begin an extensive orientation period during which he would become familiar with the company, its people, and their interrelated problems. Based on his perception of the situation and what he understood to be his assignment, the training Director could select an appropriate management development program, and administer it.

Plan C—Engagement of a Professional Consulting Firm

The third alternative solution considered by the task force would involve identification of the qualified professional consulting and/or management development firms. Having selected a firm whose capabilities best match the specific needs of Buzzy, the company would then contract for services including the following:

- Confidential interviews with a representative sample of management and supervisory personnel.
- An analysis of the results of these interviews to verify the previously identified problems.
- Identification of other problem areas revealed by the interviews.
- Proposal of a management development program.
- If acceptable to the company, the execution of the program.

Evaluation of Alternate Solutions

Having defined the alternative solutions described above, the task force then evaluated each of these in terms of advantages and disadvantages, their respective probabilities of successfully achieving the specified objectives and an analysis of required investment of resources versus the expected returns.

As seen by the task force, Plan A offered the unique advantage over the other plans that a qualified individual selected from within the company may already be well aware of the problems facing the company. Also, it was felt that such an insider would probably be more personally concerned than an outsider because of his established involvement with the company.

Several disadvantages were also recognized by the task force. It was generally conceded that it was not likely that the task force would find a man employed by the company with the required qualifications. Even if identified, making this person available for this assignment would probably require the hiring of an individual to fill the slot vacated by the man so released. Also, the reluctance on the part of potential trainees to respond openly during interviews would still exist to some degree and thereby diminish the effectiveness of the interview.

In general, it was believed by the members of the task force that Plan A had a low probability of successfully achieving the required objectives. Also, while the investment needed to implement the plan was thought to be the lowest, the expected results were similarly valued low.

Adoption of Plan B would afford the company an opportunity to more closely match the capabilities of the selected individual to the requirements of the job, thereby improving the probability of successfully achieving the objectives. Also, it was noted that this approach would have less impact on the existing operation than if an existing employee were transferred out of a critical position into the new slot.

On the minus side, the task force recognized that Plan B would require a considerable amount of time just getting to the point where the program could begin. Preparing the job description, advertising, screening applicants, selecting and hiring, orientation—all of these activities would have to precede the actual planning and execution of the program.

In considering the level of investment required for Plan B, the task force concluded that it probably would cost slightly more than Plan A and would more than likely yield a better result.

The advantages of Plan C were seen to include the following:

- The resulting management development program would be specifically tailored to the needs of Buzzy by qualified experienced professionals trained to recognize the critical problems and needs of the company.
- The time required to prepare and plan the selected management development program would be considerably shorter when compared with Plans A and B.
- Probability of successfully achieving objectives would be high based on the proven performance of the particular consulting firm selected.
- Minimal disruption of the routine company operations would occur since most of the effort would be performed by people external to the operation.

The only disadvantage seen by the task force was the somewhat higher ongoing cost of conducting the program compared with what it would cost using one of the so-called in-house plans.

Selection of Best Solution

Based on the foregoing evaluation of the alternative solutions considered, the task force selected Plan C, stating the following reasons orally to Mr. Topman at the next staff meeting:

- Shortest time to implement the program.
- Highest probability of successfully achieving program objectives.
- Least impact on routine company operations.
- Most reasonable investment based on expected return.

After considering several possible consulting firms for the Plan C assignment, the task force selected Need to Know Corporation based on their earlier involvement and their acknowledged reputation as a leader in their field.

Implementation of Selected Solution

Having arrived at a conclusion, the task force then wrote its report to Mr. Topman. The substance of their assignment was summarized briefly, followed by the problem definition, alternative solutions considered, their evaluation of the alternatives, and the conclusions and recommendation for subsequent action.

Mr. Topman accepted the conclusions and the recommendation of the task force, thanked them for their participation in this special assignment and relieved them of any further responsibilities. He then directed Mr. Peoples to proceed with the approach recommended by the task force.

Shortly thereafter, in response to a request from Mr. Peoples, Need To Know submitted its proposal for instituting a management development program at Buzzy. The program, to be coordinated and administered by the Industrial Relations Department, was designed for individuals responsible for developing strategies for human effectiveness within their organization. The program addressed five major areas of interest and concern:

1. Communication Laboratory. A one-day session which aims at solidifying the work group into a team. The method includes both structural and non-structural techniques. Communication barriers are to be examined and approaches to alleviating the problems are developed.
2. Managing Management Time. A one-day seminar which examines the content of a manger's day as opposed to the efficiency with which he carries out his activities. Special consideration to include the art of delegation, the rightful assumption of responsibility, and the use of leverage in time management.
3. Motivation and Job Enrichment. A one-day seminar exploring a basic philosophy of management relating to people. Consideration to be given to those needs which on the surface appear to be motivational but are not. The actual motivation needs are to be explored with an eye to immediate practical application. The application of motivation concepts to the task of job enrichment will be featured.
4. Managerial Performance Standards. During this one-day seminar, managers will learn the technique of writing managerial performance standards. They will study the methods of determining with their supervisor how they will be quantifiably measured before the performance takes place. Specific emphasis on effective performance review and controlling performance standards will be discussed.
5. Development Sessions. This series of development sessions will be conducted every fourth Friday covering such items as problem analysis, decision-making, conference skills, managerial skills, technical skills as related to budgeting and finance, organization structures, etc. These seminars will be given by individuals having expertise in these categories.

After reading this proposal, Mr. Peoples smiled to himself and began to prepare the necessary internal papers to begin the program.

39. Kandor Corporation*

Karen Rice took a deep breath while seated at her desk. The morning's events left her incredulous. She mentally recounted the incidents that led to disciplinary action against her.

Karen began her career with the Kandor Corporation two years ago. She graduated first in her MBA class at Stanford. In addition, she brought with her four years' experience in financial analysis gained through her family's CPA firm, which she joined after completing a BS in Finance at the University of Southern California.

Upon joining Kandor, Karen was impressed with the company's aggressive culture. The perfect environment for a new employee to demonstrate entrepreneurial skills, abilities, and talents!

Kandor processes natural gas for itself and for several other gas producers, owning and operating three gas plants in West Texas. One gas plant uses a refrigeration process to separate and distill hydrocarbons. The two newer plants use a cryogenic, or super-cooling, process to separate the hydrocarbons. Dehydrated gas arrives at the plants through pipelines and once processed, flows through on-plant metering stations. Kandor charges the producers a fee for processing but elects not to purchase their gas as it enters or leaves the plants.

Kandor has long-term contracts with several pipeline companies who own, or share, pipelines at the metering site. Once processed, Kandor directs the gas into the pipelines indicated by the gas producers. For example, a gas producer may indicate that processed gas be piped into the Texas Pipeline Company's line that flows to Houston from the metering site.

Keeping track of these transactions requires an elaborate accounting system. While 100 mcf of natural gas may enter the plant for processing, the end products are methane, ethane, and butane. The processing fee is based on the level of refinement required by the gas owners (or, in Kandor's situation, on the requirements of long-term contracts). Thus, the accounting staff must work closely with the process staff to track the gas and determine the volume of refined product.

Due to this complexity, Kandor developed an intricate accounting system to track the gas it processes for itself and for other gas producers. Karen's initial responsibilities required completing a detailed one-year forecast for volumes and revenues. Monthly updates compare year-to-date actuals with year-end forecast and year-to-date forecasts. According to her supervisor, this assignment would provide value training in the Company's accounting procedures and form a solid foundation for financial analysis for Kandor's operations.

Karen enthusiastically tackled the project, poring over accounting procedures manuals and reviewing the files from prior years. Eager to learn, Karen devoted time after hours to recalculating previous years' volumes as a check on her

*This case study was written by Isabel Cordova and is printed by permission. A graduate of the University of South Carolina, Ms. Cordova is now Supervisor of Employee Relations at Howmet Turbine Components Corporation in Wichita Falls, Texas.

knowledge of the procedures. She reviewed any questions with her supervisior, Bill Lynch, and completed the project by the November 1 deadline. The project was successfully reviewed, and Karen had only minor changes to make before going final. Pleased with her knowledge of the system, Karen hoped that she would soon apply this knowledge in the Financial Analysis Department. While willing to develop a strong foundation in Kandor's accounting procedures, Karen was eager to move into her area of expertise, financial analysis.

During her one-year performance review, Karen asked Bill Lynch about her chances to move into Financial Analysis. Bill avoided the issue, citing personnel levels and a slowdown in cross training opportunities. He praised Karen's enthusiasm and perseverance, and explained that the surest way to succeed was to excel in the work she was currently performing. Bill diplomatically encouraged Karen to begin managing her time better, and to focus her efforts on producing a higher volume of accurate work. Karen was receptive and attentive, but was disappointed with her 5.6 percent raise.

Nonetheless, Karen heeded Bill's advice, determined to eliminate areas of deficiency. She attended two Kandor schools on forecasting and completed a one-day time management course. Applying her skills on the job, Karen discovered she could complete her work in short order and could devote one to two hours per day to extra projects.

On her own, she decided to develop improvements in the forecasting procedure and to review these with Bill upon completion. She devised a plan that would not only simplify the process but that was also easily computerized. Again, enthused about her project, Karen began devoting after-hours effort to the project. She performed computer simulations and experimented with several computer graphics programs. Convinced that her project would increase productivity, Karen scheduled a one-hour session with Bill Lynch to review her planned recommendations.

Bill listened attentively to Karen's presentation, making notes and reserving questions until she had finished. Karen noticed that Bill appeared apprehensive and impatient. She quickly answered his questions and asked for feedback on the project. Bill suggested a review on Thursday at 10:30 A.M., allowing time for him to review the project in depth.

Confident that Bill would be pleased, Karen relaxed and entered his office Thursday morning right on ime. Bill invited her in and he put her at ease immediately with his friendly grin. They reviewed her recommendations and Bill praised her initiative and resourcefulness. He diplomatically indicated that while he appreciated her diligence, keeping him abreast of her activities was desirable for several reasons. First, he could direct her efforts toward meeting his departmental objectives or could assign her to a high priority, short-fuse project. Secondly, he could keep her informed on matters not readily apparent to a "newer" employee. For example, similar recommendations two years earlier were vetoed by the Accounting Manager. Thirdly, he had been worried that Karen was spending an excessive amount of time achieving her objectives, assuming that she had been working only on her regularly assigned tasks.

Calm during the review, Karen could hardly wait to get home that day. All her diligence and commitment resulted in a verbal reprimand! To top it all off, she found herself frustrated because her known talents were not even being tapped. Her extra efforts, in addition to being fruitless, caused Bill to perceive her as a slow performer. Accustomed to independence at her family's CPA firm, Karen was shocked to discover that she had to clear everything with Bill before taking action.

Karen accepted the counseling and buckled down. She made sure that Bill was apprised of her commitments and even suggested a fifteen-minute meeting each Monday to keep Bill informed and to allow Bill to clarify his priorities.

Within six months, Karen felt that the meetings had served a useful function. She became more aware of Bill's goals and organizational requirements. Yet she was beginning to feel stifled. Bill began praising her work and she started receiving both verbal "Atta Girls" as well as complimentary notes attached to completed work.

At this point, Karen was completely baffled. In her opinion, Bill was not reinforcing entrepreneurial activity or creative thought. She began to wonder if choosing Kandor had been a wise choice.

At that moment, her phone rang and Bill asked her to come to his office. As she entered, Bill's friendly grin appeared somewhat strained. He decided to level with her. After two years, in his opinion, Karen was not successfully competing with other employees in her rating group. While he had seen many areas of strength, including diligence and commitment, he did not feel that she would achieve the growth she expected in her career with Kandor. While extremely bright and capable, she had not mastered the Kandor approach to meeting business objectives.

He handed her a letter outlining these points, and noting areas in which her performance was lacking. These areas for improvements included improving her time management, a need to work with less supervision, and a need to strengthen communications skills. She read the letter incredulously. Almost speechless, she took a deep breath and tried to plan a course of action.

She thanked Bill for his candid appraisal and asked for time to let it sink in. Bill agreed and Karen managed a faint smile. She returned to her desk wondering how events had led to this.

40. Relying on Aptitude Testing*

William Lightfoot was born and raised on the Anadarko Indian Reservation about seventy-five miles west of Oklahoma City. He was a full-blooded Sioux Indian who grew up determined to live in the "white man's world."

Bill was always level-headed and usually tended to be somewhat stoic in his reactions. He maintained a "B" average through high school, played varsity football, graduated, and joined the Army. He was sent to Vietnam, where he rose to the rank of Sergeant E-5 and was decorated for valor. Bill considered the idea of reenlisting, since Army life at times appealed to him. Finally he decided against it and returned to Anadarko in April 1974. He soon discovered that getting a good

*Bruce Evans, Associate Professor of Management at the Graduate School of Management, University of Dallas. Printed by permission.

job was difficult. Being a veteran he decided to use his G.I. benefits to go to college. In September 1974, Bill entered Oklahoma State University. He enrolled as a full-time day student and took a part-time job at night.

On campus, after a successful first semester, Bill met Sue Waters. She was a native of Lawton and part Indian herself, although Sue looked less the part than Bill did. She was in her last year of Nurses' Training at the O.S.U. Hospital. That spring Bill continued through his first year at school during the daytime, worked nights, and dated Sue whenever he could. In June, she graduated and began working full-time at the University hospital.

Bill took the summer off and decided to find another job which would allow him more time to see Sue and incidentally pay more. He went to work at the New Moon Mobile Home Plant just outside the city as a production line worker. When he began his new job his intent was to work all summer and return to school in the fall. After about a month, however, a different idea began to grow in his mind: He was making good money on the production line since the wage rate was based on a set amount plus a bonus. Bill's group was "making full bonus" (about $6.00/hour). Not only that, but his group could finish their daily quota and go home early, sometimes as early as 3:00 in the afternoon. Bill reasoned that he could marry Sue (a prime objective), continue to work days, and go to school nights (the go-home-early arrangement would help provide study time). By combining their two incomes (total take-home pay between them would probably be over $14,000/year), life as he saw it would be pretty good. Bill convinced Sue of this and in August they were married.

The arrangement worked fine for several years. Bill was soon moved up to "Lead Hand" on the crew and given ten cents/hour raise. In late 1980, Jim Day, the Production Manager who had hired Bill, called a general plant meeting to announce that the New Moon Company was initiating an Employee Aptitude Test Program. Very shortly all employees, hourly and salaried in all four company plants across the country, would be asked to take aptitude tests. Jim assured the employees that this test would not jeopardize anyone's job but that it was "just for the record."

Plant scuttlebutt, however, quickly had many people worried, although Bill showed little concern. About ten days later, on a Friday afternoon, Bill's crew was given their aptitude tests.

One week later, Jim Day came up to Bill and asked him to "stop by my office before you go home this afternoon." Right on the dot at 3:00 Bill knocked on the door of Jim's office and went in.

"Sit down, Bill," said Jim from behind his desk, not wasting any time. "I called you in here today to congratulate you. You had one of the highest scores in the plant on your test . . . even higher than some of the office people. You're Lead Hand on the Sidewall crew, aren't you?" said Jim, apparently changing the subject.

"Yes, sir," replied Bill.

"Well, Bill, my Material Handler Foreman quit a few days ago, and I need a bright fellow like you to replace him. Do you want the job?"

Bill was stunned; he didn't know what to say. "It would mean a raise and you would still be eligible for bonus. Frankly, Bill, I've always thought you were a cut above the average line worker and this test proves it to me. I think you've got a good future in front of you."

"Thank you, sir," replied Bill, a bit bewildered by the whole thing. "Yeah, I'll take the job."

In the weeks that followed, Bill worked into his new position easily and really enjoyed it. Jim was very pleased with his choice of Bill for the job.

Several weeks later, Jim Day's promotion and transfer to New Moon's Alma, Michigan, plant was announced. Jim was moving to understudy the General Manager. It was rumored that eventually he would become general manager of that plant.

Alma was the home office of the corporation as well as the site of its most prestigious plant. Two other smaller plants were located in Pennsylvania and Nebraska. Bill was sorry to see Jim go. They had become friendly; Jim had become sort of a father image to Bill. The plant grapevine had it that Jim had also scored well on the aptitude test and was destined for better things. It seemed to make sense as Bill saw it.

Jim left in the spring of '81. Bill's work life seemed to continue going quite well. Sue was proud of her husband's abilities. His schooling was slowly but satisfactorily progressing. Sue's hospital job was also working out well. Things continued that way until last October when Fred Sherman (Bill's new boss) called Bill into his office. Fred told Bill that there was an opening for an assistant Material Manager (really a training position for Material Manager) at the Michigan plant. Fred added that Jim Day, who had now taken over as General Manager in Alma, had asked for Bill. Bill and Sue talked the decision over. It would mean a move to Michigan, which neither of them really wanted. It would mean leaving school, which didn't bother Bill as much as it did Sue. She had wanted him to finish but he had become tired of the grind. However they felt that opportunity had knocked and they decided Bill should take the job. Bill trained his successor and awaited the move.

One month later they found themselves in Alma, Michigan, a small town of about 20,000 people, forty miles west of Saginaw. Jim Day had welcomed Bill warmly and was openly pleased to have him "on board."

Their world abruptly began to change. People in Alma were not used to having neighbors and co-workers of Indian descent. Unfortunately Jim failed to notice that other New Moon employees were covertly hostile to Bill at work. Jerry Murphy, the Material Manager and Bill's immediate superior, had come up from Flint and was barely tolerant. The Production Manager, Ed Wheeler, was a life-long Michigan resident who displayed unmistakable hostility toward Bill. Neither man would mention their feelings to Jim, however, as both believed Bill to be "Jim's boy."

Sue found matters no better at Alma General Hospital when she applied for a job. Despite being a competent R.N., she was told there were no openings and given the very distinct feeling that even if there were, an Indian nurse would not be welcome.

During the months that followed they found themselves isolated from the community. They had no friends and Sue became bored and restless staying at their mobile home all day long. Bill sensed that he was not performing on the new job. Jerry pointed to Bill's under-par performance as his inability to do the work. In plant conversations Ed reinforced Jerry's evaluation. Whenever Jim Day saw Bill in the plant, however, and asked him how it was going Bill always replied, "just fine." But soon even Jim became aware of Bill's sub-par efforts and was puzzled.

He could not believe his Materials Manager's evaluation that Bill "just wasn't smart enough to cut it." After all, hadn't the same aptitude test which had been responsible for his promotion to General Manager of this plant also proved that Bill Lightfoot had the ability?

The situation continued to deteriorate rapidly. Bill even began to drink a little which was something he was never able to handle well anyway. Finally one morning in late April, Bill had come to work badly hung over. He immediately got into an argument with one of the Line Foremen about some material not being ordered on time and it ended up in a fist fight. It was stopped but not until Bill had bloodied the foreman's face pretty badly and the man had to be restrained from coming after Bill with a hammer. Immediately after the incident both Ed and Jerry stormed into Jim Day's office and issued an ultimatum: "Either you get rid of that red-necked Indian or we've had it!" After the two angry men left his office, Jim tried to decide what he should do.

Part VII

Employee Rights and Collective Bargaining

Cases Outline

- Microware
- Whose Rights Are Right?
- Who Should Drive the Wagons?
- Washington County Hospital
- How Big Is a Small Knife?
- Quality of Work Life: Getting Started
- A QWL Startup: Is the Formula for Success Always the Same?
- Dealing with Organizing Problems Via the Bargaining Table: The Case of "Neutrality Agreements"

41. Microware*

Microware is a small, aggressive, and fast-growing computer software company located on the outskirts of Boston. Within the last three years, Microware has grown from a two-person to a 150-person operation. Business has boomed for Microware because from the very beginning the company has carefully delineated its product line. Staying away from arcade games or highly competitive business software, Microware has zeroed in on the education market. Its best selling programs to date consist of a series of sophisticated statistical packages capable of running on any microcomputer. The programs are unique because they are simply formatted. Even novices or computerphobics can use the programs with a minimum amount of difficulty.

Because demand for these products has risen so greatly, Microware recently decided to launch a series of new educational products. The firm's marketing research department had determined that within five years approximately 80 percent of all major universities would have microcomputer facilities and demand at least some minimum level of computer literacy from all students. The researchers also determined that there was a great need for other simple-to-operate computer-based instruction modules. While the academic community is supportive of the use of computers in the classroom, most professors are not programmers. Nor are they interested in becoming programmers. What they need and want, the market survey showed, are pre-packaged programs that can be used in the classroom to supplement the basic lecture format mode of instruction. While software is needed most in the sciences (e.g., biology, chemistry, statistics, physics), demand is also growing for products in personnel, business, labor relations, English, and the humanities. Microware's objective then is to capture as much of this market as possible.

To meet the increased demand for products, Microware has tripled its current staff within the last year. Because the company is a wage setter, they have been able to attract some of the best young talents in the industry. In some cases, they have even stolen people away from larger competitors. Additionally, the company has actively and aggressively recruited potential rising stars from top-notch universities along the eastern seaboard. One such bright prospect recruited by Microware was Sara Jones.

*Vandra L. Huber, Assistant Professor, University of Utah. Printed by permission.

Background of Sara Jones

At twenty-two, Sara Jones was a young, assertive, confident junior executive. A year ago, after completing a dual major in computer science and marketing, she had accepted the position at Microware. Because she had internships with IBM and Data General while in school at Cornell, she had had numerous job opportunities. Rather than going with one of the larger, more established computer firms, Sara chose Microware because she felt she would have more responsibility and be able to move up more rapidly. Her gamble had paid off. By working diligently, she had risen from marketing research specialist to the position of product manager within one year. Assigned to Microware's newest unit, Business Education, Sara's current product line consisted of a series of educational programs for use in personnel and labor relations courses. Thanks to the courses she took in Cornell's School of Industrial and Labor Relations (that is an editorial comment by the Professor), she had a solid grasp of the subject matter for which she was developing programs. This put her head and shoulders above new product managers, some of whom knew nothing about their product domains prior to their job assignments.

As a product manager, Sara was responsible for keeping her current project on track and on time. Additionally, she screened new products for possible development. Aspiring young programmers or faculty members seeking tenure would submit educational software ideas and concepts to Microware. Sara screened all ideas relating to personnel and industrial relations. If promising, she ordered a market survey to determine the demand for such a product and to identify the potential market. If the market survey indicated that there was a potential market, there were not existing programs available, and the demand was high, Sara assigned the project to a matrix team.

Matrix management is designed to give research and development agencies maximum flexibility. A team of resource persons is pulled together to work on a project. Once the project is completed, the team disbands. In most cases, a software team consists of a technical writer, programmer, subject area (e.g., personnel, biology) expert, psychologist, and graphic artist. An important part of Sara's job, then, was to keep group members working together to produce a quality product. Additionally, Sara had to coordinate her unit's research and development efforts with package design, disc production, and marketing to ensure that once the finished product was developed, it was marketed immediately.

In sum, Sara liked her job because it combined her interests in business personnel and computer technology. Because she had a great deal of latitude over operations, her opinions and ideas mattered and she was more than happy with her job at Microware.

The Interview

When Sara arrived at work Monday morning, a phone message was already on her desk from Bob Ryan, Microware's personnel manager. All the message indicated was that he wanted to see her in his office around 10 A.M.

As 10 A.M. grew near, Sara still didn't have any idea what the meeting was about. Knocking on Ryan's door, she decided she'd just let him call the shots.

"Come on in, Sara," Ryan immediately responded, busy shuffling papers at his desk. "Here, why don't you sit over here," he said, directing her to a chair at his left.

As if he had read her thoughts, Ryan immediately began talking. "I guess you're wondering why I've called you into my office. Let me first assure you that we are more than pleased with the quality of work you've been doing. In fact, that labor relations simulation you developed was really top notch. Marketing tells me they've already got big orders from Wisconsin, Utah, Cornell, and Ohio State," he said, smiling as he sipped his coffee.

Impatient with Ryan's beating around the bush approach, Sara interjected, "I'm glad the company likes what I'm doing. I really like my job here. But I sense that's not what this meeting is all about. I wonder if we could get down to what's really on your mind?"

A startled look crossed Ryan's face. "Well, okay," he stammered. "Because we are pleased with your work, we want to take some precautions to ensure that you stay with us. As I guess you are aware, in the past three months our turnover rate has increased from about 12 percent, the industry average, to double that figure.

"It's really been a problem for us because it's difficult to replace employees. What's particularly bad about the situation is that our employees are quitting and taking ideas about our products with them, and using them to develop their own products and business. Over the long run, we're going to lose a lot of business over this."

At that point Ryan stopped talking. Still wondering what all this had to do with her, Sara asked, "I still don't see where I fit into the picture here. Since I've been here, only one person in my unit has quit. That's pretty low turnover if you ask me. And I'm more than satisfied with my job, so I'm not planning on quitting."

Ryan nodded in agreement.

"Well, I'm getting to that now," he said, pulling a file folder out of his drawer. "The president of Microware has asked me to call all product managers in one at a time to talk with them. Our attorney Madaline Rayburn has drafted an employee contract. We're going to require all new employees who come aboard to sign this agreement as a condition of employment.

"Additionally, we're also asking, but not requiring, all present employees to sign the agreement. Basically, the agreement just spells out what the company expects from its employees and what the employees will get in return.

"We're calling product managers in first because we want you to set an example for the other employees by signing the agreement first. Then we want you to encourage the employees in your unit to sign the agreement as well," he continued.

"Again, let me reiterate that the contract is not required, but employees who do sign it will be accorded additional privileges and benefits that won't be offered to those who aren't committed to the company."

At that point, Sara interrupted Ryan, "Could you spell out more completely what you mean by benefits?"

"Sure, take yourself for example. When we hired you, you indicated that you wanted to return to college to get your MBA. Well, if we know you are on Microware's team, then the company is willing to help you reach that objective.

We're setting up a new tuition reimbursement program. Not only will we cover tuition up to $2,000 a year, but we'll give you release time to take one course per semester," he said, adding that the course must be job-related.

"Of course, employees not committed to Microware will not be entitled to this fringe benefit."

At this point, Sara interrupted Ryan again. "Well, tuition reimbursement is nice for me, but what about other employees? What's in it for them?"

"In addition to the employee tuition program, we're also implementing a new daycare program. The company will pay up to $100 a month per child for daycare. That should help a lot of employees. And any employee who wants to buy a microcomputer for home work can receive an interest-free loan from the company," Ryan said, grinning broadly.

"As you can see we're really offering employees quite a lot in exchange for a little loyalty. "Not only that, but employees who sign the agreement will have layoff protection should financial conditions ever reverse themselves."

At this point, Sara just sat dumbstruck.

"Well, I can see I've said enough for now," Ryan said, interrupting Sara's thoughts. "Why don't you take a few days and read the contract over. I'd like you to get back to me on Friday about this," he said, handing her a copy of the contract (see Exhibit 1) and a memorandum concerning the employment clause (see Exhibit 2).

After reading the contract over, Sara sat at her desk trying to decide what to do. She had to admit that having the company pay for her schooling and giving her release time was certainly appealing. Still she wondered what rights she would be giving up if she did sign the contract. Additionally, she wondered if it was legal to give extra benefits to employees who signed the contract versus those who did not. She also was concerned about trying to enforce compliance of this agreement among her subordinates, when she herself was so uncommited.

With so many questions racing through her mind, Sara just didn't know what she would do.

Exhibit 1. Employee Agreement

I. Sara Jones, of Boston, Massachusetts, in consideration of my employment by Microware, and for other good and valuable consideration agree that:

1. Employment

    The Company has hired me to work in the position of Market Production Manager. This employment is not for any particular period, and may be terminated with or without cause at any time. I acknowledge that, as a part of my employment, I am expected to create inventions and/or ideas of value to the Company.

2. Definition of Proprietary Information

    As used in this Agreement, the term "Proprietary Information" refers to any and all information of a confidential, proprietary, or secret nature that concerns the present or future business (including research and development) of the Company. Proprietary Information includes, for example and without limitation, trade secrets, processes, formulas, data, know-how, improvements, inventions, techniques, and software programs, marketing plans and strategies, and information concerning customers or vendors.

3. Proprietary Information to Be Kept in Confidence

    I acknowledge that Proprietary Information is a special, valuable, and unique asset of the Company, and I agree at all times during the period of my employment and hereafter to keep in confidence and trust all Proprietary Information. I agree that during the period of my employment and thereafter I will not directly or indirectly use Proprietary Information

Exhibit 1. Employee Agreement *(continued)*

other than in the course of performing duties as an employee of the Company, nor will I directly or indirectly disclose any Proprietary Information or anything relating thereto to any person or entity, except with the express written consent of the Company. I will abide by the Company's policies and regulations, as established from time to time, for the protection of its Proprietary Information.

4. Other Employment

I agree that during the period of my employment by the Company I will not, without the Company's prior written consent, directly or indirectly engage in any employment, consulting, or activity other than for the Company relating to any line of business in which the Company is now or at such time is engaged, or which would otherwise conflict with my employment obligations to the Company.

5. Disclosure to Company: Inventions as Sole Property of Company

I agree that during the period of my employment by the Company I will not, without the ments, trade secrets, formulas, techniques, processes, and know-how, including software programs, whether or not patentable or copyrightable and whether or not reduced to practice, that have been conceived or learned by me during the period of my employment, either alone or jointly with others, and that relate to or result from the actual or anticipated business, research, or investigations of the Company or any Subsidiary, or that result, to any extent, from use of the Company's premises or property (the work being hereinafter collectively referred to as the "Inventions").

I acknowledge and agree that all the Inventions shall be the sole property of the Company or any other entity designated by it, and that I hereby assign to the Company my entire right and interest in all the Inventions; the Company or any other entity designated by it shall be the sole owner of all domestic and foreign rights pertaining to the Inventions. I further agree as to all the Inventions to assist the Company in every way (at the Company's expense) to obtain and from time to time enforce patents and/or copyrights on the Inventions in any and all countries. To that end, by way of illustration but not limitation, I will testify in any suit or other proceeding involving any of the Inventions, execute all documents that the Company may reasonably determine to be necessary or convenient for use in applying for and obtaining patents thereon and enforcing same, and execute all necessary assignments thereof to the Company or persons designated by it. My obligation to assist the Company in obtaining and enforcing patents for the Inventions shall continue beyond the termination of my employment, but the Company shall compensate me at a reasonable rate after such termination for time actually spent by me at the Company's request on such assistance.

6. Non-Competition

Upon termination of my employment with the Company, I shall not directly or indirectly, within any of the restricted territories specified in Schedule A attached hereto (embracing territories in which the Company is at present conducting business and also territories in which I know the Company intends to extend any carry-on business by expansion of its present activities), enter into or engage in the software business or any branch thereof, either as an individual for my own account, or as a partner or joint venturer, or as an employee, agent, or salesperson for any person, or as an officer, director, or shareholder of corporation or otherwise, for a period of two years after the date of termination of my employment, whether this termination is with or without cause. Solicitation or acceptance of orders outside the restricted territories for shipment to or delivery in any of the restricted territories shall constitute "engaging in business" in the restricted territories in violation of this Agreement. This covenant on my part shall be construed as an agreement independent of any other provision in this Agreement; and the existence of any claim or cause of action on my part against the Company, of any kind whatsoever, shall not constitute a defense to the enforcement by the Company of this covenant.

MICROWARE

Dated: _____   Dated: _____

By: _____   _____
(Signature)

_____   _____

(Typed or Printed Name)   (Typed or Printed Name)

Exhibit 1. Employee Agreement *(continued)*

Schedule A

Restricted Territories

For purposes of the non-competition covenant of this Agreement, Restricted Territories shall be defined as:

1. The area within a one hundred (100) mile radius of company headquarters in Boston, Massachusetts.
2. New York City, San Francisco, Denver, into which the company is currently considering expansion.

Schedule B

This Agreement is signed at a date subsequent to my first employment with Company. I acknowledge, however, that the present writing simply codifies policies of the Company that have been in existence, and known to me, since I first became employed by the Company.

Employee Signature

TO: All Employees   DATE: April 15, 1985

FROM: Bob Ryan

SUBJECT: Clarification of Employee Agreement

Several employees have asked me for a clarification of Section 6—Non-Competition in the Employee Agreement. Although it may not be possible to cover every situation, I will attempt to amplify what is meant by "software business or any branch thereof" as found on the last page of the Agreement.

This section of the Agreement is intended to protect the Company from situations in which an employee might go to work for a company that directly competes against our company in wholesale or retail computer software business.

This employment prohibition includes any position at a directly competing company, but a position at any other non-competing company is completely acceptable. It is important to remember that most people's skills are actually quite broad. The job skill is really electronic repair, not computer repair. For example, technical sales, not microcomputer software sales, or programming, not educational software programming.

Some examples might make the issue clearer:

--A technician might leave to work for Wang, but could not make discs for softtech because the softtech statistic packages are computing products similar to ones that we sell.

--A sales person could sell IBM mainframe computers but could not work for McGraw-Hill because McGraw-Hill sells computer education software in competition with ours.

--An administrative aide could work for MIT, Computer Services, but not Digital Equipment because Digital markets services and products that directly compete with those offered by our company.

--A product manager could work for mainframe computer companies or software companies except those that produce educational software.

Of course, any person may take any position at a company that does not do any Massachusetts, New York, San Francisco, or Denver business.

All these prohibitions end two years after the date of the employee's termination.

I hope this memo clarifies this section of the Agreement. If you have any further questions, please let me know.

Exhibit 2. Memorandum on Employee Agreement

42. Whose Rights Are Right?*

Jim Stone had been the director of the human rights commission in Vernon City since its inception six years ago. The Vernon City commission is one of six locally based human rights commissions. This commission has been in existence for three years. The Vernon City's commission on human rights was created to protect individuals from employment discrimination. Its main function is to investigate individual complaints filed with the commission. The basis for these complaints is employment discrimination based on race, national origin, religion, sex, or handicap. Typical issues for the discrimination charges range from hire/fire decisions to transfers, promotions, and salary disputes. The commission refers to Title VII of the 1964 Civil Rights Act as its primary source of enforcement power for workplace discrimination.

This particular commission has been recognized statewide for its overwhelming progress in the fight for human rights. Within the past year alone, Vernon City's commission returned nearly $600,000 to employees in the form of back pay and back benefits. The current governor of the state, Gordon Willis, is an ardent human rights advocate and the Vernon City commission's human rights achievements have not gone without his notice. Governor Willis had delivered numerous campaign speeches touting the benefits of human rights protection. Upon completion of a successful gubernatorial campaign, he decided to create a statewide human rights commission to make good on his campaign promise. Although the governor was told he would receive opposition from the business community, he believed a state human rights commission could be developed to serve both employees and employers of the state. Jim Stone had been very supportive of the governor during the previous election. Based on this support and on the Vernon City Commission's amazing progress, Governor Willis determined that the best individual to appoint as executive director of the new state commission on human rights would be Jim Stone.

Jim felt honored when the governor asked him to head the newly created state commission on human rights. He also knew this appointment would give him the opportunity to advance his career goals. He would now have a chance to make a real contribution by helping the people of his state. Jim was anxious to get started in his new position.

The development of the statewide commission was being carefully planned by a specially appointed legislative committee. This process took a great deal of time. The delays were primarily due to the opposition of the business community. Many business leaders believed the commission would cause them difficulties and increase their expenses through costly settlement of disputant claims. After several debates, the special committee denied to include a provision in the charter of the state commission on human rights. The provision required the commission to offer the opportunity to negotiate an informal no-fault settlement between employee and employers before the initiation of the formal complaint

*Marybeth DeGregorio, Texas A&M University. This case was written for class discussion and is not intended to illustrate either effective or ineffective organizational behavior. Names of individuals and organizations are fictitious, but the events as described are real.

process. This stipulation, to attempt a preliminary no-fault settlement between the parties, was the innovative product of many committee meetings. The compromise satisfied the business community, and subsequently the bill to create a statewide human rights commission passed.

Jim Stone was officially appointed Executive Director of the State Commission on Human Rights on June 1, 1985. Jim's first duty as executive director was to hire and train staff in a very short amount of time with a limited budget. Despite delays due to the political concerns about a statewide human rights commission, the legislative committee overseeing the commission expected a fully functioning commission by July 15, 1985. This prompted Jim to hire Bob Cole as his assistant director. Jim and Bob had worked closely together in Vernon City; hence, Jim trusted and respected Bob's work.

Bob and Jim immediately began the task of interviewing a variety of applicants for the twelve positions of case investigators. (An investigator's starting salary is $22,000 and as a result over 100 people applied for the dozen openings.) An investigator's duties include receiving calls from clients, contacting relevant witnesses, contacting and questioning employers against whom a complaint has been filed, and rendering a final opinion. Jim and Bob sorted through the applications and chose thirty well-qualified applicants to interview. The interviews were structured and applicants were allowed to review the interview questions prior to their interview. Jim developed a point system based on the number of correct responses the applicants provided. He personally conducted all thirty interviews within two weeks. By July he had selected twelve people who had received the highest point ratings.

The investigator training had to be conducted quickly if the commission was going to be in operation by July 15. Jim, Bob, and Equal Employment Opportunity Commission (EEOC) specialists from Washington began two weeks of intensive training. The investigators were trained for six days a week, eight hours per day. Jim discussed the purpose and philosophy of the commission with the newly hired investigators. The EEOC specialists presented several lectures regarding the legal aspects of case handling. Investigators also viewed a variety of films on employment discrimination. Bob taught the investigators how they were expected to handle a case investigation. He brought in several examples of cases handled at the Vernon City Commission. The investigators were then asked to role-play interactions with employees and employers. They were also given short quizzes on how they should conduct an investigation step-by-step. The investigators learned many procedures including the need to contact all witnesses the client provides, informing the employer that a complaint has been filed, and learning to attempt a negotiation of an informal no-fault settlement. Bob explained that a no-fault settlement is often to the advantage of both employee and employer because it reduces the time and money that otherwise could be spent in a court battle. He described the circumstances under which the commission was enacted and the probable consequences should the business community become unhappy with the commission. At the very worst, the business community could pressure the governor to repeal the enabling legislation that created the commission in the first place. If this were to happen, they would all lose their positions with the commission. Despite this less than auspicious beginning, the training was completed on July 15, 1985, as scheduled.

Several months later, the legislative committee overseeing the commission requested that Jim Stone provide a report regarding the commission's progress. This committee wanted a detailed report indicating the number of cases processed, the outcome of the decision, the amount of back pay and back benefits awarded, and a survey of employee and employer attitudes toward the commission. Bob went to work gathering case and back pay/benefit information, while Jim decided how to conduct the survey. Jim remembered that a few weeks ago management students from a nearby university approached him inquiring about internship opportunities. He called the university to find out if these students would be interested in conducting the employee and employer survey. He explained that he was short on staff and if the students conducted this survey satisfactorily, he might be able to arrange future internships. The management students enthusiastically accepted his offer.

The students interviewed investigators to get background information on the cases. The investigators were assured that the results of the survey would be reported in summary form only. The investigators were very helpful after receiving the assurance that their names would not be specifically reported. The survey was quickly mailed to employees and employers involved in the cases. The students received approximately 70 percent of the mailed surveys and upon analysis reported the results to Jim Stone.

When Jim reviewed the report findings, he noticed that despite assurances of confidentiality, the students had inadvertently broken down the case load data by investigator.

Upon further examination Jim discovered that one investigator, Jean Byer, received significantly more dissatisfied ratings by employee clients. Jean Byer's clients thought she had not contacted all the appropriate people. Jean had presumably, learned from the training sessions that her duties included contacting all the witnesses provided by the client. Nonetheless, the clients she worked with said via the survey responses that she had not contacted them. Similarly, many employers on Jean's cases said they had *not* been informed that an investigation was being conducted. Finally, employees and employers both stated that Jean often failed to attempt to negotiate a no-fault settlement. Jim was disturbed by these findings, particularly in light of the emphasis that this step of the investigation had received during the training program. Jim knew that if these allegations of Jean's improper investigatory behavior were true and if they leaked back to the governor, funding for the commission could easily dry up. Jim agonized over what to do with the survey information. He knew he should never have seen this data in the first place. On the other hand, if Jean was not doing her job properly and important steps were being overlooked, the future of the commission could be jeopardized. The ramifications for human rights advocacy in the state weighed heavily upon Jim; he knew that he needed to do something, and soon!

43.   Who Should Drive the Wagons?*

COMPANY: Bethlehem Steel Corporation, Shipbuilding Department, Beaumont,
Texas

UNION: International Brotherhood of Teamsters, Local 920

On August 7, 1974, a salaried employee who was not a member of the bargaining
unit drove a group of employees who were members of a union other than the
Teamsters to an off-site work area in a company-owned station wagon. A grievance was filed the same day, contending that the driver should have been a
Teamster. When no settlement was reached at the third step of the grievance
procedure, arbitration was invoked. The parties agreed that the matter was
properly before the arbitrator and that the issue in dispute was:

> Did the Company violate any agreement by allowing a salaried employee to drive
> a Company station wagon on August 7, 1974?

Background

The primary function of Bethlehem Steel's Beaumont yard is building and
repairing ships and offshore oil drilling platforms. Repair is done in the Yard and
at off-site (field) locations. Men, tools, and equipment are transported to off-site
work in two ways. The first is with Transportation Department trucks driven by
members of the Teamster bargaining unit. The Teamsters have exclusive
representation rights for employees in this department.

The second source of transportation is General Manager's Department
vehicles, which include two station wagons. These wagons have generally been
driven to the field by supervisors when both a supervisor and two or three
bargaining unit employees were being transported.

Relations between the Company and the Union are governed by the August
18, 1972, Agreement between Bethlehem Steel and the Beaumont Metal Trades
Council, with which Teamster Local 920 is affiliated. Pertinent contract provisions
are reproduced at the end of this case.

During the 1969 negotiations the Union raised the question of supervisors
driving bargaining unit personnel in Company station wagons, and introduced the
following language for inclusion in the new agreement:

> Transportation of tools, material, and crafts will be made by personnel of the
> Transportation Department, inside and outside the plant, whether by car, bus, or
> truck.

---

*This case was prepared by I. B. Helburn, Bobbie and Coulter R. Sublett Centennial Professor,
Graduate School of Business, The University of Texas at Austin, and Darold T. Barnum, Associate Professor of Management, University of Illinois at Chicago, as a basis for class discussion rather than
to illustrate either effective or ineffective handling of an administrative situation. Real names of
individuals in the case have not been used.

No agreement was reached on this provision and it was not included in the 1969 Agreement.

On February 27, 1970, the Union filed a grievance because two individuals who were not Teamsters used a Company wagon to transport themselves and their hand tools to the field. The Union Business Agent, Parson, dropped the grievance after the first step because he considered the incident an emergency.

The 1972 Agreement was negotiated with no changes in the language regarding work assignments. However, the Union alleges and the Company denies that Mr. Lincoln, the chief Company negotiator, told Union members during conversations that if supervisory personnel were doing bargaining unit driving, the practice would stop.

On September 26, 1972, the Union filed a grievance after a salaried employee had transported a non-Teamster member of the bargaining unit to Lake Charles, La. Business Agent Parson dropped the grievance after the first step, considering the incident an emergency.

On April 30, 1973, Don Hughes filed a grievance because a supervisor had transported a machinist and an electrician to an off-site job in his own car. This grievance was withdrawn by the Teamsters when Hughes picketed the Yard in violation of the Agreement. (The Union did not sanction the picketing, and withdrew the grievance because of it.)

On February 21, 1974, an hourly-paid leaderman, a union member other than a Teamster, drove a Company wagon with other bargaining unit men and their tools and related equipment to an off-site job. As a result the Teamsters filed a grievance and ultimately invoked arbitration when no third-step settlement was reached. Prior to the actual hearing the parties reached agreement on their own. The settlement of the grievance, which did not involve back pay, was stated in a June 25, 1974, letter signed by A. B. Julip of Bethlehem Steel and confirmed by Parson for the Union. The letter stated:

> This will confirm our agreement to enter into with you contemporaneously herewith concerning certain work performed by truck drivers.
>
> In the future on jobs performed outside a radius of fifty miles of the Yard when only hourly employees are involved it is Management's intent to transport these employees in a Transportation Department vehicle, when such a vehicle adequate to the task is available, with truck drivers. This does not preclude the use of commercial transportation, when applicable.

In the past, some jobs have been within and others outside the fifty-mile radius. On August 7, 1974, the current grievance was filed as noted previously.

Union Position

The Union argues that bargaining unit work cannot go unprotected and that the Company wrongfully assigned bargaining unit work outside the unit. By this action the Teamsters have been deprived of the work and of the double-time pay specified for off-site repair work.

The Union points to language contained in Article XIII, Section 10 and paragraph 3 of the appended letter as specific support for the grievance. They argue that the contract requires the assignment of work to the appropriate craft, in this case the Teamsters, and that the letter prohibits supervisors from doing bargaining unit work. The Union further argues that all Company-owned vehicles are included in the term "equipment" when bargaining unit personnel are transported in them. The grievances filed in 1972, 1973, and 1974 are offered as proof of the Union's intent to protect its contract rights.

The Union contends that in the June 1974 letter from Julip, the Company agreed not to assign driving of bargaining unit personnel to other than Teamsters. To construe the letter in such a way as to continue to allow supervisory personnel to drive would mean that the Teamsters settled the grievance without truly gaining their objective. The Union Business Agent testified that this was clearly not the understanding he had when the grievance was settled. He understood the settlement to require that only Teamsters would drive the station wagons when bargaining unit personnel were being moved.

Finally, the Union says that an oral commitment had been given by the Company's chief negotiator during the 1972 bargaining. Parson testified that when he returned in August 1972 from convalescing from a heart attack he was briefed on the progress of negotiations by Braxton and Fonda. Included in the briefing was the information that Lincoln had said that driving by supervisors rather than bargaining unit personnel would stop if it was occurring.

Local 920 President Braxton and Steward Fonda both testified that Lincoln had indeed made the statement they reported to Parson, and Union counsel spoke of non-Teamster members of the bargaining committee who were also present when the remarks were made. The Union does not dispute the right of supervisors to use the wagons by themselves, or to transport members of the bargaining unit for medical attention or for other true emergencies. However, the Union does claim that when passengers are bargaining unit members and there is no emergency, the wagon driver should be a Teamster.

Company Position

The Company argues that the practice of allowing supervisors to drive members of the bargaining unit in station wagons dispatched from the General Manager's Department is an established past practice which has not been changed by anything that the Company has written, said, or done. Article II, Section 1, refers to work "normally performed" as covered under the Agreement. The Company claims that the grievance does not involve work "normally performed" by the bargaining unit.

The Company says that Teamsters have never driven the station wagons. Even Parson, under cross-examination, said that he could not recall a Teamster ever driving a wagon, although he thought it may have occurred. The Company also claims that the Union's attempt to introduce new contract language in 1969 showed that they knew the existing language did not give their members the right to drive the wagons. When asked to define "equipment," Julip included trucks but excluded station wagons. Richardson, the supervisor who drove the wagon resulting in the present grievance, testified that he had fifteen to twenty trips in the fifteen years he had been a member of the Yard supervisory force, and that his experience was typical of most supervisors.

The Company notes that those grievances filed prior to 1974 do not establish past practice in the Union's favor, since the three were all withdrawn prior to the second step of the grievance procedure. Neither is the June 25, 1974, letter from Julip viewed as serving to establish the right of Teamster members to drive the station wagons. The Company points to specific wording granting the right of Teamsters to drive only when hourly-rated employees alone are involved and when the work is outside a fifty-mile radius from the Yard. The claim is also made that the absence of back pay indicates no wrongdoing on the part of the Company.

Lastly, the Company disputes the Union contention that an oral agreement was made by Lincoln in 1972. The Union did not mention the agreement during the earlier stages of the grievance settlement process. Julip testified that he too represented the Company during the 1972 negotiations and to the best of his recollection was present each time Lincoln was. Julip stated that he did not remember Lincoln making an agreement such as that described by the Union. Furthermore, according to Julip, he was responsible for local issues, Lincoln for national issues. Thus Julip and not Lincoln would have been the likely negotiator on issues which were local, such as this work assignment issue.

1972 Agreement Selected Provisions

Article II, Section 1. This Agreement covers the bargaining unit at the Beaumont Yard consisting of hourly-paid employees, except watchmen and clerical, supervisory and building trades construction employees.

This includes work as normally performed by the various classifications in accordance with shipyard practices. . . .

Article XIII, Section 10. In accordance with past practice of the Company, supervisors shall allocate the work to the craft which normally performs such work as recognized by the Unions involved.

Article XIX, Section 7. The arbitration procedure shall not be used to change or modify any of the provisions of this Agreement in any respect.

Letter, Appended to the Agreement, Paragraph 3. Salaried supervisors will not work with tools or operate equipment in the performance of their duties or replace other employees, except to instruct in the use of tools or equipment or methods or performance of work, except in cases of emergency.

Also, Appendix 1 of the Agreement includes job classification descriptions for Chauffer, Bus Driver, and Truck Driver. The language of Article XIII and paragraph 3 of the appended letter has remained unchanged since before the 1966 contract.

Washington County Hospital is a county mental institution caring for patients with a variety of mental illnesses. A typical unit of the hospital houses about eighty patients and is staffed by seven Nurse Aides and one Licensed Practical Nurse (LPN). The LPN oversees the operation of the unit and administers a variety of nursing procedures. A Registered Nurse (RN) is responsible for several such units and checks periodically to make sure they are functioning properly. LPNs are not paid as supervisors and have no formal supervisory authority, but they informally direct the unit when the RN is away. Washington County Hospital employees below the rank of RN are represented by the American Federation of State, County, and Municipal Employees. AFL-CIO (AFSCME), the exclusive collective bargaining representative as certified under state law pertaining to public employees.

On April 2, 1971, Mary Schneider, a Nurse Aide at the hospital, was discharged for " . . . being an unsatisfactory employee." As a result, the AFSCME local filed a grievance in Schneider's behalf. When union and managment failed to resolve the dispute, the grievance was submitted to arbitration under the existing agreement. At the hearing, the parties agreed that the issue to be determined involved the question: "Was the grievant, Mary Schneider, discharged for just cause?"

First Year of Employment

Schneider was hired on December 11, 1968, as a Nurse Aide. As was required of all employees in the bargaining unit, she served a six-month probationary period. During that period, she was evaluated twice by RN Feltz. Both evaluations were reviewed by Ganton, the Director of Nursing. An evaluation dated March 14, 1969, was done on a standard Performance Rating Report and rated Schneider "Good" as an overall rating on a scale of Unsatisfactory, Fair, Good, Excellent, and Outstanding. The Aide was rated "Good" on Quality of Work, Quantity of Work, Work Habits, Initiative, and Dependability; "Unsatisfctory" on Relationship with People. Nurse Feltz commented on the rating form:

> Does nursing procedures well and does physical care for residents—has difficulty adjusting to various personalities of residents. *MUST* establish better working relationships with co-workers—should do more listening and less talking. Will be rotated to area in hospital and observed for ability to get along with others.

Schneider was shown the evaluation and signed it.

The second evaluation, dated May 27, 1969, and also signed by Schneider was based on her first five months of employment. All categories noted above were checked "Good" as was the overall rating. Written comments noted general

*This case was written by Edward B. Krinsky, Director of Academic Personnel, The University of Wisconsin—Madison, and I. B. Helburn, Bobbie and Coulter R. Sublett Centennial Professor, Graduate School of Business, The University of Texas at Austin, as a basis for class discussion. It is not designed to present illustrations of either correct or incorrect handling of administrative situations.

improvement in all areas but indicated necessity for continued improvement in relationships with others. In June 1969 Schneider successfully completed her probationary period and was given permanent employee status.

In October 1969, RN Hunt verbally reprimanded Schneider for being "loud and bossy" and "sassy" with patients. The reprimand came after the RN counseled Schneider about this several times, but the Nurse Aide did not correct her behavior to Hunt's satisfaction.

In December 1969, Schneider was given her one-year evaluation by RN Wallace, under whom she had worked since August. Ganton again reviewed the report. The evaluation was made on a revised form which no longer included an overall rating, but included revised categories for which ratings of Unsatisfactory, Satisfactory, or Outstanding were to be used. Schneider was rated "Satisfactory" on Quantity of Work, Quality of Work, Work Habits, Initiative, Dependability, and Acceptance of Responsibilities. The categories Relationship with People and Communicative Skills were checked on the line between Satisfactory and Unsatisfactory. Wallace wrote:

> You are a willing and capable worker and are thorough in your care of the patients. You are very observing but at times seem to be too critical of other personnel, almost looking for someone to make a mistake. You should make an effort to speak in a more quiet manner and also to use more acceptable language.

Again Mary Schneider reviewed and signed the evaluation. At the arbitration hearing, Wallace testified concerning the evaluation that she did not consider Schneider completely unsatisfactory but felt there was much room for improvement. Wallace also testified that Schneider used "profane language" to patients and employees, although she neither defined "profane" nor gave examples.

January 1970 through Suspension

The one-year evaluation was the last until the final rating preceding discharge. However, several incidents occurred in the intervening period, with each noted in Schneider's personnel file.

In January, Schneider restrained a patient with a "seclusion belt" because the patient was standing in an unauthorized area. This was reported to supervision because the Aide had taken the action on her own initiative without checking with nursing personnel. No counseling or discipline resulted from the incident.

In March, RN Hunt claimed that Schneider cleaned some wall heaters in the Day Room contrary to specific orders that this work be left for Maintenance. No counseling or discipline was given.

On April 21, 1970, Schneider was verbally reprimanded by Hunt for loud and inappropriate language and for refusing to follow LPN Green's order to perform a "foot soak" on a patient. Schneider acknowledged the counseling but testified that she did not understand that she had been given a verbal reprimand.

On May 8, Nursing Director Ganton issued Schneider a written reprimand for her "attitude displayed while on duty." The reprimand stemmed from a complaint by the brother of patient Allen that Schneider had used loud and abusive language and was rude to the patient. No grievance was filed protesting the reprimand.

On July 2, Schneider was given an eight-day suspension as the result of two incidents which had occurred in late June. According to LPN Hyman, Schneider told patient Allen in loud, harsh tones to sit at the first table in the dining room or be put in seclusion. Allen had previously been required to sit at the first table so that her smoking habits could be observed since she had a problem with careless disposal of cigarettes. Hyman later testified that this requirement had been removed at the time and that Schneider should have been aware of the change. The Aide claimed that she thought the requirement was still in effect.

In the second incident, Allen crushed a container in which cigarettes were held after Schneider refused to give her a second cigarette. The Aide then began shouting at the patient. LPN Hyman intervened, asking Schneider to given Allen a cigarette, and was told by Schneider that she would do so only under orders as she thought Allen was not supposed to have additional cigarettes. Hyman did not give such an order.

Hyman did not counsel Schneider about the incident because she felt that "you couldn't talk to Mary, she wouldn't listen," and because she thought RN Reynolds would do it. However, Reynolds did not do it since she was going to inform RN Wallace of the situation the next day. There was no evidence of a counseling session between Wallace and Schneider, and two days later the Nurse Aide was suspended. Schneider grieved the suspension and the appeal was denied by both the Superintendent and the Board of Trustees. The union did not exercise its right to appeal the suspension to arbitration.

July 1970 to Dismissal

In July, after the suspension, LPN Green reported that Schneider had called a patient a "pig" after discovering a piece of meat in the patient's purse. Green's memo to her supervisor about this incident was not shown to Schneider. Neither disciplinary action nor counseling was given.

On November 7, 1970, Schneider refused patient Jackson's request for a second cup of coffee because she thought that the patient was allowed only one cup. After Jackson took the second cup anyway Schneider, in an effort to get it back, threatened and then took back a pair of slippers she had earlier given to Jackson as a gift. According to LPN Royal, she went to get Nurse Hunt after Schneider refused three orders by Royal to return the slippers. The Aide claimed she returned the slippers.

One week after this event, Wallace with Hunt in attendance held a conference with Schneider. Wallace noted the incidents which had been reported to her and told Schneider that, "if she was unable to control her emotions in dealing with patients, perhaps this was not the best work for her to be in . . . that she had already been given a suspension for her behavior and if she did not control her emotions properly, further disciplinary action would be taken."

At the Christmas party in December, Schneider yelled at two other Aides in front of the assembled patients, telling the Aides to "get your asses back up on the unit." The Aides gave no explanation for their presence to Schneider since they felt she was too upset to talk to. They did note that such language was commonly used among Aides, but not in front of patients. Schneider testified that she might have used the language and that it was inappropriate. No discipline resulted from the incident.

On February 20, 1971, an incident occurred involving Schneider and patient Wise. RN Phillips reported that Wise was very upset because she was in a phone booth talking to her boyfriend when Schneider ordered her out of the booth, using harsh language. Schneider then dragged Wise out of the booth, causing the patient to hit her head in the process.

When Phillips talked to Schneider at the time of the incident, the Aide admitted removing Wise from the booth, but only after repeatedly asking the patient to leave for over 30 minutes because a hospital employee wanted to use the phone. Consistent with her talk with Phillips, Schneider testified that she did not drag Wise from the booth or cause her to hit her head. Phillips had not witnessed the event and neither Wise nor the other employee contributed their versions of the incident during the arbitration hearing.

The following memo from Phillips to RN Ransovitz indicated considerable confusion about the use of the phone booth: "What I really want to know is are patients allowed to use the phone booth on the first floor? . . . Just thought we needed a decision on this."

The day after the phone booth happening, Schneider was transferred to a unit where an RN or LPN had supervision at all times. Ransovitz explained to Schneider that the transfer was necessary because the Nurse Aide "was not able to understand and cope with patient behavior and needed constant supervision." At the hearing, Schneider acknowledged the explanation of the transfer.

On March 10, 1971, LPN Norman of Schneider's new unit requested that her own (Norman's) schedule be changed to coincide exactly with that of Schneider. Norman testified that, "While I was on the unit with her the work she did was satisfactory. The reports from other Aides indicated this situation did not occur on my days off. Therefore, I felt in fairness to the hospital and to Mary it would perhaps be best for me to have my days changed." While no other testimony was offered, Norman said the reports of Schneider's work when the LPN was not there showed the Aide did too little and that "her interpersonal relationships were not satisfactory."

On March 23, 1971, Wallace filled out Schneider's performance rating report for the period December 11, 1969, to December 11, 1970. Schneider was checked "Satisfactory" on Quality of Work, Quantity of Work, Work Habits, and Dependability; "Unsatisfactory" on Relationship with People, Initiative, Communicative Skills, and Acceptance of Responsibility. Wallace further wrote:

> Because of your reprimands with regard to your behavior and attitude, you are considered unsatisfactory in these areas. You still seem to feel it necessary to defend your actions with regard to patients. You have apparently tried to improve in the area of self-control, but still react in a very immature manner toward patients and co-workers. Therefore, I am recommending that your employment with Washington County Hospital be terminated.

The evaluation led to an April 1 conference at which it was decided to terminate Mary Schneider the following day.

APPENDIX A

Article VI: Disciplinary Procedures

The following disciplinary procedure is intended as a legitimate management device to inform employees of work habits, etc., which are not consistent with the aims of the Employer's public function, and thereby to correct those deficiencies.

Any employee may be suspended or discharged for just cause. As a general rule, the sequence of disciplinary actions shall be oral reprimands, written reprimands, suspension, and discharge. Any reprimand sustained in the grievance procedure or not contested within the first five (5) working days after the date of the reprimand shall be considered a valid warning. Except for patient care warnings, no valid warning shall be considered effective for longer than a nine (9) month period.

APPENDIX B

Cast of Characters by Title

Director of Nursing:	Ganton
Registered Nurses:	Feltz
	Hunt
	Phillips
	Ransovitz
	Revnolds
Licensed Professional Nurses:	Green
	Hyman
	Norman
	Royal
Nurse Aide:	Schneider
Patients:	Allen
	Jackson
	Wise

45.   How Big Is a Small Knife?*

COMPANY: Atlantic Richfield, Houston, Texas
UNION: Oil, Chemical, and Atomic Workers International Union, Local
             No. 4-367

On July 25, 1976, Mr. J. D. Johns, the grievant, and co-worker, Mr. Mills, were
involved in a fight on company property. The fight started when Mills provoked
Johns by his use of profanity. Johns actually threw the first blow and later pulled a
knife and made a threatening remark before the fight ended. Both men were
suspended pending investigation and ultimately discharged. No grievance was
filed over the Mills discharge. The union did file a grievance on behalf of Johns,
claiming that the discharge was too severe given the provocation by Mills and
Johns' thirty-one years of employment with the company, all without other black
marks on his record.

When the grievance could not be settled in the earlier stages of the grievance
procedure, the discharge was submitted to arbitration. The hearing was on
October 27, 1977; the decision rendered on December 27, 1977. The agreed-upon
issue follows:

> Was J. D. Johns discharged by the company for good and sufficient cause? If not,
> what is the appropriate remedy?

Background

Article XXXI of the collective bargaining agreement, the Management Rights
clause, gives the company the right to make reasonable rules governing employee
behavior and the right to discharge "for a good and sufficient cause." The
company had issued a set of work rules in a booklet termed "Employee
Information." Each employee was given a copy of the booklet. Under the section
titled "Violations of Code of Conduct" is a list of penalties for conduct which is
considered "Acts or threats of violence against others." The minimum penalty for
a first offense is a fourteen to sixty day suspension; the maximum penalty is
discharge. For a second offense discharge is the penalty.

Mr. Johns was a Stillman in the refinery, responsible for directing six to eight
men. Stillman is a bargaining unit classification, just below Foreman, which is not
in the bargaining unit. Johns' immediate supervisor testified that he was a good
employee who had caused no problems in thirty-one years with the company.

Prior to the fight, Johns had complained to Mr. Cornelius, Area
Superintendent, about Mills saying, "I have had just about all I can take from Mr.
Mills." Mills was known for his use of profanity, which was often directed at fellow

---

employees in a quite personal manner. This conversation, which took place on Wednesday, July 21, ended with a warning from Cornelius to Johns not to do anything rash or to get in a fight which was likely to result in discharge. The Superintendent also said he would talk with Mills, intending to get the two men together to see if they couldn't work out their problems between themselves. In fact, before the weekend Cornelius did tell Mills that Johns had had all of him he could take, though Mills received no warning and the two men were not brought together.

The fight occurred on Sunday, July 25. Johns and some of his crew were waiting in the "bull-pen" for the next shift to relieve them. The "bull-pen" is an area about seventy-five yards from the control room where smoking is permitted. Mills approached some of the men and asked if they had signed a petition he was circulating about some "stupid S.O.B." who had left his gasoline-soaked pants in the control room. The reference was clearly to Johns. Mills then proceeded to direct a steady stream of extremely personal and vile language at Johns for a period of ten to fifteen minutes without interruption, according to one witness.

Johns stopped the profanity by saying he had had all that he could take and hitting Mills in the face. A series of blows followed and both men fell to the ground with Mills, by far the larger of the two, holding Johns down. The scuffle had lasted only a few minutes. The men were separated by onlookers, and Johns proceeded to pull a small pocket knife—such as one which might be used to clean fingernails—open the blade, and say to Mills, "I ought to cut you." Witnesses said that no threatening gesture was made with the knife, which Johns held at his side with the blade partially covered by his hand. Mills ran a few steps away, dared Johns to come at him and then rammed a grocery cart which was nearby into Johns' legs. Mills then ran off to the control room and Johns left the plant grounds.

Rather than going home, Johns went to the house of Mr. Boehm, the Unit Supervisor, and reported the incident, though without mention of the knife. This was the first report of the fight to a member of management. Later that day Johns was told not to report to work the next night, Mills was escorted from the refinery by plant guards, and both men were suspended.

After investigation, both men were discharged. At the time Mills had ten years' seniority and a clean record. Johns, with thirty-one years, was allowed to take early retirement at a reduced monthly annuity and to maintain his group medical and life insurance coverage. He also retained the right to receive an employee discount on company products.

Company Position

The company claims that the rule against violence is proper and enforceable, that the grievance should not be sustained because of the mitigating circumstances, and that proper procedures were used in investigating the incident and deciding on the penalty.

The rule against fighting is part of the company work rules. This particular rule is well-known by all employees, who are aware of the company's feelings about fighting and of the discharge that will follow. Penalties for fighting are not unduly harsh in view of the considerations of safety and well-being for both employees and property. This is particularly true in a petroleum refinery where the potential for serious accidents is high. The company contends that the arbitrator's failure to up-hold action taken against Johns will irreparably damage the impact of the plant rule and the effect it has had in virtually eliminating fighting among employees.

Johns' termination was fully justified because he threw the first punch and because he drew a knife and threated Mills, despite the grievant's thirty-one year history with the company. Other arbitrators have ruled that seniority is not enough to set aside a discharge for fighting. Arbitrator Turkus has written, "Good conduct is a continuing obligation and condition precedent to continued employment—not an exemption from discharge." (*Harry M. Stevens, Inc.,* 51 LA 258 [1968]). Arbitrator Roumell notes that "Length of service alone is not enough to mitigate discharge for physical assault of a co-worker." (*R. J. Tower Corp.,* 68 LA 1160 [1977]).

W. P. McCoy, in *Kelly Springfield,* 37 LA 704, 706 [1951], states:

> Ordinarily the man who voluntarily engages in a fight on company property cannot hope to have a discharge set aside. Many years of seniority alone will not save his job. Nor will provocation, ordinarily. Nor will a previous good record.

And, Arbitrator Shipman, in upholding a discharge, writes "Twenty-nine years is not given force and effect to reduce the penalty." (*Allegheny Ludlum Steel Corp.,* 22 LA 255, 258 [1954]).

Johns cannot use his complaint to Cornelius prior to the fight as a defense, particularly since the Supervisor warned Johns not to get in a fight. Given the warning, Johns' behavior on Sunday could not be described as an impulsive, uncontrolled response to provocation. Cornelius told Johns that he would discuss the matter with Mills, and this was all he could do at the time.

Finally, there have been no deficiencies in the investigation of the incident and the decision to terminate Johns. More than a month was spent investigating and considering the discipline to be applied, with all witnesses interviewed, the participants allowed to tell their stories, and individuals from corporate head-quarters in Los Angeles consulted on the final decision. All facts were considered and the impact and consequences of various alternative penalties were reviewed.

Johns' discharge was consistent with prior enforcement of the no fighting rule. Only two fights have taken place in the last several years. Two employees were discharged for a fight in which one participant produced a knife and the other used a 2 x 4 while on an operating unit. A second fight brought a four weeks' suspension without pay for two employees who were fighting without weapons at the plant gate. The Johns-Mills fight is clearly more like the first of the two previous fights since a weapon was used and the fight took place on the plant grounds near an operating unit.

In the administration of discipline management must be given a reasonable area of discretion and judgment subject only to the requirement that disciplinary action be for just cause. This was stated by Arbitrator Dworkin in *Schuler Axle Co.,* 51 LA 210, 214 [1968]. Arbitrator W. P. McCoy has also written that the arbitrator should be hesitant to substitute his judgment for that of management. (*Stockham Pipe Fittings Co.,* 1 LA 160, 162 [1945]). Thus the grievance should be denied.

Union Position

While the company rule against fighting is valid, it has been misapplied in Johns' case due to management's negligence and mitigating factors such as the location of the fight, provocation, and the grievant's work record. No penalty should be imposed because of these reasons, but in the alternative no more than a four-week suspension is called for since discharge is not mandatory for a first offense.

The fight need not have occurred if there had been an appropriate response to Johns' complaint about Mills. However, Cornelius merely told Johns that he would speak to Mills and did not take immediate action to correct the situation. Arbitrator Jaffe in *International Paper Co.,* 56 LA 558 [1971] states that management cannot condemn conduct which is the result of a situation it has permitted to continue.

Since the "bull-pen" is a relatively safe place away from the main workings of the refinery and since no operations were disrupted as a result of the fight, the company's concern for safety and efficiency will not be undermined if Johns is reinstated. This case is not similar to the earlier fight which resulted in discharge because Johns, unlike others discharged, made no offensive move with the knife and because the Johns fight did not take place in the midst of operations.

Heavy consideration must be given to the grievant's thirty-one year unblemished work record. Since the purpose of the penalty is to deter such conduct in the future or to discharge an employee who poses a threat to the safety of others, the penalty is unnecessary in light of Johns' past record. It has been written that "(A)rbitrators agree that long service records establish 'credits' for employees which should not be taken away through discharge unless there is no alternative." (*Charleston Navel Shipyard,* 54 LA 145 [1970]). Elkouri and Elkouri, in *How Arbitration Works,* 3d. edition (BNA, Inc.), p. 638, also write that an offense may be mitigated by a good past record.

Since the grievant was sorely provoked before taking action and thus did not really start the fight, he should not be given the ultimate penalty of discharge. One union witness testified that Johns remained calm "much longer than I would have." According to the union brief "almost anyone in a similar situation would have done the same thing (as Johns) to keep his own self-respect and that of the employees working under him."

46. Quality of Work Life: Getting Started*

Bill is a second-level manager in a construction and maintenance department of a large public utility. The company has a policy of hiring university graduates and "fast tracking" them through to at least the third-level of management if they show promise. Bill, with MBA in hand, started as a first-level manager two years ago, and was promoted to second-level last year. Basically, Bill believes he is a participative-style manager although lately he has felt the need to put the pressure on his first-line supervisors for more productivity particularly at one of the locations under his supervision. He knows he was given this opportunity to "prove himself" and be groomed for promotion.

Bill has seven first-level supervisors who report to him. Four of the supervisors are at a location within a large metropolitan city, and three of them are at a location near Highway 7, which is about twenty miles from the city.

The city location is in a part of the city that has some of the oldest underground utility services, which often break down and seem to require constant maintenance. This location has for years been among the poorest in the state regarding measures of productivity. The last three years it has been last in terms of productivity. Bill shares this location with four other functional departments of the utility company. The garage the employees report to is run down, dirty, and overcrowded. It is the original garage built twenty years ago when the number of employees reporting to the garage was about half of what it is now. Although company officials indicate that the congestion is only at the beginning and end of the shifts, and at other times the garage is practically empty, during these times the congestion has led to heated exchanges between supervisors and workers.

This location is represented by Local 9 of the Utility International Union. Tom, who has been the president of the local for many years, has seen a number of managers come and go. They all come with the idea of being the one to improve productivity, and have their own ideas of what was needed. Some, with specific methods of monitoring workers, managed to increase productivity for a short time, but none of the procedures had any long-term effect. The rank and file were constantly trying to transfer out of this location. Management was constantly changing and with these changes came changes in procedures. The union was seen by most rank and file as a stabilizing force. The work of Tom and the other union officials had prevented what many believed to be injustices to specific union members. For this reason, the union has solid support of the membership at this location. It was the only local in the state that could call a "walk out" (a wildcat strike) and be assured of 70–80 percent compliance. The grievance rate was high and on occasion the walk out had proved to be an effective tool for obtaining what Tom believed to be fair resolution of a grievance. Tom had worked for the company for eighteen years as a repair person and had always been active in the union. He enjoyed his job and was known as a hard worker. He never used the

*James W. Thacker, University of Windsor and Mitchell W. Fields, Texas A&M University. Printed by permission.

power of his union position to obtain special favors. He was liked by the rank and file and respected by most of the managers he dealt with, although they did wish he wouldn't use the "wildcat" strike as a tool. If pushed, however, many of the managers would admit that he did not use this tool very often, and even then only after all other avenues had been explored. Tom sometimes had a difficult time controlling the chief steward and stewards at the city location. They are definitely more militant than Tom, but this is to a certain extent a function of having to work at a location fraught with problems. At the present time, Tom had a grievance filed regarding contracting out. He had met with Bill about this and indicated that past practice had been to only contract out jobs *after* giving employees the opportunity to do the work on overtime. Tom had attached to the grievance a letter of agreement signed by the second-level manager who had Bill's job six years ago. This letter indicated that employees would be given priority if they would like to do the job on overtime. The contract indicated contracting out was at the discretion of management.

The second location, twenty miles outside the city, was labeled the "country club" by employees of the company. It was built on a hill overlooking acres of farm land. The building was five years old and had all the modern conveniences. Bill did not know much about this location as he only visited it twice since becoming the manager of construction and maintenance department. This location was also shared by other functional departments but had been built expecting expansion and was still larger than needed. Productivity here was about at the mid-point when compared to the state.

The "Country Club" was represented by Local 12 of the Utility International Union. The president of this local also did not know much about the "country club" location, as he was situated forty miles from it. His chief steward and stewards at that location seemed to be able to handle any problems that arose. There were few grievances, and those that were filed were handled at the first step.

The company and international union had recently formally embraced the Quality of Work Life (QWL) concept and had formed a corporate steering committee of top management personnel and union officials. One of their first charges after developing a charter was to urge everyone to become involved in the process, although in theory the process is voluntary.

At the last bi-monthly meeting, Bill's supervisor said, "Times are changing, and we must also change. The company wants us all to become actively involved in the QWL process and so we shall. I'll expect to hear a progress report from each of you at our next bi-monthly meeting."

Bill met with his first-line supervisors to discuss implementation of QWL at his two locations. He was surprised to hear what they had to say on the subject. Supervisors from the city location had the following comments: "Our measure of productivity is the lowest in the state and with pressure to improve, I'll need all my workers out doing work, not discussing problems." "It may be OK to work on QWL efforts with a union that is responsible but the local union we deal with would just take advantage of this type of cooperation." "Cooperation, you've got to be kidding. It might work out at the country club—they have a good relationship with the union, but we can't sit down with the union screaming at each other." "All this will mean is the union will have another way of airing their complaints; and with this union, the grievance procedure is enough." "If we try this, will the company get off our back regarding productivity long enough to make this work?"

The supervisors at the country club location were no more enthusiastic about QWL, but for different reasons. Comments from the country club supervisors included: "Things are fine the way they are." "The nickname for our location is the country club." "We already have QWL."

Bill was surprised at the resistance of his supervisors at both locations, but believed that he should go ahead any way. Before doing so, however, he decided to meet with the union officials who would be included.

Bill thought he should meet with the representatives of each local separately to see how they felt regarding QWL implementation. Tom, the president of Local 9, indicated he would not meet with Bill until the grievance on contracting out was settled. He was aware of corporate policy and pressure on managers like Bill to get involved in QWL. This was just what he needed to win the grievance.

In the meeting with union officials from Local 12, Bill soon discovered that they were not enthusiastic about the QWL process. The chief steward suggested that it was a management idea designed to weaken the union. Management, according to the chief steward, wanted to develop a structure in which problems could be dealt with without the formal grievance procedure. The chief steward commented that "this would be designed to get around long-standing union-management agreement on how the work should be done." A steward suggested that it was just a way to increase productivity. The president of the local said that he attended a conference on QWL at a local college and thought it could be a positive thing if implemented properly.

While Bill was driving home, the following thoughts were almost subconsciously passing through his mind regarding the QWL issue. If I am to move up in the company, I would have to demonstrate that I'm a progressive manager. This would definitely mean having my subordinates involved in QWL process. There is no way that the company will ease up on productivity especially when you are in last spot. I should just announce that we are entering into a QWL process and schedule training at both locations for those interested. Once the union sees that the rank and file want it they will have to go along. Do they really need QWL at the country club?

47. QWL Startup: Is the Formula for Success Always the Same?*

Alan is a third-level manager at a large public utility. In his organization, the Midwest Utility Company, Alan is a relatively young manager for somebody at the third-level of management. He received an MBA from a prestigious New England school where his training emphasized the development of non-traditional views regarding the role of management. Alan's job entailed responsibility for delivering his company's special services to the public. Customers would call Alan's offices and place orders for special services. Alan directly supervised four second-level managers who in turn supervised five first-level supervisors each. Each first-level supervisor had ten non-management, union-represented employees reporting to them. This resulted in a total of 20 first-level supervisors and 200 non-management employees within Alan's district. All these employees worked at one job site located in the suburb of a large metropolitan area. The non-management employees were represented by one local union of the Public Service Workers International (PSWI).

One chief steward represented all Alan's non-management employees. This individual, Rita, came from a largely blue-collar, unionized background. When news spread of Alan's appointment, Rita was concerned. Having heard rumors about Alan's new ideas, she felt that Alan could create problems in an otherwise stable situation. The manager previous to Alan had been from the old line. He expressed much mistrust of the union, which was echoed by Rita in a mistrust of management. Both had learned to live together in a highly competitive atmosphere with a fragile truce. Under this truce, grievance activity was high as was the number of disciplinary actions filed by management.

Alan entered this job assignment with a perspective that varied from that of his predecessor and the majority of managers in his company. He believed that the only sensible approach to employee relations involved cooperation between union and management. Within the first week of this job assignment, Alan learned the history of the relationship between his predecessor and Rita. He determined that the most effective way to overcome the previous pattern of relationship would be to begin immediately with a new set of ground rules. As a first step, Alan invited Rita to a meeting, at a neutral off-site location, to become better acquainted with each other.

Rita was one of the few female chief stewards in her local union. She had moved through the union hierarchy by watching management carefully out of the corner of her eye. This behavior resulted in Rita winning several strategic victories on disputes with Alan's predecessor. In one instance, Rita won a grievance that shortened the workday of her employees by fifteen minutes through the implementation of a time allowance for travel to work. This particular victory entrenched Rita so firmly in her position that she had run for reelection uncontested in the last union election. Rita viewed any form of cooperation with

*Mitchell W. Fields, Texas A&M University, and James W. Thacker, University of Windsor. Printed by permission.

management as a pitfall that could undermine the support she received from her constituency. Yet she did agree to Alan's meeting so as not to appear closed-minded to the new manager. Rita felt that she could use the meeting to probe Alan for weaknesses that could be used to her advantage at a later date.

At the meeting, Alan surprised Rita by not suggesting any radical changes in the operations of the department. Instead, Alan focused the meeting on pleasant discussion, with Alan probing Rita for her reactions to some of the more pressing problems employees experienced at the workplace. Rita was surprised to find that she and Alan shared some common perceptions of problems and the most effective solutions. The entire meeting went by without either party proposing any changes in the relationship. Both individuals felt positive about the experience but realized that the demands of the job could prevent any additional movement. At the conclusion of the meeting, Alan did suggest a follow-up meeting between himself, Rita, and the president and vice-president of her local union. Rita indicated that she would propose this to her officers but could not make any promises as to their receptivity.

Later that day, Rita met with her local officers and briefed them on the details of her meeting with Alan. Rita was surprised to find her officers receptive to pursuing this matter. In response to Alan's invitation, these officers found themselves in an unusually precarious situation. In the most recent contract negotiation, the international union negotiated a clause into the collective bargaining agreement urging cooperation between union and management to improve the quality of working lives of all employees. It had been a year since the contract was signed and no activity had been initiated anywhere in the company. The international was placing much pressure on the various locals to begin exercising this clause. These officers felt that they could win considerable points with their international by becoming the first local to move ahead with Quality of Work Life (QWL) efforts. Another factor pressing in favor of Alan's invitation concerned the financial state of the Midwest Utility Company. The company was undergoing a financial crisis, tied to an economic recession, which was soon to result in a loss of jobs because of changing human resource needs. The officers realized that the maintenance of existing jobs could depend on changing the strategies they employed when dealing with management.

On the negative side, these officers were scared of QWL. They had become comfortable in their old patterns of behavior and the idea of changing created stress. Traditionally, these officers had resisted any form of cooperation between labor and management. They believed that any perception on the part of the rank and file that the officers were cooperating with management would undermine their authority. There was a very stiff anti-management contingent in the local that would pounce on any management cooperation. Already there were rumblings in the local about "selling out" to management that might strengthen the opposition in the upcoming union election.

It was with some degree of mixed emotions that the officers agreed to at least meet with Alan to hear what he had to say. The meeting took place at an off-site location. Ground rules that had been set in advance prohibited the discussion of particular problem issues (i.e., unresolved grievances) and encouraged discussion only of issues of mutual concern not specifically governed by the collective bargaining agreement. Rita was particularly uneasy regarding this meeting because she was seeing her officers in a different light. When she agreed to suggest the meeting to her officers, she expected a flat refusal. Instead, the offer was met with an almost immediate acceptance.

The actual meeting turned out to be more positive than any of the parties had expected. A number of areas of mutual concern that could be resolved through joint action were raised at the meeting. It was unanimous that further action was warranted and positive benefits to all parties might result. A tenative plan was developed to continue meeting and to hold further discussions. All parties agreed that no actions would be implemented immediately but future discussions would move slowly and involve more people.

The local officers decided that they would leave all future matters in Rita's hands. She was chief steward and the people involved looked to Rita for leadership. These leaders were playing a cautious hand by leaving themselves out of the direct action for several reasons: First, their direct involvement might be interpreted as an attempt to undermine and usurp Rita's authority. Second, if the attempt at QWL improvement turned into a disaster, they were leaving Rita to take the blame. Finally, if sentiments in the local ran anti-QWL involvement, they could claim that this was Rita's territory and they had not right to interfere. Rita thoroughly understood the vulnerable position she was being placed in and agreed to these terms. Rita was willing to risk the possibility of failure in return for the high potential payoff. Rita realized that since her people were involved, she should be the one to take the political risks. Rita reluctantly agreed to move ahead with further discussions. In return, the officers left all responsibility with Rita and agreed to act as unofficial resource people providing whatever informal support they could. Alan agreed to these terms and further proposed that sometime in the future a steering committee be established, jointly chaired by Rita and himself with an equal number of union and management representatives. His proposal was unanimously accepted.

Although reluctant, Rita treated this new change as a challenge. She felt that if successful this process could have a permanent and positive impact on her constituency. After several future discussions, Alan and Rita felt that it was time to move ahead. They determined that the next step would be to invite several "key people," both management and union, from the work district to a familiarization meeting. They invited all second-level managers, assistant chief stewards, and stewards to this meeting. In all, fourteen persons attended the meeting. Alan and Rita jointly presented the concept of QWL and their vision concerning what this might entail. Of the fourteen present, ten elected to move ahead and pursue the matter further.

Throughout a slow and arduous process lasting about eighteen months, Rita and Alan developed what many considered to be the organization's "showcase" QWL effort. QWL committees and teams had been established at all levels of the district. Employees became actively involved in the process. Many changes in work procedures were implemented that saved the company considerable money and made the work more interesting and challenging. Morale among employees was high and employees from all over the company were requesting transfers into the district. Alan gained a positive reputation as a manager who was willing to take risks and who could deliver results. Rita found herself besieged with requests to act as a union spokesperson for the benefits of QWL.

At this point, Alan received a change in job assignments. A new and unique position opened up in the company that called for a manager with new ideas who was not afraid to take risks. Because of his success with QWL, Alan had become quite visible and was placed in this new assignment. His new assignment entailed responsibility for 300 non-management and 45 management employees dispersed widely over a geographic region entailing an entire state. Alan was charged with supervising the work of twenty different offices with employee counts ranging from 5 to 50 employees at each location. These employees were represented by eight different local unions. This involved a significant job change for Alan, who had previously managed employees at one office who were represented by one local union.

Consistent with his past success, Alan decided that the most effective manner to approach his present job assignment was to implement QWL as a mechanism for managing his employees. This situation presented a unique challenge to Alan. The function his people were performing involved the marketing of new product lines to new customers. These services were recent additions to his company and had come about as a result of some technological advances. All the employees were new to their jobs. There were no standard practices, nor was there any type of history of union-management relationships. Alan was literally starting from scratch. His company did not even have the expertise in these services to provide training for his employees. Alan had to contract with an outside vendor for these services.

As a first step, Alan invited a representative of each local union to a preliminary meeting. Two of the locals refused to attend, wanting no part in any cooperation with management. Six locals did send representatives. In some cases, the president of the local attended, in other cases a chief steward attended. In addition to the union representatives, Alan invited his nine second-level managers, all of whom attended. These managers had just begun working for Alan and had heard of his penchant for union-management cooperation. Although several were distrustful and would rather not have attended, they did not want to risk making an unfavorable impression on their new supervisor. Total attendance at this meeting included twenty-two individuals.

From the very beginning, Alan encountered a host of problems that thwarted his progress. Even the scheduling of the initial meeting presented problems. With the wide geographic dispersion of his work locations, some locals represented as few as ten members while others represented as many as seventy employees. Ideally, Alan desired to create a steering committee with representation from each local. One of the smaller locals, representing ten employees was located over 150 miles from the meeting place. This required the union representative to travel considerable distance and to spend considerable time to attend a meeting at which he represented only ten employees.

There was a wide variance among the locals in terms of their experience with QWL. Some locals were old hands while others were relative newcomers. Among those present at the meeting was Rita who represented twenty employees in Alan's new district. Alan and Rita immediately started conversing and remarking at their excitement about working together again. The remainder of the initial meeting consisted of a two-way conversation between Alan and Rita concerning what they felt could be accomplished with this new and unique job situation. In their enthusiasm, Alan and Rita failed to notice that the representatives of the other locals were remaining quiet and not participating.

By the conclusion of the meeting, Alan and Rita had developed an action plan that included the development and administration of an extensive survey to measure the relevant attitudes of employees in the district. Within sixty days following the meeting, each employee would be asked to complete a survey. This data would then be used to facilitate the implementation of joint union-management QWL efforts. One of the union representatives present, Mark, was very upset at the pace of the meeting. Mark was a union president from an outstate location and had traveled 100 miles to attend this meeting. Only fifteen of his members actually reported to Alan. Under normal circumstances, Mark would have sent his chief steward, but in this case he wanted to hear everything that transpired. He decided way in advance of the meeting that QWL and labor-management cooperation represented an unacceptable mode of operating. He attended the meeting because management was paying the expenses for his trip and he wanted to be informed concerning all goings on.

At the meeting, Mark only became more firm in his anti-cooperation attitudes. He believed that Alan was pressuring those in attendance into action before they had the opportunity to investigate alternatives. He was dismayed at the relationship between Rita and Alan. Upon leaving the meeting he was heard to comment that Rita's union had sold out to management. After returning to his local, Mark sent Alan a note indicating that his local would have no further involvement in QWL activities.

Aside from Mark, the other members of the steering committee agreed to go ahead with the implementation of QWL and specifically the survey. Many in attendance felt that Alan was moving too fast but did not express these sentiments. The chief steward of one of the larger locals, Steve, had no direct experience with QWL. He was friends with Rita and had heard many positive comments from her and from other local officers. Steve had been interested in getting started in some QWL activity for several months. Upon first receiving Alan's invitation to the meeting he was pleased that the opportunity to begin had presented itself. Although he voted to move ahead with QWL, Steve's enthusiasm fell off by the end of the meeting. He left feeling railroaded and disappointed that his input at the meeting had not been sought to a greater degree.

After the meeting Alan and Rita met for a debriefing. Both felt that something at the meeting was missing. They were disappointed and could not explain the unenthusiastic attitude expressed by those in attendance. Several months later Mark changed his negative attitude about QWL. He had come around to a more positive way of thinking about union-management cooperation. By the time he was ready to participate, the survey had already been administered and fed back. The steering committee was moving ahead with other projects. Mark's local had been left out of the action and nobody wanted to slow down to allow them to catch up.

48. Dealing with Organizing Problems Via the Bargaining Table: The Case of "Neutrality Agreements" *

The leadership of the United Tire Workers Union (UTW) has begun growing increasingly frustrated in its attempts to get new workers to join the union. Workers no longer seem to have the same interest in being union members that they had in the union's earlier days. Moreover, employer resistance to union attempts to organize employees has grown sharply. Indeed, there has been a dramatic increase over the past decade of instances of unlawful employer "discriminatory discharges," i.e., cases in which employers have unlawfully fired employees who are involved in union organizing activities.

Such "discriminatory discharges" are, of course, unlawful under the National Labor Relations Act, and the union has pressed claims before the National Labor Relations Board, the administrative agency established to administer the Act. But it often takes over a year for a case to be decided by the NLRB, and NLRB cases are automatically appealable to the federal courts, where it can take years for a final decision in a case to be rendered. In addition, the penalties imposed on employers for engaging in such illegal actions are relatively small, so small in the opinion of some observers that there is little incentive for employers to actually obey the law.

To help rectify this situation, in 1977 the UTW and other unions sponsored legislation in the U.S. Congress to amend the National Labor Relations Act. Under the union-proposed legislative amendments any employer that consistently engaged in illegal "discriminatory discharges" would, among other things, have any contracts it had with the federal government taken away. Because many of the tire companies had large contracts to supply tires to the federal armed forces, the UTW felt that this amendment would help ensure company compliance with the labor laws. This labor law reform legislation, although passed overwhelmingly by the U.S. House of Representatives was successfully defeated by way of a filibuster in the U.S. Senate.

The UTW, now more frustrated than ever, decided to start seeking solutions to its organizational problems through the use of its clout at the bargaining table. The union proposed a new provision, known as a "neutrality agreement," for inclusion in the labor organization's new collective bargaining contract with the Goodwrench Tire Company. The proposed provision stated as follows:

> In situations where the UTW seeks to organize employees in a Goodwrench Tire Company plant which is not presently represented by a union, the company management or its agents will neither discourage nor encourage the UTW's efforts to organize these employees, but will observe a posture of strict neutrality in these matters. . . .

*Leonard Bierman, Texas A&M University. Printed by permission.

> The UTW will conduct itself in such organizing campaigns in a constructive manner which does not misrepresent to employees the facts and circumstances surrounding their employment.

Goodwrench's negotiations first balked at the inclusion of this provision in the parties' new three-year labor contract but, reflecting on the need for better long-term relations with the UTW, ultimately agreed to incorporate the neutrality language in future contracts.

Six months later Goodwrench established a new subsidiary called Goody Muffler Company. Goody Muffler was comprised of one hundred muffler shops throughout the country. The UTW quickly decided to attempt to organize the employees at the forty Goody Muffler shops in Ohio, Michigan, Indiana, Illinois, and Pennsylvania. Goody Muffler Company, not particularly excited by the prospect of its employees being represented by the UTW, comes to you, an expert outside consultant in the personnel area, with the following questions:

1. Is Goody Muffler bound by the "neutrality agreement" reached by its parent company Goodwrench Tire Company with the United Tire Workers Union? What if all labor relations decisions are made independently by Goody without consultation with Goodwrench?

2. Assuming that the "neutrality agreement" does apply to Goody Muffler as a subsidiary of Goodwrench, what, if anything, can Goody management *say* in response to the UTW's attempts to organize its mid-western employees? Can Goody print and distribute a fact sheet presenting the pros and cons of joining a union but taking no formal position on the subject? To what extent is the union limited in terms of its campaign propaganda by its agreement to conduct its campaign in a "constructive manner"?

3. What happens if Goody Muffler ignores the Goodwrench-UTW "neutrality agreement" and wages a vigorous campaign against the union? How can the union enforce the agreement? Can the union take the company to federal court under section 301 of the National Labor Relations Act? What happens if there is a grievance arbitration clause in the Goodwrench-UTW contract?

4. Is there a possibility that the "neutrality agreement" between Goodwrench and the UTW is illegal? Does not section 8(a)(2) of the National Labor Relations Act outlaw "collusive" union-management behavior? What are some of the arguments in favor of and against the legality of "neutrality agreements" of this kind under section 8(a)(2)?

5. What happens if at the end of the current three-year labor contract the UTW wants to renew the neutrality clause, but Goodwrench flatly says "no" and refuses to negotiate at all over the issue? Can Goodwrench lawfully do this? Assuming the legality of such agreements, would they be categorized as "mandatory" or "permissive" subjects of bargaining? What implications might such categorization have in terms of a union threat to take economic action, e.g., strike, with regard to this issue?

6. What implications does Congress's enactment of section 8(c) of the National Labor Relations Act in 1947, and its enactment at section 8(b)(7) in 1959 have on the legality and viability of "neutrality agreements"? Could one successfully argue that such agreements are legal, but violate the "laboratory conditions" standard for labor elections set forth by the National Labor Relations Board in its seminal 1948 *General Shoe Corporation* case?